Edith Garnett

Susan Soley

Bag and Baggage

Bag and Baggage

*Moves and Memories of an
Army Daughter and Wife*

Edith Garrett

The Pentland Press
Edinburgh – Cambridge – Durham – USA

First published in 1999 by
The Pentland Press Ltd
1 Hutton Close
South Church
Bishop Auckland
Durham

ISBN 1 85821-671 0

Typeset in Bell 11/14
by Carnegie Publishing, Carnegie House, Chatsworth Road, Lancaster
Printed and bound by Bookcraft (Bath) Ltd.

To my husband and children with gratitude for the happiness they have given me

Contents

Illustrations

Foreword

MRS GARRETT HAS WRITTEN A FASCINATING and nostalgic account of an upper middle class English military family, reaching back through the tales of her elders of the last century, to her own remarkably clear memories of her earliest days between the Wars, living in the English countryside with the support of the numerous servants, which are now a distant memory.

Crucial to the story was her decision on leaving school, supported by wise advice from friends, to take up teaching. This led, after posts in England, to a time in Cyprus, then still a British Colony. There, her ever lively interest and sharp observation of the local scene, and a new found interest in archaeology, will remind readers of the attractions of an island they once knew. Coming home after the loss of her father, she enrolled as a teacher at the Westminster Abbey Choir School. This proved to be the climax of her scholastic career culminating in her involvement in the Coronation of Queen Elizabeth II. Although an attachment to the school has remained, her teaching career thereafter ended. Through the loving machinations of a mutual cousin, she met and married Anslow, an Army officer and distant cousin, who has made her happy ever since. The Abbey hierarchy and the Army co-operated to produce a wedding which must have been of well-deserved splendour, and which united two characters well suited to their subsequent career together.

Before long Anslow was promoted to Lieutenant Colonel and appointed to a post in the Army Headquarters in the still colonial Nigeria. Both here and subsequently in Zambia, they were both involved in the 'Wind of Change', and he in the organization of the ceremonies of British withdrawal, and the inauguration of independent States. In the midst of all the work involved, and the adjustment to life in the tropics, the Garretts were able to fit in much travel, some in the luxurious conditions available to a senior officer, and to see much of 'Africa south of the Sahara'. Mrs Garrett's acute powers of observation and botanical knowledge lend colour to her descriptions, while her sense of humour ensured her philosophical acceptance of the clash of cultures brought into her day-to-day living by sometimes wholly untrained servants.

An aspect of this picture of an already bygone age, is the nostalgic account of sea travel, that leisurely but officially accepted means of long distance travel, when air travel seems hardly to have attracted official notice. The comfort and luxury of those liners plying to Africa and the Far East is unforgettable, even though the latest cross Channel ferries exceed their size by several thousand tons.

The climax of this story is Anslow's further promotion to Brigadier, as Defence Attaché to the British Embassy in Turkey. Sensibly prepared by a year's study of the Turkish language, the Garretts made a large circle of Turkish friends from the Commander-in-Chief downwards. They travelled out overland exploring Venice on the way, and taking ship to Izmir. From there they began their exploration of Turkey, which they thereafter pursued with their customary resourcefulness and imagination.

A characteristic of Mrs Garrett was her decisiveness, which aroused admiration and even awe among her friends. She found the domestic staff, which she was to inherit from her predecessors, were not only dishonest on a heroic scale, but also dissolute. She sacked the lot and withstood a month's seige operated by the local unofficial trades union. Had they any experience of the opposition, they would not have wasted their time! An appeal for reinstatement was naturally rejected, and a satisfactory staff recruited in due course.

This story is crowned by Anslow's share in the organization of the State Visit of the Queen to Turkey, accompanied by Prince Philip and Princess Anne. In particular, Anslow had co-operated in arranging the Royal visit to Gallipoli. For this the Queen arrived in the Royal Yacht. After the visit, all those involved were invited to lunch on board. Afterwards, Anslow was invited to step forward and was handed by the Queen the insignia of a Commander of the Royal Victorian Order (CVO), and Prince Philip presented a signed photograph of the three royal guests.

The account of the Garrett's time in Turkey and their visit to Iran

Foreword

constitutes little short of an ideal guide to the most attractive sites in the two countries, both for holidays and for the pursuit of the endless and important archaeological remains covering some three thousand years of history, all this spiced with many tales of adventure due to climate and primitive roads, and adorned by the unfailing kindness of the local population to any traveller in difficulties. Mrs Garrett rightly attributed their success to a knowledge of at least some of the local language.

This book is not only an entertaining story, but one of the author's unfailing courage and humour, passing over as she does the personal tragedies and difficulties which are the inescapable part of an adventurous, and an increasingly historic career.

Sir Roderick Sarell, KCMG, KCVO
Ambassador to Turkey 1969–1973

Preface

HAVING BEEN BLESSED with a good memory, and with persuasion and encouragement from my family, I have written this book in the hope that it may be of interest to my potential readers. It is not a story of great drama and excitement, but more of a diary which starts with a record of a way of life long since passed, which perhaps some readers of my generation may have experienced. Also the accounts of travel and friendship which I have been privileged to make, may appeal to those with a curiosity about places beyond these shores.

One always regrets not having questioned and sought more information from parents and grandparents in their lifetime. Let us hope that at least my grandchildren and other young people will be mindful of this when they read this book. I have found it difficult, even after all these years, to write of my personal tragedies, but felt that, as they were part of my life, they had to be mentioned, albeit briefly, for without them, my life might have taken a very different course. Who knows?

Where necessary, the names of my family, close friends and some others have been changed to protect their privacy. Otherwise I have tried to be as accurate as possible, and everything I have written is as I remember it, or as it was told to me.

Edith Garrett. 1998.

Acknowledgements

I WOULD LIKE TO THANK Sir Roderick Sarell for his generous Foreword. My friend, the writer Miss Veronica Thackeray for her wise counsel and suggestions. My sister Elizabeth for helping to gather old family photographs. My family for helping me to master my word processor and for reading my manuscript, and finally my publishers for their enthusiasm, attentiveness and professionalism.

Part I
The Backdrop 1886–1925

The Backdrop 1886–1925

IT WAS A SPRING DAY and tall yellow tulips were shining like sentinels in the warm sun, beside a long straight path which divided them from a square apron of lawn. My eldest sister toddled unsteadily down the path oblivious to all around her except those yellow blooms which had caught her eye. She stopped and studied them and then, slowly and deliberately, she stooped and put her index and second finger on either side of the stem, ran them up to the flower head, and with a determined effort popped the bloom off the stem like a head being guillotined from its neck. Slowly many of the tulips met the same fate before she was discovered by a horrified nanny who ran out, snatched her up and hurried her inside.

All this I saw from an open window above, as I stood in my cot in my parents' bedroom where I had been put to sleep. It is my earliest memory, together with a vivid recollection of that bedroom and its furnishings, my parents' twin beds with green silk covers decorated with a raised appliqué design of purple flowers and green leaves in the centre. I remember too the sash window open at the bottom, and how I threw my toys out to attract attention. I must have been one and my sister just over two.

I was born into an itinerant Army family, but because my mother would not go abroad, my poor father had to content himself with postings in England after his marriage. Quite a changed way of life after service in China, India, Ceylon and Malta, but I never heard him complain, though it must have scuppered his hopes of promotion beyond Major. My parents were first cousins and were truly devoted to each other, and they gave us an idyllic and secure childhood. After nine years of marriage, they had produced five girls and, although money was always short, there was Nanny, a housemaid, cook and other staff, before the 1939 War anyway. My paternal grandmother certainly gave my father a generous allowance and I am sure, like many grandmothers, she helped in other ways too.

I never knew my paternal grandfather. In the 1880s when she was a young woman, my grandmother went out to India to stay with one of her brothers who was resident out there. On board ship she met two young men who both fell in love with her and before the end of the long voyage, they had both proposed to her. She accepted one, subject to her family's approval, and tragically the other suitor threw himself overboard in his despair and was drowned. This must have put a bit of a damper on the happy couple, who, I may say, were heavily chaperoned by my great Aunt Jessie who was travelling with her younger sister. After family approval and visits on both sides, they eventually married. My father was born in 1888, but tragically when my grandmother was pregnant with her second child, my grandfather died of a severe attack of asthma, leaving Grannie, as we always called her, with a memory of only three years of marriage. Uncle Harold was born posthumously and, of course, neither of those two little boys ever knew their father. One can only begin to imagine how Grannie coped with this tragedy, but she was one of a large family and the grand-daughter of a prominent Suffolk family who helped out financially and gave her lot of support.

Within a few years Grannie had met and married my step-grandfather who proved to be a good husband. He took on those boys as though they were his own. He was quite a bit older than Grannie and there were no more children forthcoming. I remember him as a gruff and rather humourless old man in the 1930s, but Pa always spoke of him with gratitude and respect. Their relationship was formal and he called him 'Sir' and spoke of him as 'the Old Man'! But at that time it was normal to do so in such families. When I was about seven years old, we used to go over to see them in Guildford where they were living, and looking back, I could hardly imagine a more ill-matched couple, as Grannie was such a warm, loving, jolly person, but they were happily married for more than forty years, and he was certainly a generous man at heart.

My father went to Repton School in Derbyshire while Uncle Harold went to King's School, Canterbury. It has often puzzled me that they didn't go to the same establishment, but later on they did not get on well together, so perhaps this antipathy started much earlier. As a young teenager my father would be taken by the family horse and carriage from his home in Brislington to Bristol Station. All his life he was always late for everything and very bad at leaving his bed in the morning, and even in those early days, he would complete his dressing in the carriage and there would be a scramble for the school train. My grandmother, ever indulgent, arranged for a sustaining hamper to be put on the train when it reached Crewe. There a porter walked down the platform calling out 'A hamper for Mr Wyndham, a hamper for Mr Wyndham'. Young Mr Wyndham put his top-hatted head out of the carriage window to claim his booty. Immediately a bevy of boys fell upon this unexpected windfall and 'helped' him to demolish it. In his first term at Repton, he had to undergo a rather alarming and daunting ritual which all new boys in his house, The Priory, were put through. This consisted of placing a splayed hand, palm down, on a well-worn piece of wood and then a senior boy, with a sharp penknife, would jab the blade backwards and forwards between the fingers as fast as he could. History doesn't relate how often he missed the gap between the fingers and pinned down his wretched victim. This initiation was supposed to test the nerve of the new boy.

From Repton, Pa went to Sandhurst and subsequently he was commissioned into The Somerset Light Infantry in 1910. His first posting was to join his chosen regiment, who were in Peking guarding our legation there. It must have been a fascinating time to have been in China. While there he trekked with servants and laden mules a great distance into eastern China as far as the mountains on what is now the North Korean border. He also took advantage when he could to buy a number of Chinese artefacts. In our various homes many years later, I remember paintings on rice paper in attractive maple frames, a large embroidered picture of fighting cocks, cloisonné dishes and little jars, a seated Buddha with an enormous tummy who was known as 'the fat man' who had pride of place on our drawing-room mantlepiece.

There were also very heavy metal and stone incense burners in various shapes which were used as garden ornaments by my grandmother. My sisters and I discovered in the forbidden territory of Pa's dressing room, an album with some gory photographs of a public execution in Peking, showing a Chinese uniformed figure with a long sword flashing through the air, decapitating a kneeling figure, and the head severed and still falling to the ground. We were both horrified and fascinated by it.

1. Father (centre) with his servants and laden mules on trek into Eastern China circa 1911.

Today's child would probably not turn a hair. It is difficult to imagine in these days of air travel, but there was no problem in those days in bringing the most unlikely baggage by sea, bulky and heavy as some of Pa's possessions were.

After China, Father went to India, and was there when the First World War broke out; at first he was stationed near Bombay and so was not far from his English relatives whom his mother had journeyed to visit over twenty-five years earlier. From what he told me years later, he travelled fairly widely within the country, and in Ceylon as it was called then. Uncle Harold served in The Royal Scots, but later when he left the Army after the 1914–1918 War, went out to Ceylon, where he was a tea-planter.

I envy Pa his time in Agra and the hill-stations further north. As in China, so in India he acquired Indian mementoes. He was one of generations of British in India who shot antelope, leopard, panther and tiger, and their skins adorned our floors at home. It was while he was in India that Father had the batman who served him so faithfully for many years. His name was Cummings, but more of him later on in my story. Other faithful companions were his mules and a horse called Betty. During the early part of his time in India, he married his first wife, an Englishwoman, in Bombay Cathedral in 1915. Sadly it all ended in tears after a comparatively short time, as she had an affair with a brother officer and they were drummed out of the regiment and went to a farm in Kenya. When Pa was in Agra, and other places later on in his time in the sub-continent, he wrote many love letters to my mother. Being cousins, they had known each other since childhood. My mother had always adored him, and I think the realization that their feelings were mutual came to him after the break up of his marriage.

My father left India finally in the 1920s having served many years abroad, but it was quite normal for regiments to be away for years in those days. After India, Father went to Valetta on the island of Malta, being there for some two years, and I know from what he told me that he very much enjoyed his time on the island. It was a complete change for him after so many years in the Far East. The climate was pleasant and there was much of historical interest for him to enjoy, besides the feeling of being nearer home.

While Father was at Repton, Grannie and step-Grandfather had moved from Brislington to a lovely historic old manor house near Keynsham. Among her papers when she died in 1948, Pa and I found her old housekeeping books for the period before the Great War. They made fascinating reading, particularly the wages of the servants. Her cook was paid £30 per annum, the parlourmaid £15 and the house-maids and maids in the kitchen £10! It all sounds amazing to us now, but they lived in and were 'all found' and uniform provided, and had one afternoon off every week. The house, Queen Charlton Manor, was supposed to be haunted by the ghost of Catherine Parr, and one of my aunts said it had a very spooky chapel, and like many houses in England it had a bed in which Elizabeth I was supposed to have slept. They lived there for nearly twenty years, and Grannie indulged in her interest of gardening. She was also a very keen salmon fisherwoman, and in this period she used to fish alternate years in Norway and on the River Shannon on the west coast of Ireland.

They were comfortably off then, but later in the 1930s step-grand-father lost money in the slump. By the time my father came back to England, they had moved to another house, in Surrey, called Chantry Dene. I remember it well from visits made there in the 1930s. Grannie had chows, a breed of dog like a large poodle. As was the fashion then, they were clipped in a certain way, so that to my young eyes they

2. Grannie with one of her beloved chows on the steps of Chantry Dene.
Mid 1920s.

looked very peculiar, and hers always had a blue bow tied on the top of the head. She adored them, but I thought they were snappy little dogs. The move to Surrey meant she was nearer to the Royal Horticultural Society's gardens and, as a member she went there often. On one of her visits a new rose had been bred, and was waiting to be named. It was named, in her honour, Mrs Herbert Nash. Unfortunately it was never a commercial success, and after some ten years it was no longer available. For sentimental reasons I would dearly have loved to have it in my garden, but all my efforts at tracking it down came to nought. I even contacted the curator of the famous rosary at Sangerhausen in Germany, and had a charming letter back which said that they had the rose until 1956 when it was lost with hundreds of others in a very severe winter. I was bitterly disappointed.

My mother was the middle of three daughters born to my grandfather, who was a banker with Coutts Bank all his working life, and who in the mid-1880s married my paternal grandmother's sister. To put it more simply, my two grandmothers were sisters! Grandpa was a dear gentle man, who was indulgent and kind beyond belief. My maternal grandmother died in 1910 of a stomach complaint. This must have devastated Grandpa and his three young daughters. The eldest, my Aunt Kathleen, was 22 and she took on the task of looking after her two young sisters, who were 14 and 12. From all accounts she was a fairly bossy elder sister, and I heard many years later from my mother of the strict régime which prevailed under her rule. All three sisters had very strong personalities, which I think they must have inherited from their mother, who in her lifetime had certainly ruled the roost. Although very little about this grandmother has come down to me, one story my mother told me about her perhaps typifies her character. She once took her daughters out for a walk in the Essex countryside, and, in spite of pleas from the girls, she insisted on walking across a field in which a fierce bull was grazing. Needless to say the bull charged, the girls scattered, while my grandmother stood her ground, opening and shutting her flimsy parasol as the bull approached, as though she were some sort of female matador. She was known for her grit and determination, although it was sometimes misplaced. They were lucky and escaped and lived to tell the tale, though the children had a nasty fright.

She and her sisters were educated largely at home in Essex where they lived. They had cats and dogs, kept bees, and they all had little Dexter cattle partly as pets, though they had to learn to look after them and milk them. They lived in a large old rectory which had a bit of land, and thus were sown the seeds of a love of farming which my mother always had. She was sent to a finishing school in Belgium for a spell. Strangely she was the only daughter to go off and do this, and this was the only time in her life when she went abroad, while her sisters later became great travellers in spite of missing out on the Belgian experience. My eldest aunt, Kathleen, married when she was in her 50s and the youngest aunt, Armorel, never married, and so I suppose they were free of family responsibilities when they were young, and could pursue more adventurous lives.

My mother was a forthright and, some might say, an autocratic person. She held very strong views on many subjects and once her mind was made up, she rarely deviated. She was also a great home lover and the family meant a great deal to her. I think the circumstances of their childhood made the sisters capable, self-sufficient and full of initiative. They were all very competent artists, and my mother in particular was a very proficient sculptress too. Some of her work was sent up to the Royal Academy for assessment; years later I found the letter which she received back which said 'This pupil shows great promise and should certainly pursue a career in sculpture.' It was signed by a member of the Lascelles family. There were several artists of the Suffolk School in my grandfather's family, so it was not surprising that she inherited this gift. As time went by, the three sisters pursued their various 'careers'. I put it this way because young ladies at that time were really not trained or qualified to do anything in the way of earning their living, but were expected to stay at home and wait to get married. As there was not a lot of spare cash around, it was a necessity that they should try to support themselves.

On the outbreak of war in 1914, Aunt Kathleen became a nurse with the Red Cross, or the British Red Cross Society as it was called then. She found herself in France nursing the wounded, which must have been a harrowing time for her and many young girls straight from home, to see the true horrors of the wounded from the trenches. My mother freshly back from Belgium stayed at home to keep house and look after her father, and sometime after the war, she was taken on to run the pedigree Guernsey herd belonging to the head of a well-known firm of publishers. Sir Hubert and Lady Longman had a very grand establishment at Lavershot Hall in Surrey, and my mother lived with them and they treated her like the daughter they had never had. They became lifelong friends and I remember Lady Longman coming to stay in the 1930s. Mother was very happy there, as she was in her element with her beloved cattle, and she led a very social and comfortable life with the family. She must have had quite a wardrobe of clothes as they changed into evening dress for dinner every night whether there were guests for dinner or not. My youngest aunt, who was 16 when the war broke out, went to live with a friend whose husband was away in the war. She also was welcomed into this very jolly family. They became life-long friends, and later in the 1930s I had many happy holidays with them and their five offspring.

In 1916, when she was only 18, Aunt Armorel followed in her eldest sister's footsteps, by serving her country. She joined the Red Cross ambulance service as a driver, and was also sent to France for a time, and then by 1917 she was sent to Italy as part of the Italian Expeditionary Force. It was January and very cold and the female drivers all had rather long bulky coats belted round the waist and with fur collars. On their hands they wore leather gloves with long gauntlets, and to top the lot a peaked uniform hat with a badge on the front. Judging

3. Armorel (second from right) with some of her drivers in Italy in 1917.

by the photographs of her, she had a quantity of warm clothing on underneath the outer layer.

After the war she became General Lemprière's driver, and drove his Morse car. He was a distinguished soldier who at one time had been ADC to Lord Napier of Ettrick, the 10th baron who had held a number of diplomatic posts. Armorel and the General got on like a house on fire. I think he enjoyed and admired her spirit. My grandfather and Armorel became great friends of his and they used to go and stay at his house in Camberley, called Collingwood Mount. He died sometime during the twenties and left Armoral a legacy which she decided to spend by going round Africa in a Dutch coaster, ending up in Kenya.

She spent a year out there based in Nairobi, and while there she had various adventures while on safari with a few companions. On one

4. Armorel at the wheel of General Lemprière's Morse car. Early 1920s.

occasion they had a journey of hundreds of miles to do, and it necessitated camping overnight. They had tents, which they duly pitched in a circle near their camp fire. My aunt had a tent to herself, and strangely, although much was very primitive for all of them, she had managed to have a strip-wash in a tin bath in her tent before turning in for the night. She was sleeping soundly on her camp bed with the flap of her tent open for air, and a rifle on the ground under her bed, when she was awakened by a sound of a loud splash. She opened her eyes and, to her horror, she saw the outline of a lion against the sky, standing with it front paws in the tin bath, which she had left in the entrance to her tent. She very slowly put her arm down to feel for her rifle, when to her relief the lion turned away and left without more ado. Her relief was somewhat short-lived when she realized that she had to get up, go out and wake the others and tell them to tie up the flaps of their tents knowing that the lion was probably still in the vicinity. On another occasion she was walking in the bush when she was charged by a rhinoceros and to escape she had to shin up a tree, and, as the rhino was still in evidence, she stayed up there all night until a search party rescued her at dawn!

By 1925, my mother had left Lavershot Hall, married my father who was by now back in England, and prepared to settle down to life as an army wife.

Part II
Childhood and Adolescence
1926–1945

Chapter I

Following the Drum

Y ELDEST SISTER, Patricia, was born within the first year of my parents' marriage. She was the only one of the five daughters who was not born at home. Pa was commanding the regimental depot at Taunton by the time of my arrival, thirteen month later, my parents having rented a cottage in a tiny village in Somerset, and it was here that I was born. My sister called me Dede, pronouncing it Deedee, and from that day on I always answered to that name. With the birth of each child a maternity nurse came and lived in for a month and took complete charge of the new arrival. By all accounts some of these nurses ruled the roost, and expected to be waited on hand and foot. I remember one we had a few years later who insisted on having her meals sent up to her in her room; I can imagine such a person intimidating a new mother with her firstborn! From Somerset we moved to Tidworth, very much a traditional army environment. Again my parents took a rented cottage, and again another baby arrived. It seemed to me that there was always a baby in the nursery. She was known as Beth and was a bubbly fair-haired child. She inherited her colouring from Mother who had been ash-blond with a fair freckled skin. Mother's hair had turned white when she was in her twenties, almost without anyone noticing, and she used to be very annoyed when people thought she was our grandmother and not our mother just because her hair was white! After Tidworth we moved to Sunningdale and again another unfurnished house. This house was considerably larger, which was necessary for the growing family. I remember the garden well and in it the little building – one could hardly call it a cottage, just two rooms – which my father's batman, Cummings, had as his retreat when he was with the family and not on duty in barracks.

My life and that of my eldest sister Patti revolved round the nursery. We had all our meals there presided over by Nanny. We were taken for bracing walks daily, and occasionally went out to tea, sometimes with Nanny, and sometimes with Mother. On one occasion, when I was about five years old, Patti and I were dressed up in specially pretty little dresses, both the same, made by Grannie. She was a wonderful needlewoman and I remember those frocks so well, especially the lovely smocking. We were being taken out to tea by Mother, to one of her friends. After tea, we were sitting like little mice and on our best behaviour, being seen and not heard, when our hostess brought in a large carved box rather like a Bible box. She opened the lid and inside was ball after ball of different coloured knitting wools in great quantity, the leftovers of a prolific knitter, I imagine. Anyway we were invited to choose a ball each, and I remember being torn between a violent purple and a very bright orange. After some deliberation I chose the orange. We were given some large thick bone knitting needles, and after saying our thank yous, off we went home.

The next day I wanted to be shown how to knit and Cummings offered to teach me. I learnt to cast on and do ordinary plain stitches and I was very proud of my first efforts, but by the time I had done about an inch, it was becoming more and more difficult to put the needle into the stitch and to slide the stitches along the needle. I had been clutching the wool so tightly that the whole thing had become immovable. I was desperate, so off I went down the garden to find Cummings. He couldn't move it either, so Nanny was consulted and a decision was made to cut it off the needles. I was heartbroken, particularly as my sister had had no trouble at all, and had produced a thoroughly presentable piece of work. This was my first memory of being annoyed and jealous of Patti.

It was while we were living in this house that we kept rabbits, and we had quite a number of these creatures and of various different breeds. There was a row of cages on legs about three feet from the ground, and Patti and I were allowed to help to feed them. Although some of them were pets, the others were kept for their pelts. History doesn't relate what happened to the flesh. The skins were scraped and pegged out on boards to dry, they were then softened, though I don't remember how this was done, before being made up into gloves. I particularly remember having a pair of grey chinchilla mittens. I also still have a scar across one of my index fingers, the top of which I nearly lost through poking my finger through the wire of the cage of one hungry rabbit!

It was while we were living in Sunningdale that my Father had a disturbing experience while driving our car. Mother, Patti and I were with him, and we were driving along at a moderate speed, when suddenly, it seemed from nowhere, there appeared a female figure who threw herself across the bonnet of the car as though she was trying to commit suicide. We heard afterwards that she was mentally unbalanced and had not known what she was doing, poor thing. It made a deep and lasting impression on me, and must have been upsetting for everyone concerned, though thankfully she was not badly hurt.

By 1933 we had moved yet again. This time to Blackdown but into an unfurnished army quarter, an uninspiring red brick house and again faithful old Cummings had his domain in a separate building at the back of the house. There seemed to be plenty of people to look after us. There was Mrs Ellis, the cook and a parlourmaid under her called Rose, and I remember a young housemaid called Ellen who kept the house clean. Pa used to get very annoyed with her because she would leave her brushes and dusters all over the place when she was working. She was only sixteen and completely untrained until she came to us, but later on she left under a cloud when it was discovered that she had stolen one of Mother's brooches. Cummings used to wait at table and he would also don a green baize apron once a week and clean the silver, sitting at the kitchen table. Of course he was in charge of my father's uniform and polished his Sam Browne belt, leather gaiters and shoes daily, as well as looking after all our footwear. In the nursery, we now had a different nanny. She was older than her predecessor and far more strict. She had been passed on to us by great friends whose children had out-grown her. Under her was a nursemaid called Margaret whom we all adored.

My third sister Mary was born in 1934 in this same house, and it was soon after her arrival that I went to stay with my youngest aunt, Armorel. It was to be the first of many visits. She was living on Hayling Island at that time and it was on this visit that I met the children of the Llanmorris family whom she had known since the Great War. There were five children now, four boys and a girl ranging in age at that time between eleven and eighteen and so they were quite a bit older than me. They were all very good-looking and great fun to be with. To accommodate all these large numbers of people, my aunt turned her garage into a dormitory, with rails fixed up, over which were draped old curtains for the females in the party to have some privacy when dressing and undressing. We had old iron beds to sleep on and everything was pretty basic but adequate. It must have been a dry summer because we seemed to have all our meals outside including breakfast, but I think that one tends to remember the nice positive things of the past and all those that gave us pleasure, and one's mind blots out the rainy days.

Aunt had an old Morris car with a dickey at the back, and the older boys in the party had cars too, and so we would all pile in and set off on some expedition. These were often combined with bird-watching, exploring churches and historical ruins; in fact there was always an educational side to the outing. It all seemed so carefree and natural, and of course at the age of seven one never thought of what went on behind the scenes, about who produced the meals and did the shopping, and generally organized everything to make our holiday so enjoyable. One great excitement for me was being taken down to the beach for a moonlight swim. To have been allowed to stay up for such a treat was unheard of to me coming from my well-ordered existence at home. When I returned to my family after this visit, I remember being astounded at the change in the newly-arrived sister. She had been a new-born dark-haired scrap when I left, and on my return she was fair-haired, chubby and quite different. I was convinced that my mother had changed her for another baby!

By now Patti and I had started school, having been educated at home until we were seven. I remember so well that first introduction to school. I had been left-handed and naturally enough I picked up my pencil in that hand, only to be told to change it to my right hand. Can one imagine such a thing being done nowadays? Anyway I dutifully did and I can honestly say that I don't think it affected me in any way afterwards. This was the first of a number of schools we went to, necessitated by Father's profession.

Periodically friends and relatives came to stay. When Lady Longman came there was always a great kerfuffle. She arrived in her chauffeur-driven car with her maid, and my parents turned out of their bedroom for her, and her maid had to be accommodated too, so there was quite a lot of doubling up. Besides this she always had breakfast in bed, and took ages to get up and dress and would appear halfway through the morning. Grannie used to come over for visits from Chantry Dene, in a Rolls Royce driven by her chauffeur who was called Martin. I think that was his surname, not his first name. She used to sometimes take Patti and me to dancing classes in Camberley, and I remember her tapping on the glass window between us and Martin to give him his instructions. The aunts turned up from time to time too. Aunt Kathleen was by far the more severe of the two. She had very straight hair which we discovered she henna-ed regularly. This intrigued us no end. I got to know her much better when I was older and came to like her no-nonsense approach to life. I think my mother got on better with Aunt Armorel; after all they were much closer in age and had spent more time together as children. Both the aunts were very good to me, and I used to go and stay with them a lot during my childhood and after I had left home. I learnt a great deal from them over the years and have always been grateful for that.

At this time we had a large old touring car called a Bean. Needless to say it was called 'the old bean' by all of us. It was a spacious car with three leather sofa seats in it and was a rather dreary grey colour. It seemed to me to have an enormously long bonnet, and there were running boards, on one side of which could be strapped spare petrol cans. Whenever we went out as a family, Father always drove and Mother sat beside him. The current baby was put in a drawer from one of our chests of drawers! It was lined with a blanket and made into comfortable bed and little Mary was deposited in it, and the whole thing put on the middle sofa seat of the car with Patti beside her. I always envied my eldest sister being given this position in the car for two reasons. Beth and I sat at the very back on either side of Nanny, who was dressed in severe grey uniform and wearing a grey felt hat, which matched her somewhat strict demeanour, as she watched us with an eagle eye; as I also suffered dreadfully from car sickness, I was sure this was always much worse where I had to sit at the back.

We were not a great family for going away on holiday. I suspect the cost of doing so with a large family was one of the reasons, but Mother did take us all to some furnished rooms in Bildeston in Suffolk one year. Pa didn't come and nor did Nanny. I suppose the former was busy with his regimental duties; he was second-in-command of his battalion at that time, and the latter was probably having her annual holiday. The name of the owner of this house in the village was Mrs De'Ath, pronounced death! This amused the older members of the family as you can imagine. It was on this holiday that I was introduced to the book *Black Beauty* by Anna Sewell. Another year we went again into furnished rooms in a farmhouse near Haverhill. I think that both my mother and my father were drawn to Suffolk as they both had family connections with the county.

By now Father had served nearly twenty-five years in the army. In those days retirement came even sooner than it does now, and my parents were faced with a growing family to bring up and educate. Besides this, Mother had never been profoundly happy in her role as a service wife, as, inevitably, it had prevented her from pursuing her farming interests; so the decision was made that, when the time came for Pa to retire, he would commute part of his pension, and with this money, they would buy a farm and Mother would at last do what she had always been happiest doing. It was farewell to a chapter in our lives, where we had been very cushioned from the outside world, and although we didn't know it then, we were to be launched into an environment where we had lots of freedom, as well as having our eyes opened to a very different way of life.

Chapter II

Kent

FTER LEAVING THE ARMY in 1935, the search began for a suitable property at a price my parents could afford. They finally found and bought a farm in Kent which was on the North Downs and on the highest point in the county. On a fine day we could see across to the Isle of Sheppey. The farm was certainly in a wonderful position with good views, though the house was not particularly attractive to look at. It was two cottages thrown into one, with two front doors, two staircases and no way of getting from one half to the other on the first floor, as well as having an awkward drawing-room with a fireplace in the middle of the room where the dividing walls had been taken down. It looked like a Victorian house with a pillared verandah tacked on to the front, which made the drawing-room very dark. I think it must have been built on the site of an earlier house, as there was a large walled kitchen garden built of nice old mellow brick, and the walls were covered with neglected cordon and espalier fruit trees. In the middle of this garden there was a large old Robin pear tree which had lovely little rosy-cheeked pears on it, but oh, the disappointment on biting into these tempting little fruits. They were as hard as bullets and designed to give one collywobbles! There were also apples, pears, damsons and greengages which were a great favourite with Mother.

This move must have been particularly difficult for my mother as she was heavily pregnant with her fifth child, but in spite of this, Father and Mother set about stocking the farm. They had decided on a dairy herd and chose Guernsey cattle. This breed was chosen because the milk has a high butter-fat content and my parents wanted to be able to make and sell butter and cream. The foundation of the herd were bought from a farmer in Somerset who was retiring. As the herd was pedigree, the cattle all had a herd name, which had to be registered with the breed society ours being Ashdown after the name of our farm.

I can still remember the names of many of the milking cows – Cowslip, Clover, Golden Gleam, Buttercup, and Jessica who was frightfully greedy and took every opportunity she could to get out, but could always be found with her head in the big butts of pig swill, slurping up the unappetizing mixture until she was thoroughly blown and uncomfortable. She moaned and groaned with discomfort afterwards but never learnt her lesson! Eventually in desperation, when Jessica was put out in a field, she had a four foot length of wood, attached in the centre, to a collar she wore round her neck. This went some way to stopping her from pushing her way through a weak point in the hedge, and making for the nearest stolen meal! We also had South Down sheep and Middle White pigs and Light Sussex chickens. All the animals were 'free range' in those days of course. The whole farm was pasture with some woodland, which consisted of two beech woods known as the Little Beeches and the Big Beeches and a copse of mostly hazelnut with quite a bit of spindleberry. There were three hundred and eighty acres in all.

My youngest sister, Frances, put in an appearance in September of that year. Aunt Armorel came to stay to give a hand with the family, while Mother and the new baby were looked after by a maternity nurse who stayed for the customary month. It was this nurse who wanted her meals to be sent to her room, which annoyed my aunt somewhat, as she found herself waiting on her. I think the feathers flew on more than one occasion. In the nursery now, we didn't have Nanny. She had retired on our move to Kent, but we had Margaret who moved with us and settled us in our new surroundings. She washed and ironed and gave the little ones their meals when they got to the high chair stage, as well as keeping the nursery clean and tidy. But this happy arrangement was not to last, as, after a time, she left to get married. Margaret was replaced by a nursemaid called Gladys who was the daughter of Mrs Tanner the cook. They both came in daily on bicycles from a nearby village. Mrs Tanner was a fairly formidable woman with iron grey hair dragged back into a bun. We stood in a certain amount of awe of her, and sometimes when we wanted something at the dining room table, which perhaps she had forgotten, one of us would be sent out to ask for it, whereupon Mrs Tanner would say 'You are as full of wants as a dog's full of airs'. We never knew if she meant airs or hairs! She was a real Cockney who in her younger days had lived in the East

End of London, and she and her family used to go down to Kent and pick hops in late summer. She eventually married a Kentish husband and brought up a family in her adopted county.

As a family, we were very self-sufficient. We grew all our own vegetables and we had our farm produce, and we always had homemade bread. Our meals were simple and wholesome, and we only ever had cake on birthdays and special occasions, and were never allowed both butter and jam on the same piece of bread, in spite of the fact that we made our own butter on the farm. Mother obviously had strong views on what we should eat, because when we went to school she wrote to the school giving them a long list of things which she didn't want us to have. I remember pork, ham, and sausages in particular being on the banned list. The school must have found this extremely tiresome, and often we ended up by having eggs for our lunch.

Mrs Tanner must have been fairly industrious. Not only did she do the cooking but she cleaned the downstairs of the house, so she was really a cook-general. Large quantities of jam and marmalade were made every year to satisfy the needs of the family. It seems a colossal amount to us nowadays but 400lbs of jam and 200lbs of Seville orange marmalade were made at the appropriate season, but one shouldn't forget that we were a large, hungry family and we could easily demolish 1lb of jam at teatime everyday. The marmalade was stored in large 7lb stone jars which one sees nowadays in bric-a-brac shops being sold as antiques! Among the jams were marrow and ginger, rhubarb, plum and damson. Besides all this activity, much of the surplus fruit was bottled and stored away for winter use. It was also a ritual with us to put our fruit stones on the sides of our plates and say 'Church, Bar, Sea, Sword, Squire, Artist, Doctor, Lord' an older and, I think, a much nicer version of 'Tinker, Tailor', and on which Mother was brought up in her childhood.

Outside there was a cowman who lived in a small four-roomed chalet-style wooden bungalow on the farm, who helped Mother on the cattle side while the other workers came in daily. My mother managed the pigs and chickens, and we had a shepherd and sheepdog. The latter lived outside entirely and in no way was she a pet. My father's input was in keeping the books and generally doing the paperwork. Pa was notoriously unpunctual and as he hated getting out of bed in the morning, this was a decided drawback for a farm where the days starts at dawn. In many ways he was fairly unpractical, while Mother had a very good business head and was thoroughly down-to-earth, but, to give him his due, he backed her to the hilt and always deferred to her on the practical running of the farm. For instance we were often secretly amused that when we were out in the car, Pa always knew a 'quick' way home, which invariably entailed going round the mulberry bush for miles and ended up in getting lost and taking twice the time! Another frequent occurrence when we were out in the car were punctures. We seemed to have more than our fair share of them, and when this happened, Father would change the wheel, but he had a habit of putting the spare wheel on the top of the car. When we were ready to set off again, he forgot all about it and the reminder came when there was an ominous thud as the wheel rolled off. There was an occasion when it was not discovered for some time, and in spite of going back to look for it, the wheel was never found. It was an unnecessary and expensive mistake.

At haymaking time in early summer a team of people turned up. It all seemed to be quite a family affair, and relatives arrived to help, and large baskets were brought full of food to be eaten in the fields and we all joined in. After the hay was cut and partially dried, it was turned by a machine called a hay kick, to dry further. Then the sweep was brought into action to gather it up and bring it to where the haystack was being built. The sweep was a machine with long wooden poles with metal tips coming out of the front at ground level, and the whole contraption was propelled forward by attaching it to the front of a tractor. The tractor drove into the lines of turned hay and gathered up as much as it could hold, and then took it to where it was needed, dumping it by backing away and leaving the hay behind. The haystacks were made up of this loose hay, and later a thatcher came in to cover it with thatch made of straw, to give it weather protection until it was needed.

The cows were all milked by hand, and in the dairy there was a separator which was a machine which separated the cream from the milk. This was necessary because we made butter from the cream while the skim milk was used to feed the pigs. Any spare full-cream milk was cooled and put into churns, collected from the farm and sold. Mother made all the butter, and if she wasn't in a hurry, we would be allowed to turn the handle of the churn. The butter was made into 1lb and ½lb packs with our special pattern on the top of each pack, made with the edge of the scotch hands, and it was then placed carefully in a large wicker basket to be taken to market with the cream which we also sold.

As well as the cows, we had a very fierce pedigree Guernsey bull. He terrified everyone and only Mother could handle him. He had to be kept firmly under control when he was in at night, and was put on a long tether when he was out during the day. He rumbled away angrily whenever anyone went near him, including the time that Pa sat us in turn on his back when he was tied up in his night quarters. I remember Mother being displeased with Father for doing this, because it was really teasing the old bull. She used to put the bull on a long staff, the end of which clipped on to his nose-ring, and lead him out daily to his wives in the field. On one famous occasion, although it was unintentional, he got the better of her. She took him to a trough to drink on the way in for the night. As he didn't want any, he suddenly tossed his head up impatiently, and caught the end of the staff in my mother's mouth. It knocked her to the ground and the bull, seizing his advantage, gored her very badly. Father and the cowman heard her screams and ran to her assistance. Somehow one caught the bull and the other rescued my mother. I think the cowman deserved a medal for catching the bull, because he was terrified of him and normally wouldn't have gone near him. We children didn't know what had happened at the time, but I remember seeing Mother being carried back to the house by Father. There was a vacant stare in her eyes, her head was lolling over Pa's arm and blood was pouring from her mouth. I was probably ten years old and I remember thinking in a very matter of fact way that she might be dead. But my mother was made of stronger stuff, and, although she was badly bruised and stayed in bed for several days, she made a full recovery.

We led a very free happy sort of life on this farm. There was lots to amuse and occupy us. There was the sight of Pa sitting in the middle of a barn with a sheet round his neck, while Mother cut his hair with the sheep clippers. There were a lot of farm cats, so there were nearly always litters of kittens hidden away in the barns. We would search them out and try to count them all; there were forty-one on one of our counts. These cats were never allowed near the house. They were purely for mice and rat catching on the farm. I am sure that, unbeknown to us, there must have been a periodic cull of these litters of kittens in order to control the numbers. When the weather was very frosty and cold, and there had been a litter of piglets, we were given little tins of vaseline to grease their tails to prevent them getting frost-bitten. One of the old sows was called Gloriana, and her claim to fame was that she always had enormous litters, for she would regularly produce seventeen, eighteen or even, on one occasion, nineteen piglets. The sows, who were farrowing, were in special pens with a low rail round the perimeter which enabled the piglets to escape from being lain on when the sow lay down, as they are sometimes rather careless mothers. We seemed to go in for rather fierce animals; we had a boar who had to be treated with a certain amount of respect because he had some fairly sharp tusks and he knew how to use them when he was annoyed. One day he went for Mother and ripped into her gumboots, putting a nasty gash in her leg. We children never went into the field if he was out there.

All this was a great education for us, but Patti, Beth when she was old enough, and I went to a day school in Ashford. Getting there and back was quite an expedition. We were taken the four miles to Lenham by Pa in the farm car, an old and somewhat unreliable Morris Cowley, to catch a bus to take us the nine miles to Ashford. When Father was on the school run, we often arrived late, screeching into the square in the village with the bus waiting for us, or to find that it had left, and then we would chase down the main road towards Ashford to catch it at the next stop! All the regulars on the bus knew us, and a cheer went up on our belated arrival. On very rare occasions, we were taken to the bus by one of the farm workers, which meant we actually arrived early. This allowed us the luxury of going into a little sweet shop to buy a quarter pound of dolly mixture for 1d. We then legged it like mad along the bus route to the next stop, so that our bus fare matched the money we had left in our pockets. For our return journey, we came on the bus again, but this time, on alighting, we had to face a four mile walk, a lot of it uphill, to get home. We were told that we must stay together and never to accept a lift from a stranger. Nothing changes!

During this walk home, we passed a wood in which some Romany gypsies lived. We were fascinated by the way of life that they followed and would creep along a lane towards them to try and get a look without being seen. They looked bronzed and unwashed with tangled hair and very ragged clothing. One of the women had very dark hair drawn back into a bun and on one occasion she came to our house selling wooden clothes pegs, which were called dolly pegs. I remember having in the back of my mind the fear that gypsies stole little children! Beth was about six and seven at the time we were doing this. I think it was a long way to walk daily at that age, but it does illustrate that we were not mollycoddled and were also trusted to be responsible and sensible. There was an incident though which rather blew that trust out of the ground. Beth had been attracted by some bright red berries in the hedgerow, and ate some. A few hours later she was very ill, and a doctor was called. After some very unpleasant treatment of salt and water to make her get rid of the poison, she mercifully recovered. She had eaten the very poisonous berries of the plant Lords and Ladies.

On one occasion when we were in the old Morris going to Lenham, the car became overheated and burst into flames, and that was the end of that. We also had a large family car which had replaced the Bean. This was an Austin 24 Tourer, and it was used for all family outings. Again I never remembered the hood being put up, but it must have rained sometimes! It was in this car that Beth used to become very car sick and from the back she relayed her problem to me. I didn't dare tell Pa direct as he could be pretty intolerant of complaints of this nature. Mother was informed and when she told Father, he called out 'Put your head out of the window'! Not a lot of sympathy there. By now it was little Fanny who was bedded down in the drawer for our outings.

I was always very happy at school, but likewise I loved the freedom of the holidays. We used to go for quite long walks, gathering wild flowers and interesting ourselves in our surroundings. Living on chalk downlands, there were a lot of special species growing wild on our land including the rare bee orchid, and interesting butterflies which were reasonably common then, but alas have become quite rare now. We learnt to identify them, and to name the different wild birds.

Discipline was pretty strict at home, and for serious misdemeanours we would get a caning from Father. This was always administered with his silver-knobbed regimental pace stick. Beth and I discovered where he kept it. It was behind the cistern in the upstairs lavatory. We debated whether we dared remove it and hide it, but just didn't have the nerve to carry through such an audacious act. Pa was famous for his quick temper which blew up just as quickly as it subsided, so we wisely refrained.

Once on a very hot summer's day, Beth and I were feeling particularly hot, and we longed to have somewhere to go for a swim, so we undressed down to our cotton knickers and took a dip in the sheep dip. It was the first of a number of occasions when we sneaked off and did this. Looking back on the event, I can't think how we could have done such a thing. The dip was a murky, slimy green and dirty, and I believe had arsenic in it. We had the added complication of washing out our underwear and trying to get it back to its normal colour of pink check cotton. We never told our parents what we had done at the time, but many years later I did, and Mother was duly horrified.

Another incident which had a more lasting effect was the time when three of us got cattle ringworm. Some of our herd had become affected, and unwisely, I think with hindsight, we were allowed to help to rub sulphur ointment on their infected places. I had ringworm on my head and had to have my head shaved in order to treat it. This meant losing a term of school, and when I did finally go back, I had to wear a beret to cover the dressing and conceal my lack of hair. It was a painful moment to walk into that schoolroom and to face the questioning stares of my friends, who thought I had forgotten to take my hat off.

During this time in Kent, my parents decided that we should have a pony. They answered an advertisement in *The Times* from a woman near Tenterden, who had a grey for sale. We were all highly amused when this woman wrote to my mother and signed the letter, 'Yours sincerely Mrs Boddington'! Patti and I went with Mother to look at him, and to try him out. A price was agreed – only £15 – and he was ours. He was very dappled and true to his looks he was called Dapple, but we renamed him Puncy, and he was always called that by us. My father taught me to ride on him. I had to learn bare-back, with only the bridle on him at first, and until I had mastered this, I was not allowed to saddle him up. As I became more confident, I tried jumping a fence and took a very nasty tumble into a ditch, including a bed of nettles. Not only was my pride dented but I was slightly concussed. I was brought in and put to bed and a doctor called. This incident showed me the unexpected tender side of Pa, who fussed over me in a way that I hadn't met before. He also proved to be just as caring when I woke up with the hideous nightmares which plagued me in childhood.

I would only allow him to comfort me. I also remember another occasion when my parents came up to the nursery late one evening and woke us up, so that we could see the Aurora Borealis or Northern Lights in the sky. I can see that wonderful warm pinky-red glow in the sky to this day. It was the only time I have ever seen them.

Puncy proved to be a very amusing pony and he had all sorts of tricks up his sleeve. He was extremely difficult to keep in a field and could clear a five bar gate with no trouble, and so was more out than in, but when on the loose, he invariably came to the back door. He would press the bell with his nose and wait expectantly for it to be opened, and to be given some sweets. Mrs Tanner was not amused! Even less so when, one day when she wasn't in the room, we walked him round her kitchen table and he left his calling card! He always nuzzled our pockets for something to eat, and when we fed him his oats in a wooden half-barrel, after finishing he would turn the container over and stand on it with all four feet close together on the base. He refused to get down without a 'clever boy' reward. Then one day a woman with her teenage daughter turned up. They had seen Puncy in the field and thought they recognized him, and they came to ask us where we had got him from. It seemed that he had belonged to them once, and they had bought him from a circus. This explained all!

Although we had a telephone at Ashdown, we didn't have mains electricity. Many an evening we would be reading or playing cards, when the lights got dimmer and dimmer, and finally petered out. There would be a scramble for candles, while Pa took out a torch to get the generator going again. We also had a very deep well which supplied all our water. It was 485ft deep and went down to where the River Stour flowed underground. The motor which pumped the water was at the bottom of the well, and when it went wrong, which was frequently, an engineer had to come out from Ashford to fix it. This meant him being lowered in a box on a cable attached to our tractor 485ft away. The tractor, on a signal, edged forward very slowly, lowering the engineer and his tools, to the bottom. I remember being allowed to look down the well, being held firmly by a parent, to see the tiny dot of light from his torch. On one occasion, the box lowering the man caught on some iron bars criss-crossing the well a little way down, and he was in danger of being tipped out. There was much shouting and panic to stop the tractor which was some distance away. Fortunately all was well, but this particular man refused to go down again, quite understandably I think. In fact after this incident, we had difficulty in persuading anyone to go down and repair the pump.

During the winter evenings, we were encouraged to read or amuse ourselves in a worthwhile way. Pa invented a card game called 'Muggins' which was long and complicated, and the more people who played the better. He was also very good at story telling, which he made up as he went along, giving us a new instalment every evening. One of these was his answer to Snow White, and was called 'Soot Black and the Seven Giants'! Bedtime reading was nearly always from one of the Fairy Book series, i.e. *The Pink Fairy Book* and *The Blue Fairy Book*.

In 1936, we had another visitation from Lady Longman. It was on this occasion that she gave Patti and me our first watches. They were silver and had black straps. Patti's had a red twelve and mine a blue one, on the face. I was thrilled to be given such a grown-up present. Looking back, I cannot think how my parents, who were very busy with the farm, entertained LL as my mother called her, or how they accommodated her now that there were seven of us in the family. She came from a completely different world in our eyes, and every time we looked at her, she was wearing a different outfit, and was a strange misfit among our farm surroundings.

In the summer holidays of 1937, I went to stay with Aunt Armorel again. I was put on a train for London, and met by my aunt who was living in London at that time. We went to see my grandfather, who lived in Kensington, and he took me out to lunch which was a treat in itself, and in doing so we went on an open-topped double decker bus. There were lots of them on the ordinary bus routes in London at that time, though possibly they were only used in fine weather. From there we went to see a cousin whom I had never met, before going down to Tonbridge to stay with the Llanmorris family whom I had first met on Hayling Island. I remember so well being given a needle and thread and helping to sew on what seemed like hundreds of name tapes for their daughter Meg who was off to Roedean that September. Another visit which I made at about this time was to go and stay with Grannie in Surrey. Grannie was a widow by now and she was living in Ripley. When I arrived, I found Great Aunt Jessie was staying there too. This was especially nice for me, as I had not seen much of her over the years. One of the expeditions on that visit was to go to Hampton Court Palace. It was a lovely experience. We went round some of the State Rooms, and then sat in the garden and ate a picnic. I must have worn out my grandmother because after lunch she suggested that I should go into the famous maze while she sat on a bench and had a little rest. I remember being a little worried in case I got lost and couldn't find my way back to her, but in fact I had no trouble at all.

By 1938 war clouds were gathering in Europe. We, as children, were quite oblivious of this of course, but I think that it did have some bearing on my parents' plans, but the worry nearer home was that the farm was not supporting the expenses of the family. They had had a certain amount of bad luck with the cattle getting ringworm, and after that the herd got Johns Disease, which was an added blow as it affected the income from the dairy products. Johns Disease was a wasting illness and the cattle got terribly thin and some died. I remember large deep pits being dug on the farm into which the carcasses were tipped and buried. I will never forget the stench of rotting flesh. I have never understood why, but Father had one of his famous flights of fancy earlier that year, and decided to build a loggia on to the side of the house. By the time they were ready to sell up, this building had been finished, but we never moved into it. The builders had left it in a bit of an untidy state, and the door into the house had not been made. It did seem a dreadful white elephant.

The whole place went on the market, and the furniture went into store. Mother moved into the cowman's bungalow with Mary and Fanny while Patti, Beth and I were shipped off to Aunt Kathleen who was managing a sort of Health Clinic/Christian Community near Doddington, for a Doctor of Divinity who was the owner. It was an odd place altogether. There were patients there for 'the cure', I am not sure if this was physical or spiritual, as there was a chapel which played quite an important part in the daily routine, as well as stoned-lined baths in which the inmates sat in wheelchairs and had douches. We, very naughtily, used to peep through the cracks in the door to watch these rotund ladies having their treatment. The whole place was strictly vegetarian. It was a strange environment for three young children, but I suppose my parents were desperate to know what to do with us, and we were able to continue to go to Ashford School from there. This time we bicycled to a point where we could catch the bus, leaving our bicycles somewhere arranged by aunt. At least at school we had a good square meal in the middle of the day. I think the ban on sausages must have been lifted by then, because I remember coming back to Margaret Manor, as the community was called, and saying teasingly to Aunt Kathleen how much we had enjoyed our sausages for lunch. This was done deliberately to annoy her. We knew meat-eating disgusted her. Poor Aunt Kathleen. She had no experience of looking after children, except her own sisters some 25 years earlier, and I am sure we were a great trial to her. She was very strict with us, and consequently, I expect, we were naughtier than usual. We had to attend Chapel regularly, and had to learn the collect each Sunday. No harm in that. Dr Josiah Oldfield the owner of the whole set-up, expounded the Gospel from the pulpit. In my childish eyes he looked like God. He had pure white wavy hair down to his collar, a flowing white beard and piercing blue eyes.

Chapter III

Norfolk

WHILE ALL THIS WAS GOING ON, Pa had joined the Royal Air Force, partly to do his bit for his country and more urgently to support his family. He was posted to Norfolk as an Intelligence Officer to an RAF Station of Bomber Command. He was fifty years old and I think he knew that the army wouldn't want him at that age for active service, while in the RAF he could enjoy a static and worthwhile job not too far from home. In fact he did a very valuable and interesting job all through the war, and was twice mentioned in dispatches and wore the oak leaf on his medal ribbons.

The farm eventually sold and Mother moved up to Norfolk, adding Mary and little Fanny to the brood with Aunt Kathleen. Mother lived for a time in an hotel in Swaffham while she and Pa desperately house hunted. Temporarily they settled for furnished rooms in a farmhouse in a village near King's Lynn. The great day came for the parents to come back to Kent and collect us. We were all very thankful to be together again, though I don't think any of us suffered from home-sickness during this period. We knew it had to be and so that was that! As a family we were undemonstrative and accepted completely the arrangements which were made. Patti was very much the eldest sister and had tried to keep us in order. Although I was only 13 months younger than her, I seemed to knock about with Beth more. Patti was rather goody-goody in my youthful eyes, while with Beth I was 'in charge'!

The biggest snag about the furnished rooms was the fact that Mother had to share a kitchen with the owner of the house. It cannot have been easy. Again I was lucky in having an invitation to stay with Aunt Armorel, so off I went once more, this time by train to London. On these journeys, I was always put in the charge of the guard, and my mother's cousin, John Boyes, met me and gave me lunch in a restaurant, which made me feel very grown up. I was then delivered to my aunt who was living on the outskirts of Camberley, and what I especially remember about this particular visit was being taken to my very first opera, in fact it was my very first visit to a theatre anywhere. The opera was Verdi's *Rigoletto* performed by the Carl Rosa Opera Company; I was enchanted by the whole outing. The eldest of the Llanmorris boys arrived in army uniform, in preparation for the war ahead. In fact there was a noticeable number of young men about wearing uniform. The smell of war was in the air.

It was while we were in these furnished rooms, that we used to occasionally go to King's Lynn to shop. On one of these outings Fanny, who was nearly four, got lost between shops. There was a frantic counting of heads but to no avail. Mother left Patti in charge of Mary and Beth, and hauled me off with her to retrace our steps. After a fruitless search we went to a police station in the town. There behind the counter, so to speak, was little Fanny sucking her thumb and looking quite calm and in control. The sergeant behind the desk said they had found her outside the door and had brought her in, and questioned her. He said they had asked her her name and how old she was, to which she had answered quite correctly. On being asked where she lived she said 'Where it is all green'. The sergeant then asked her whether her father was a clean man or a dirty man! This he hastened to explain was because they thought they might get a clue as to whether he was an office worker or perhaps a coalman! Anyway the conversation had come to an abrupt end when Fanny drew herself up and said 'My father is a gentleman'. Everyone was very amused, while Mother, in her 'here you are, my good man' sort of voice, asked the police how much she owed them. They pushed a charity collecting box towards her. I never knew what she 'paid' to redeem Fanny, but no doubt she was relieved to have her back safe and sound.

After some time in our cramped furnished rooms, my parents found a furnished house in the market town of Watton. They were still looking for somewhere suitable to buy but nothing had turned up so they bought themselves a little breathing space by this move.

The house in Watton was an uninspiring Victorian villa, in fact it was called York Villa. It had a thick laurel hedge screening us from the road, a bit of garden at the front, and a bit more at the back. Inside there was a sitting-room, one couldn't call it a drawing room, which had black horse-hair armchairs and sofa, which prickled one's legs when sat on. There was a morning room off this room, and a small dining-room and kitchen. Upstairs we somehow all managed to fit in. I remember the bathroom had pale green-painted tongue and groove wood all round the walls. We had a maid called Phyllis who was pleasant enough, but a bit of a scatterbrain, who was 'walking out' with a young man in the airforce. It was later on, while Phyllis was in our employ, that there was a General Election. Mother arranged to take Phyllis to the polling station and no doubt telling her who she should vote for on the way. On the return journey Mother, in her rather autocratic way, asked her who she had voted for. To which Phyllis replied 'Oh I voted for the Labour candidate, I would always vote for Mr Churchill's party!' Mother, being a true blue Conservative, was furious that she had actually taken a misinformed Labour voter to the polls.

During that summer at York Villa, the question of where we were to be educated had to be sorted out. My parents had discussed the various possibilities and had decided on a small dame school started up by the Honourable Mrs Richard Coke at Weasenham Hall. She had started this school really because she had her own children to educate and wanted to have some other suitable children to join them. This was to be Patti, Beth and me, but I rebelled. It really was the last sort of school I wanted to go to, as I had always wanted to go to a large school where there were plenty of opportunities and facilities. Even then, at the age of 12, I had wider visions and ambitions. I think my parents were non-plussed and they tried hard to make me come round to their way of thinking, but no, I would not be placated. Anyway after much sighing, and, I expect, penny counting, they gave in and Patti and Beth went to Weasenham, and I went daily by bus to Norwich High School. I remember at Christmas time, our all going over to the Cokes at Weasenham Hall to a party, and in the hall there was a roaring fire with a leather-seated fire guard round it, called a bum-warmer! I was amused at the vulgarity of the name!

By the summer of 1939, war was very imminent, and on the fateful day – September 3rd, we all sat round a hired wireless to hear the announcement that we were at war with Germany. Soon after the outbreak of war, we were issued with gas masks. They were in cardboard boxes with a string attached for carrying on one's shoulder. At first we dutifully carried them wherever we went but as the months went by we became much less conscientious about them, and eventually, we used to wear them when we were peeling onions and grating horseradish! – though we did have to take them to school every day. By now we had a Rover saloon car, the first we had ever had without celluloid windows and a collapsible hood, which Pa had to have to get him to and from his work, while we all had bicycles or we walked.

We stayed in the Watton house for some months and we didn't see much of Pa, who appeared from time to time, but we later discovered that his work was briefing and de-briefing bomber pilots before and after their raids on Germany, and so he was very much on duty at night. Where we lived, we were surrounded by airfields, and later, during the Battle of Britain, we would lie in bed and hear our planes setting out on their missions, and in the early hours before dawn we would often be awakened by the overhead drone of their return. I think it wasn't until we were subjected to the Germans bombing us, that we began to realize more fully what it was all about.

Every Sunday evening we settled down, and Mother and the older sisters read aloud from one of the classics, or from some other suitable book. I remember one such book being *The Discretions of Decima*. We read perhaps a chapter a week. We made our own entertainment and used to get up performances of poetry reading, plays, singing and piano playing, especially at Christmas time when we entertained our parents. We only listened to the wireless to hear the news, never for anything more pleasurable.

Again I loved every minute of my time at school. I was able to do far more than my sisters, but they seemed quite happy with their lot so we were all suited. My mother took us out for walks and picnics. She was a very competent watercolourist and often had a sketch pad with her. She had had little time for such pursuits when we were in Kent, but now she had a little time on her hands and could indulge in this hobby. She was also a dab hand at modelling with plasticine, as one might expect from someone who might have been a sculptress, but she always modelled animals, usually cattle; I loved to watch her creating in this way.

During our time at Watton, whenever there was a house to look at and the opportunity to do so, we would set off in the Rover to view properties which were on the market. I think Mother's original idea was to have a house cow and a few chickens to ease the rationing and thus help to feed a growing and hungry family. I don't think they were looking for a full-blown farm, but more a smallholding with outbuildings and a bit of land. In fact something which my mother could manage without employing labour. My parents looked at some pretty hopeless places but I do remember one lovely old place we looked at, which was really a proper farm but it was very tumbled-down and we would never have had the capital to put it in order, so it was sadly not for us.

Meantime I was settling down in my new surroundings at school. The large Regency-style house had been considerably enlarged when it became a school, and the whole building stood in spacious grounds. There was woodland, and playing fields for lacrosse, hard and grass tennis courts and netball pitches. Lacrosse was the chosen sport, because some years before a girl had been killed on the hockey field, and the school had vowed never to play that sport again. It was ironic really as one was perhaps more likely to receive a blow on the head in a game of lacrosse than in hockey. Inside there was a fine library, which particularly appealed to me, as I was an avid reader. Looking back, I can say that the teaching was excellent, though some of the staff were a little elderly, because they had stayed on after retirement age, because of the war.

Inevitably the subjects which one enjoyed most were the ones which were taught the best. My particular favourites were Languages, History, English Literature, Art and Music. My retentive memory even in those days stood me in good stead as I found it easy to memorize poetry and Shakespearean speeches and to revise facts for end of term exams. I was in the school choir and had piano lessons too. Our English Mistress was D. K. Broster, the writer of historical novels such as *The Flight of the Heron*, who was quite well-known in her day. We also had a Royal Academician as our Art Mistress. We were very privileged, and I certainly blossomed with all these opportunities and I hope I can say that I appreciated and made the most of what was on offer.

Chapter IV

The War Years

EVENTUALLY MY PARENTS FOUND A PROPERTY which suited them and which they could afford. They must have been thankful that the search was over, and life in a state of suspended animation was to come to an end. It was a period house, the older part being seventeenth century, with a Queen Anne wing. The whole place was somewhat neglected, but I suspect Mother and Father couldn't afford to buy something in tip-top order. It had a large over-grown garden, orchards, and out-buildings including stables, a double coach house, with a hayloft above, and three cottages backing on to these buildings. There was a fair-sized murky pond, a large kitchen garden and a few acres of pasture. They paid £800 for the property, which seems staggering to us now, but was a fair price in 1940. There was certainly plenty of scope for Mother's farming activities, and lots of space for her five daughters. There was much basic work to be done to bring the whole area under control, as it had been empty for some time.

The house was in the middle of a village some four miles from the market town of Swaffham, in south west Norfolk. It stood back from the road with a large cobbled yard in the front, which we only discovered under gravel and weeds much later on, and surrounded by a bank and tall hedge which gave us a certain amount of seclusion. There was a railway station about three-quarters of a mile away to which we walked to catch the train to our respective schools. By now Patti had joined me at Norwich High School, while Beth, Mary and Fanny when she was old enough went to another High School a little nearer.

As the years went by, we came to look upon this house as our real and permanent home. After our itinerant life initially, and the short-lived period in Kent, it was where I lived for five years, and for a further twelve it was my homebase after I grew up. Life was certainly becoming very different, partly because of the war, and the fact that we no longer had such a team of people to look after us in various ways. It made me realize how cushioned we had been before. In spite of this, Mother was very lucky to have a maid throughout the war. She was a very able pleasant young woman called Joan. She used to arrive on her bicycle from some five miles away, getting to us by eight in the morning, and leaving again after getting the tea ready in the afternoon. We used to meet her every morning when we were walking to the station to catch our train to school. She would wave and say 'Good morning Miss Patti, Miss Edith, Miss Beth, Miss Mary, Miss Fanny,' by which time she was almost out of earshot. We also had a woman from the village who came in daily to do 'the rough' as it was called, such as scrubbing the quarry tiles in the scullery and other

5. An aerial view of our Norfolk home.

downstairs chores. Mother hated doing indoor jobs, and with this help and five daughters she was able to concentrate on the outdoor activities.

We had found a funny little dressmaker in our early days in Norfolk, and she used to run up little skirts for us and do running repairs. She was quite elderly, short and very round, and a bit like Mrs Tiggy Winkle. She was a widow and had had twenty-six children, all from one husband, which amazed us all, especially as she lived in a very small cottage in which she had lived all her married life. I think what made a lasting impression with me was the fact that one of her older sons had predeceased her when he had passed middle age, which seemed extraordinary to me. She spoke with a very broad Norfolk dialect and was quite difficult to understand to our untrained ears, but one of her favourite sentences was to say 'We'll put a little bit of petersham on it'. We used to have bets as to how long it would be before she said it when we went to see her.

When we were a little older we learnt to make our own clothes, and I remember cutting out with a pair of curved nail scissors! Mother had an old Frister and Rossmann sewing machine, which we all used. On one of Beth's sewing exploits, she had some long seams to do on the machine, and, as this was a rather boring task, she asked me to turn the handle for her. Being a keen reader, I had a book in the other hand and was not watching what I was doing. The needle jammed. Beth squawked and I looked up. I had impaled my sister. The needle had gone through her nail and finger and trapped her.

In the early years of the war, Norwich was subjected to some fearsome bombing raids by the Germans, and so my parents did not like the idea of our going by train right into Norwich station daily. To overcome this, we had to keep our bicycles at Hethersett station, some five miles out of Norwich. It was really quite a flog for us and it always meant that we arrived at school in a bit of a rush so as not to be late. As the last train in the afternoon left Hethersett at 3.20 p.m., we had to leave at 2.30 p.m. which meant that we missed nearly all the afternoon lessons. We had piles of homework, some of which we did on the hour-long train journey, and arrived home exhausted. It certainly put a consid-erable strain on us to do this daily, as well as the frustration it must have caused to those who were trying to teach us. After a year or so the school finally said that they couldn't guarantee to get us through our exams unless we became boarders, and so that is what happened –

a further strain on the family purse I am sure. Our housemistress was a real stickler for propriety and good manners, which was very good for us, though I may not have thought so at the time.

Back at home, Mother had lost no time in investing in a house cow and chickens to supplement our rations. She made butter but didn't have the equipment she had had on the farm in Kent. Now she perched on the corner of the kitchen table with a bowl of cream and a hand whisk, beating and beating until gradually the cream became butter. It was a laborious process. We used to have big blocks of salt which were broken down to salt the butter. the skim milk was used to feed to a pig owned by Bob Gage who lived in one of our cottages. This was a joint effort in that we all contributed to the pig's rations, as during the war, one was allowed to kill one pig a year for home consumption. As you can imagine, this was very welcome in such times of food shortage. Every bit of the pig was used; the fat was rendered down for cooking, and we made pig's cheek brawn. Many old houses had cold cellars where this could be kept. Other means of preserving was to smoke or salt both meat and fish. Our surplus eggs were put into waterglass which was a liquid which sealed the egg shell and thus preserved the egg. They could be kept for some months like this, though were never used as boiled eggs, but rather for putting into cooked dishes. We tried one year to dry apple rings in the linen cupboard, but it was definitely not a success. I suspect it was because the linen cupboard was never warm enough.

We had a cellar which was never used by us, because, as it was sometimes flooded, it had been boarded up when we bought the house, but we did have a very cold north-facing stone-floored dairy which we used as a larder. I don't think we knew anyone who had a refrigerator for their food and generally speaking few, if any, had central heating. All we had in our larder was a meat safe hanging from the ceiling, so the blue bottle flies could be kept off the meat, while on the shelves where the rest of the food was kept, there were muslin covers to thwart any mouse which might have had designs on our leftovers. There were also big bowls of milk which were left on the shelves overnight for the cream to come to the surface. This was then skimmed off for the butter-making when the cream was lovely and thick.

We had tenants in all three of our cottages. I have already mentioned Bob Gage. He and his wife were a sterling couple. Bob had been a teamsman all his working life. This meant that he had worked with cart-horses. He was a strong sturdy man with a good sense of humour. He had quite a tummy on him and always wore a leather strap as a belt which went under his paunch to hold up his breeches and on his legs he wore leather gaiters and he had strong leather boots on his feet. I don't ever remember seeing him without a flat cap on his head, even in his cottage. We often wondered whether he went to bed in it! He was a great character and a true countryman. He wandered round with his airgun and if asked what he was planning for the morning he said with a broad Norfolk accent, 'There is a little old gentleman with a red waistcoat who is eating the buds on the fruit trees', which meant he was going out to shoot the odd wayward cock bullfinch. On another occasion he would say 'There is a little old gentleman in a black velvet jacket who is working in the kitchen garden'. He was on his way to set some mole traps to catch the offender. Bob would skin his victims and sell the moleskins.

Once a year he would bring one of his carthorses into our kitchen garden, to plough and clean the ground for the following season. The horse he most often brought was called Prince. Prince had a curly moustache on his top lip which always amused us children, but the thing which Bob did, which amused us even more, was to say as he walked behind Prince, 'Whisst Prince, do it.' Whereupon prince lifted his tail and 'did it.' 'It' duly manured the ground and was ploughed in. Prince seemed able to oblige on command!

Mrs Gage was our 'daily' for some years. She was a portly woman who always wore high-heeled shoes. She had chestnut hair coiled into earphones on her ears, and the rest looped into a bun at the back. She always wore a flowered apron and like Bob and his cap, we imagined she slept in her apron too! One day she was cleaning the hall in our house, when she put her heel through what must have been a rotten floor board. As it was almost impossible to get repairs done during the war, we had to remember to keep a rug over the hole. This was because Mother bred Siamese cats, and when there was a litter of kittens about, given the chance, they would go down this hole and scamper about under the house, sometimes a long way from the hole. The only way we could get them out was to sharpen the carving knife at the entrance; being avid meat eaters they would rush from all corners of their subterranean playground, thinking they were going to be fed. It never failed.

Old Marshall, as we called him, came to live in one of the cottages later on in the war. He used to get in our coal, chop kindling wood, clean our shoes and do other little handyman jobs. In the third somewhat larger cottage, lived a mother and daughter. Her husband was away in the army and her sister, who was also a 'temporary' war widow, came to live with her during the war years. All these tenants paid a weekly rent for their cottages. The rents were three shillings a week for the two smaller cottages, and five shillings for the larger. My mother gave them a pint of milk daily.

When Pa was at home on leave, he and Bob would sometimes go out rabbit shooting together. The meat was a welcome addition to our war-time fare. Early on in our time in this house, Father acquired a Clumber spaniel for the odd shooting day he was invited to. At some stage this dog was changed for a black and white springer spaniel. Both these dogs were kennelled outside in Bob Gage's garden, and never came into the house. As the pressure of Pa's war work took its toll, he had little time for these pursuits, besides which Mother was really not very keen on shooting as a sport, and the dog, I suppose, was sold. They really weren't with us for very long. Mother was also very anti-blood sports. Many years later I met someone from our part of Norfolk and we talked about those early years. He asked me who my mother hunted with, to which I replied that she was rather anti such things. Being a hunting man, he was horrified and asked in a concerned way 'Oh dear, how long has she been like that?' as though it was some kind of dreadful illness. Certainly in those days in Norfolk, you were considered somewhat outside the pale if you didn't hunt.

When we were finally installed in our new surroundings, Puncy was sent for. He had been looked after by friends in Kent, until we were ready for him. He continued with his little tricks. Another very irritating thing he learnt to do was to break his girth when we saddled him up. He didn't relish being put into harness, and when the saddle was put on his back, he would take a deep breath and hold it. Without realizing at first what he was doing, we did up the buckles of the girth. The little devil would then blow out his tummy and break the strap. We got wise to this and would wait until he could hold his breath no longer, and then do up the fastenings before he had time to do anything about it. He was also very difficult to catch. We would go out into the paddock, one of the older members of the family concealing his bridle, and make a big circle round him. Then as we gradually closed in on him, he would look round, take stock and break through at the weakest spot, i.e. where my youngest sister stood, and so we had to start all over again.

Puncy loved music. This was obviously a memory of his circus days. We used to take out an old wind-up gramophone and some 78 r.p.m. records to the paddock, put him on a leading rein and he would prance round on his hind legs, turn round on the spot and get very excited and neigh loudly. He might almost have been a candidate for the Spanish Riding School! He loved the sound of the huntsman's horn and was in danger of breaking out of his field if the hunt came through the village. We used to wrap Bronco lavatory paper round a comb and blow through it to imitate the horn, and he nearly went mad with excitement.

We inevitably had all the standard childhood ailments such as mumps, chicken pox, German measles, and whooping cough. Needless to say these illnesses went on for quite a long time as each child went through the whole quarantine period. Pa made up two little ditties for us to say with our plum stones. They were 'Orange blossom, Roses, Daisies, Weeds', being what we would carry at our wedding, and 'Mumps, Measles, Chicken Pox, 'Flu' what we might contract on our honeymoon! In 1941 when I was 14, I somehow got scarlet fever. Nobody knew how I got it, and mercifully none of my sisters contracted the disease. In those days it was normal for a patient to be sent to an isolation hospital. My mother wouldn't hear of this, and insisted that I should be nursed at home. Our family doctor was no match for Mother when her mind was made up, and so it came to pass that I was put in isolation within our house. This meant being in a bedroom with a sheet soaked in disinfectant and always kept wet, being pinned over the outside of the closed door. The only people who were allowed in my bedroom were the doctor, my parents and Joan who brought up my meals. I was in bed for eight weeks and had complications. It must have been a worrying time for my parents, but as I gradually got better, Pa brought me things to help to pass the time. One was the book *The Count of Monte Cristo* by Alexander Dumas. I loved that book. I also knitted a green woollen cable-stitch cardigan. My knitting had progressed since those far off days and my first disastrous efforts. Pa also brought some embroidery for me to do. This was in the shape of an afternoon tea cloth with a transfer pattern of flowers all round the border. I finished that and still have it in my home to this day.

Another spin off of my isolation was to live through some of the frightening German bombing raids which often happened at night. I would lie in bed and see the flash of a nearby explosion, count the seconds and wait for the noise of the bomb landing. The shorter the time between the flash and the thud, the closer the bomb. I knew I must not come out of my room, and that Mother was up and comforting my younger sisters. I tried to keep control of myself, but sometimes in desperation I would ring a large brass bell I had, to attract attention. Looking back I can now imagine how lonely and hard it must have been for Mother to have to cope with this sort of thing alone.

As I slowly recovered from this long illness, I remember the real agony of having to start to use my legs again. It was like learning to walk all over again and was very painful. How very different it was in those days. We weren't great people for calling the doctor but when we did need him, he always came to the house. I don't ever remember going to a surgery for treatment. I don't think anyone did in those days.

During the war we had very strict rationing, though of course we were luckier than some in that, by living in the country, we were able to supplement our meals. We used to collect watercress from a stream near us, we picked blackberries and nuts in season, and there was an area near the church where we found a sort of ground nut which we harvested by digging down with a penknife in the pasture. They were delicious. In the warm September days we went mushrooming. We knew the best places to go, and would go armed with a large wicker basket, possibly that same basket which held our packs of butter when we were at Ashdown Farm. Then we would come back laden with pounds and pounds of mushrooms and we would all contribute our bacon ration and the necessary butter to making a wonderful feast. We grew a lot of fruit and all our own vegetables. Once a week after dark, a van came through the village with what must have been blackmarket goods, in the form of tinned sausage meat. We were so thankful to be able to buy a tin, that I am afraid we didn't ask questions. We were restricted to one small tin per household. The van and its driver disappeared into the dark of the night until the following week.

At harvest time we used to go gleaning in the stubble of nearby wheat fields. Mother used to give us 3*d* a bucket to bring wheat home for her chickens. It was the only time I ever knew her to pay us for doing a job. Another idea she had once was for us to go along the railway line and gather up any sugar beet, which were rather like enormous overgrown parsnips, which had dropped off the goods trains taking them to the sugar factory in King's Lynn. These were brought home, chopped up and put in a saucepan on the kitchen range and boiled up, in a vain endeavour to extract some sugar from them, but the resulting liquid was disgusting and tasted earthy and horrible. It goes to show how desperate we were! Another more successful gathering we did on the railway line, was to pick up coal which had dropped off the passing goods trains. This stretched our meagre fuel supplies a little further.

The Rover had been laid up for the duration, and was on chocks in the garage. Its only use after this was as a sort of smoking den. Let me explain. Pa was a cigarette smoker and whenever he stubbed out a cigarette, we would secretly collect up the stubs and when nobody was about, we would get in the Rover and have a little smoke, followed by a little munch of parsley to take away the smell. Father had acquired a small rather racy little two-seater with a soft top. It was very low on the ground and made a dreadful noise as he roared off to go on duty. We called it the Bullet because the back of it looked just like that.

This left us without any wheeled transport except for our bicycles, and so Mother decided to buy a governess cart and put Puncy between the shafts. Little did we know what we were in for when we decided to do this. He didn't like it one little bit. It was difficult enough to catch him, get him harnessed up and back him in between the shafts, but when we set off and he realized there was something 'chasing' him from behind, it all took a bit of firm management. The little traffic there was on the roads was quite a hazard in itself, but when it was raining, he saw himself in every puddle and shied at invisible bogeys in the hedge. In fact he was quite a liability, but Mother was nothing daunted and was determined to be able to go shopping in Swaffham with him. We also went to East Dereham which was some nine miles away and it took us nearly an hour to get there. As the trap would only hold five of us comfortably, on shorter journeys, one of us had to ride a bicycle. We called it 'run and tie'. The cyclist went ahead and after an agreed distance would dismount, leave the bicycle on the verge and walk. Meantime the trap when it reached the abandoned cycle, would stop to tip out a passenger, who took over the cycling while the trap continued on until the walker was picked up. It was a system which worked well and gave everyone a fair share. Although

6. Puncy and the infamous governess cart loaded up for an expedition during the war.

there were not many proper hills in our part of Norfolk, there was one steep little rise on the way to Swaffham, and then several of us would dismount to make it easier for Puncy to pull the trap up the hill.

In the early years of the war, a documentary film was made on the RAF station where Pa was working. I think it was made to show the British people how we were fighting back and to raise morale. There were no professional actors, but the actual people filmed were doing their appointed jobs. Their names were changed, and the film was called *Target for Tonight*. There was great excitement in the family when the film went on general release, and came to Norwich. Mother took us all on the train, despite the danger of bombing raids, to see Father on the silver screen. Some forty years later, I had the chance to acquire the video of this film, which was a very nostalgic experience. The only other time we ever went to the cinema, was a little time after this expedition, when we went to the little cinema in Swaffham and saw Charlie Chaplin in *The Great Dictator*.

One day Mother discovered Patti, Beth and me listening in to one of Lord Haw Haw's German propaganda broadcasts. She was very displeased and forbad us to ever do such a thing again. I am sorry to say that we secretly did so on a number of occasions, until one day we heard him talking about Father and his work. It was rather unnerving. We daren't tell Mother, and from then onwards we stopped listening in.

We had some cousins who lived about five miles away in a lovely house on a large estate. They were very kind to us and we used to go there to big parties at Christmas time. On one occasion we had quite an exciting and frightening experience. It was an evening in the autumn, when we were returning from having tea with our cousins. We were in the governess cart with Puncy between the shafts, when we saw the whole sky in one direction was aglow. We knew there was a bombing raid going on in the area towards West Raynham aerodrome. It was dusk and we were only a short distance from home, when I suddenly saw coloured lights all round us and in the hedge beside us. I pointed this out to Mother, who knew instantly that they were tracer bullets. We also became conscious of a plane overhead and flying very low. Mother shouted to us to get out and lie in the ditch running alongside the road. As we did this, the local Ack Ack unit let off an earsplitting anti-aircraft gun. Puncy, with my mother at his head was absolutely terrified and bolted. Off they went, hell for leather, while we stayed, also fairly frightened, in our muddy, cold, damp ditch. We didn't really know what was happening but realized it was serious from Mother's tone of voice. After what seemed ages, Bob Gage arrived to escort us home. Ma had got Puncy under control and home and had asked Bob to rescue us. It turned out that the plane was a German bomber that had been hit and was limping home from an incendiary raid on West Raynham airfield, and it was surmised that they had seen Puncy's white back and decided to 'have a go.' We were surrounded by airfields, which were targets in themselves, as well as being on the route the Germans took returning from bombing raids on England, when they would jettison any bombs they still had on board. On one occasion in broad daylight, a large piece of metal fell off an enemy plane on to our roof. Needless to say that was a roof repair which had to wait till the end of the war to be done properly.

As the sun went down every evening, we had a routine which we had to perform of doing the blackout. This consisted of closing the shutters in the Queen Anne part of the house and drawing the blackout curtains, specially made of black material, in the remaining rooms which we were likely to use. Some of the curtains were far from adequate, and cracks of light could be seen from outside. The village air raid warden patrolled every evening and would shout 'Put out that light there'. We were frequent offenders, I'm afraid.

During the eight weeks summer holidays from school, we used to go for long walks, picnics, bicycle rides and go out into the nearby cornfields when the harvest was being gathered in. Again these were large family affairs when everyone helped out, and the older men would stand round with guns, as the corn was cut, to shoot the rabbits which ran out, and try and get one for the pot. I well remember how we laughed when we were told of a newly-wed wife who was given one of these rabbits to cook, and she put the whole animal, fur coat and all into the cooking pot. History didn't relate what her husband had to say when faced with this for supper! The corn was cut with a machine called a binder, which as its name suggests also bound up the corn into sheaves, which had to be stooked, or stood upright in groups until they were later gathered on to a wagon pulled by a carthorse, and stacked or taken to the thresher to extract the corn.

One of our favourite walks was to a wood about three-quarters of a mile from us down a lovely grassy lane with hedges on either side. In this wood, in our early days of going there, lived an old charcoal burner. He was a funny old boy, bewhiskered and with an upside down clay pipe in his mouth. He used to sit by his fire which looked like an igloo made of sods of earth with a hole at the top for the smoke to curl out. What he did with the charcoal I don't know. I suppose he sold it to make a living. Even in those days we thought it quaint and a bit of an anachronism. Another outing one summer was to bicycle to Suffolk! This meant cycling fifteen miles south to Brandon, crossing the railway line which was the county boundary, turning round and coming back again, all in order to be able to say we had done this.

We were also given little areas of garden by Father, to cultivate. These were usually completely unreclaimed bits of 'jungle'. We worked hard digging and weeding, and saved up our pocket money to buy seeds. Clarkia was a great favourite with us, but after the first season, Father had a habit of saying he wanted that area, and gave us another uncultivated bit to deal with. Looking back on it perhaps it was his way of getting the garden under control. His particular love was roses and he designed and planted a very attractive rose garden. Mother, being the more practical of the two, was more into the kitchen garden and the orchards and their produce. I can remember the names of all those old fruit varieties to this day, and which orchard they were all in. My absolute favourite apple was called a Wealthy; it was so deliciously juicy and sweet, and when one bit into it, the juice dribbled down one's chin.

The Norfolk winters, especially in those days before global warming, were notoriously cold. There was nothing between us and Siberia. We usually had our first heavy fall of snow in January. Being a flat county with little hill protection, we used to have a lot of very cold winds. This meant the snow drifted into wonderful shapes on the hedges beside the small country roads. We used to have great fun sliding and tobogganing, and, dare I say it, we used to slide on that murky pond of ours. I am sure it was really rather risky as it often made alarming cracking noises when we tested the ice. Occasionally in a hot spell in the summer we had swum in it and there was no bottom, only mud and more mud. It would have been an extremely dangerous thing to have fallen into the ice cold water in the winter. Another uncomfortable experience for us in the winter was the fact that during the war, we only had an outside privy, so if the call of nature came after dark and in the night one had to up stick and brave the elements. I remember suffering dreadfully from the cold and having awful chilblains, but any complaints of cold during the day were met with little sympathy from Mother, who would tell us to go and saw up logs or do something energetic and useful.

We had mains electricity, but not mains water. All our water had to be pumped by hand from a well, up to tanks in the attic, before we could have a bath. I can hear Mother now, saying 'Go and do 200 pumps and have a bath'. With a shortage of fuel, we were strictly rationed on the depth of our bath, and we had to share the water too. In the winter those tanks in the attic frequently froze over and the snow drifted in under the tiles up there. It was a very cold house, as the wind and the snow used to blow through the cracks in the ill-fitting windows and doors downstairs. I saved up my pocket money and bought a bulb and a length of flex and fitted up a way of reading down my bed without showing a light. My bedding was so damp with the cold that it steamed up down there! After a cold night, the condensation from our breath would freeze on the walls, which would be covered with a thin sheet of ice. No wonder some of our generation suffer from rheumatics in our older years.

As I mentioned earlier, Mother bred Siamese cats. They used to tease

7. Mother and Mary with Siamese kittens photographed after the war.

a white cat I had unmercifully. Bud, as I called him, was a staid old thing and was only ever roused by the kittens playing with his tail. I used to dress him up in dolls' clothes and put him to sleep in a doll's pram we had. The sloppy thing would lie on his back with a little frilly bonnet on his head and his paws lying on the turned down blanket and go into a state of blissful unconsciousness. On winter nights, he used to go off to the stables and sleep on Puncy's back for warmth. The Siamese kittens were quite destructive as they seemed to have sharper claws than old Bud. They would come to life in the evening and swarm up the curtains, and sharpen their claws on the furniture. When the table was laid for a meal, it was important to pull all the chairs back from the table as they were little thieves. Being thwarted they would try to jump up on the table, but the nearest they got was to get their front paws on the edge of the table and dig their claws into the wood and swing their little bodies in mid-air, while they did a sort of Bisto Kids act in the direction of the meat.

We had a system of pocket money which gave us 1d for each year of our age. But, and this was a very big but, we didn't start until we were five and no one had more than 9d whatever their age. Even then this princely sum was not for riotous living! When we were on the top rate of 9d, we had to put 6d a week into National Saving Certificates, and 2d into what Mother called a clothing fund, out of which were bought minor items of clothing and things like toothpaste too. The remaining 1d we could spend. This meant that if we wanted more spending money we had to earn it. The older members of the family used to go fruit picking in the holidays. There were a lot of blackcurrants grown near us and we were paid 5d for a 4lb punnet. It was really hard work, and especially galling to see the professional pickers managing to pick twice as much as we could in the time. I managed to make 10 shillings a day picking cherries which was a much better bet. Sadly the season was very short but it enabled me to quickly top up my funds to have enough to buy myself a new bicycle.

The great day came when Pa took me to Norwich to make the purchase. I had £10 burning in my pocket, and with the helpful advice of my father, I chose a steed called a Coventry Challenge costing £9.19.5. It was gleaming with chrome and had metal pedals. Pa gave me a present in the form of a shiny bell for it. I thought my ship had come home!

Chapter V

Visits, Visitations and Victory

ONE COULD BE FORGIVEN for thinking with all this activity at home, and the routine of school in term time, that there would be little time for anything else, but still in the summer holidays anyway, I went on visits to the two aunts. One of these was to go to Aunt Armorel, and with one of the Llanmorris young, to walk the course of the River Arun in Sussex. This was largely a bird-watching venture, and we were armed with binoculars, notebooks and sketch pads, and packs on our backs and very basic camping equipment. Fortunately on this trek which took, I think, about a week, we had remarkably fine weather. One of the things I remember particularly was a watercress farm, and wading through the beds in our bare feet. At the end of this part of my holiday, I was taken to Aunt Kathleen, who at that time had a rather lovely house called Kester's Barn. It was near Pulborough.

On this visit, I met for the first time an Austrian Jew who was to marry my aunt. His story was very sad. His family owned large estates in Austria, but when Hitler was all-powerful in that country, the family property was confiscated. Ernst managed to escape and eventually made his way to England, where he was at first interned. He later became a naturalized Briton and served in the British Army. Meanwhile one assumes his elder brother, who was head of the family, was not so fortunate. Ernst never saw or heard from him again and was forced to presume that he lost his life at the hands of the Nazis. Ernst was a quiet cultivated man, who was shrewd and wise. Aunt Kathleen, being a very managing sort of woman, took him under her wing, and it wouldn't surprise me a bit if she had proposed marriage to him but marry they did at the end of the war, and they had many happy years together.

At school another excitement for us was a visit from Dame Myra Hess, the famous pianist, who came to give a Beethoven piano recital, dressed entirely in sombre black, but her wonderful playing more than made up for this. It was a special treat for those of us who were musically inclined. The school in the early years of the war adopted a Royal Navy destroyer, and we all had to make a knitted garment for the crew every term. I started with a scarf, which had to be 42 inches long and knitted in a certain pattern. When finished, it was inspected, and at the end of term, a large consignment was sent off to the ship. The wool was provided and there were such things as socks, balaclava helmets, pullovers and gloves on the list. After we had been doing this for some time, two Royal Navy officers came down to the school and thanked us for our efforts.

In the same year, 1942, I was dispatched to stay with Grannie who was living in Ripley in Surrey. She was still a very good-looking woman with lovely chestnut hair and with hardly a grey hair in her head. She was very game and active for her age; she was about 78 years old. She took me to the cinema in Guildford and we saw a thriller with Conrad Voigt in it, after which we had a delicious cream tea. All through the war, Grannie used to go out to morning coffee every day so that she could save the sugar which was served with it. She hoarded these little packets, and when she had accumulated a respectable amount, she bagged them all up and sent a welcome package of sugar to us in Norfolk. In the spring, we used to gather wild violets and primroses and do them up into little bunches. These were packed in damp moss and put in a shoe box, and posted to her as a sort of thank you.

Our parents had a mutual cousin who came to stay from time to time. Cousin Mildred was not an easy guest. She was always rather sorry for herself and grumbled about all sorts of things, particularly the food. We sometimes wondered if she realized there was a war on. She was a spinster and had spent many years in Uganda, and knew little of life in England. I think my parents took pity on a woman who was lonely in her old age, but I know Mother found her a great trial.

Another family visitor we had in 1943, was Grandpa, whose house had been bombed in London. He was quite elderly by now, being eighty-seven years old. He was still his dear sweet self, but his mind was going, and he sometimes got in a muddle as to who was who. In spite of this, he always knew Father, and talked away to him as though he was perfectly well and remembered everything. He also still did his little party trick with his grandchildren, which he had done years ago. This was to draw a circle round a sixpence, and write in beautiful copperplate writing within this circle, the whole of the Lord's Prayer. He stayed with us for some time until he became ill and Aunt Armorel was sent for. An ambulance was called and he was taken to a hospital near my aunt. On this journey, the ambulance was driven by a young woman, with Armorel sitting beside her. At some stage of the journey they came to a roundabout and the girl asked which way, to which my aunt replied 'Straight on'. Whereupon the driver drove the ambulance with her poor old patient in the back, up the kerb, across the roundabout and bumped the vehicle down the other side! Knowing my aunt, I would not have liked to have been in the driver's shoes. Grandpa died in 1944 at the ripe old age of eighty-eight, having survived the journey in the ambulance!

Back at school, after my grandfather's stay, we found that a Norwich boys' school which had been bombed out of its premises, had been evacuated on to us. A kind of Box and Cox arrangement was organized. We didn't really see very much of them as they were always playing games while we were studying, and vice versa, much to the annoyance of some of the older girls and the relief of the staff no doubt! Patti left school in 1944, and went to work on the land. I had another year to complete my studies. Because Norwich had been such a target for the German bombing raids, all through those years we had a difficult time coping with the daylight raids. Our lessons were severely inter-rupted by the air raid warnings, so when we came up to the year of our final exams, we only went down to the air raid shelters when there was a crash warning. This was a particular siren which told us that enemy planes were overhead. We also had to have someone we could go to in case of emergency at the school. It so happened that I had a cousin in my form, and her family stood surety for me. I had a particular friend whose family were very good to me, and I used to go and stay with them often. Her father was a retired preparatory school headmas-ter who now ran a chicken farm; later he was to advise me on choosing a career.

Now that I had my bicycle, I was ready for a trip which Pa had arranged for me. Towards the end of the war he was posted to Waterbeach near Cambridge, and his Commanding Officer, who was a great friend of his, invited me to go and stay with him and his charming family in the village of Barton a few miles from Cambridge. Off I went by train with my bicycle in the guard's van. The family were called Colquhoun and were kindness itself, and had invited Pa to stay for the week as well, so that I could see something of him. While he went off to work during the day, I cycled to Cambridge and 'did' the Colleges and other places of historical interest. I explored and sketched and had a lovely time every day, going back to Barton at the end of the afternoon. On one of the evenings, Pa took me to the Arts Theatre and we saw a play called *Random Harvest*, after which we had supper at a small restaurant.

Occasionally Pa would bring home one or two of the young officers with whom he worked. I think it was a particular kindness as many of them didn't have their families with them, and they were all living under a great strain with the work that they did, exciting as it was for them in a way. It gave them a few hours break from the strange night life that they inevitably led. A large proportion of the bombing operations were at night and this involved ground staff as well as the flying crews.

It was in 1944, when I was seventeen, that Father took me to my first ball. I don't know why I went and not Patti. Perhaps she was asked and turned the offer down. She was always rather shy. Anyway I was highly excited by such an excursion, but oh what to wear. Mother and I put our heads together to work out a plan. It wasn't going to be easy as we had clothes rationing, and I doubt very much if our clothing coupons would have run to the extravagance of a new outfit. A simple long dress was put together, and she lent me some long gloves, a stole and an evening bag, all of which she had kept from the Lavershot Hall days. I can't for the life of me remember what I wore on my feet, but I expect it was a bit of 'make do and mend'. I was heavily chaperoned by Father, and I stayed beside him while young officers came up and asked *him* if they could dance with *me*. Some of them were known to me from having been to our home, and it was the following year that one of these young men, who was a Wing Commander and a pilot, asked my parents if he could take me out, or perhaps I should say in the old fashioned way, whether he could 'court' me. Mother said very firmly 'No, I was too young', but he had permission to write to me and to come over to our house from time to time.

I became very fond of him and we wrote to each other for quite a while until we drifted apart. Tragically he was killed in a flying accident in Lincolnshire in the late 1940s.

About twice a year, Pa would put on his town suit and journey by train to London to visit Uncle Arnold. He was Grannie's brother who had lived all those years in India, and who had come home on retirement to spend his final years in England. I remember asking Mother about him and her telling me that he had a chi-chi wife, which meant she had some Indian blood, and that they were childless. I never met either of them.

By this time Aunt Armorel was living in Nottingham. She had a lovely Regency house on a road called The Rope Walk, high up above the town and looking out to the River Trent. She invited Patti and me to stay. This was a great departure from her previous invitations, to have included my elder sister. We set off together, and settled in on the first evening, but to my surprise Patti said she wanted to go home. She was obviously feeling homesick. I read to her and tried everything to help her get over the problem, but it was all to no avail, and after three days she was put on a train to go home again. She was never asked again. In my aunt's eyes, she had certainly blotted her copy book.

Back at home, Pa was still in the RAF, but some of the pressure was off now that the war was coming to the end. He had a little more time to look after the bees which we already had to supplement our rations. He always wore a veil when he handled them, but never any other protective clothing. He maintained that the odd sting cured his rheumatism. In fact he was very fit, and I never knew him to be ill except when he had the occasional bout of malaria, a leftover from his days in the Far East. I remember seeing him with a swarm of bees on his bare arm. He gently rolled them down his arm with his other hand, and shook the lump of some thousands of bees on to the hiving board, prior to their going into the hive. Although the bees gave us a welcome addition of honey to our wartime rations, in other ways they were a mixed blessing. They were always swarming, and just when we were dressed up and ready to go out somewhere, a shout would go up, and there was a delay while the bees were dealt with. We also had quite a number of hornets in the garden. They were particularly tiresome as they raided the hives in the summer, and attacked our cordon pear trees, hollowing out the ripe fruit at great speed. I don't know if they were very common then, but I do know that they are much rarer now and are a protected species.

In the last year of the war, Pa suddenly went out and bought a Willy's jeep. It was brand new and royal blue. Mother thought it was an unwise purchase because it was very extravagant on petrol. I think Uncle Arnold, who had recently died, had left him some money which enabled him to do this. It was in this vehicle that Pa taught me how to drive. It was not the easiest of machines to manage! Another thing we did together was to go to Norwich and spend a day looking at churches, some of which had been badly damaged by the bombing. I enjoyed these outings, not only for what we saw, but I felt that I was getting to know Pa much better. We also went to a beekeepers' show at Ketteringham Hall. When we got there, he discovered that the owner of this lovely house was an old regimental friend, and we were invited in to tea. I thought it was very nice for him to have this meeting, as he was so surrounded by females at home. I remember once asking my mother if she would have liked to have had a son. Her reply was, 'When the fifth daughter arrived, I decided that they were more interesting to dress than boys.' I had another excursion with Pa, to an old friend of his whose surname was Ketton Cremer, who lived at Felbrigg Hall. I was fascinated by the old house and was invited to explore the library. There were some lovely carved malachite ornaments on an inlaid table which I admired. The property belongs to the National Trust now.

During the summer of 1945, after the war in Europe was over, the dreadful bombing ceased. The war in the Far East came to an end a little later. I left school having gained my School Certificate, which was what the finals were called. Many of my friends were going to University, but I knew this was out of the question for me. The family finances would not have stood it, and there were still three sisters at a fee paying school. I had to think how I could earn a living. Throughout the country there was a feeling of euphoria that a new era was dawning, but we still had food rationing for some years after the ceasefire, in fact rationing went on in England longer than in many of the other countries involved in the war. As to my future, I decided to turn to the father of my special school friend for advice. I always called him A. K., which were his initials, and a meeting was arranged between him and his wife and my parents. We all had lunch at the Bell Hotel in Norwich. Father and Mother had met them several times before, and had always felt that they would give us good sound advice. He felt it would be a good thing if I considered going into the scholastic world and he would do anything he could to help me on my way, in this direction.

Part III
Teaching, Trials and Travel
1945–1957

Chapter I

My First Job

FTER THE MEETING AT THE BELL HOTEL in Norwich which was to decide which direction my future should go, A. K. suggested that I should try to get a teaching post, really as a sort of trainee, while I tried to find out if I was in any way cut out for such a career. He offered to help me to apply for various posts, and wrote a personal character reference for me to send with any application I should make. The result of all this was that I applied for a job at a school in Cromer. I had an interview with the headmistress and miraculously the job was mine. The fact that I had no recognized qualifications didn't seem to matter in those days. One learnt in the class room the hard way, and the idea was that I would be supervised and that there would be experienced, qualified staff about whose advice I could seek. I was to live in and was paid very little, but I had all my meals and laundry free. I was to teach English, History and Geography to boys and girls from the age of eight to fourteen.

At home I put together the few suitable clothes I had. It was all rather a shot in the dark, as I had never done anything like this before. Having got the whole business organized, I settled down to enjoy my last summer holiday. Part of this I spent with my great school friend, A. K.'s daughter, Harriet, and instead of going to her home as I had done before, we both went to stay with her aged grandfather and a maiden aunt of hers. They lived together in a house on the Norfolk coast at Trimingham. The house had been built as a summer dwelling, but they lived in it permanently, and consequently, when the weather was inclement, it could be very cold. That part of the coast was being very eroded, and chunks of cliff used to fall on to the beach and into the sea every year. Going back many years later, I remember seeing large concrete blocks lying at all angles on the sand. They were the sea defences which had been built on the top of the cliffs at the beginning of the war. I daresay if one went back now there would be nothing to see at all.

Harriet's grandfather had been an engineer with the firm who had built the famous Sydney Harbour Bridge. He was a funny old man, and had a reputation for being fairly tight-fisted, and one of the little tricks he used to play on us, was to stick a piece of black cotton on to the back of an old sixpenny piece and put it on the carpet near his chair, while holding the end of the cotton. He would then point out that someone must have dropped a coin, and when we went to pick it up, he would take great delight in jerking the cotton, so that we couldn't do so. It was all very childish and at the end he never gave it to us. Anyone who came to tea or to stay for a little longer, regardless of how they had arrived, would be hurried on their way when he got tired of their company. This he did by looking at his pocket watch very pointedly and saying, 'I mustn't keep you, what time is your train?' It usually did the trick. I don't think that either of us particularly enjoyed staying in this humourless and rather holy atmosphere, but we escaped when we could and went on some fun jaunts together on our bicycles, to get away from the rather Victorian atmosphere.

When September came, my mind switched back to my new job, and the big pack took place. I took some of my favourite books, and my paints and sketch books, though latterly I had been doing quite a lot of pen and ink drawings of historic houses in Norfolk. It is worth mentioning here that I had thought I would have liked to have gone to Art College, and perhaps to pursue a career in commercial art. It was pointed out to me that this would cost money, so that was that!

I made the journey by train, with my precious bicycle in the guard's van, and found on arrival in Cromer, that I was to sleep in a school house some distance from the school and where two other members of staff had rooms. My bicycle proved to be invaluable, as I had to cycle daily from this house to the main school building.

My introduction to my future pupils was uneventful, and I don't remember being nervous or unsure of myself. I prepared my first lessons carefully, and it would never have occurred to me to be anything else but my normal, natural self. Early on in my first term, I had a warning from a senior member of staff, that I should be very careful with one particular class, as there was a boy in that form who was an epileptic. I should definitely avoid mentioning the word blood, or anything which might conjure up the picture of gore in this pupil's mind as it made him have one of his epileptic fits. This could be pretty tricky when I was teaching mediaeval history which covered a very bloody period in the Middle Ages. I was very careful for some time, but, yes you have guessed it, one day I got a bit carried away, and there was Harrison lying on the floor. I was horrified, but obviously some of his fellow classmates had seen it all before and knew what to do, while others sent for outside help, and he was carted away for treatment by matron.

I soon learnt that the staff-room atmosphere left a great deal to be desired. The school was a large co-educational private establishment, but the majority of the staff were female. In those days, the women teachers were nearly always spinsters, and I am sorry to say that the middle-aged members were often very bitchy. I found this very tiresome and rather bewildering as I had never come across this aspect of human nature, but there was one husband and wife couple on the teaching staff, who were good fun. She was a niece of G. K. Chesterton, and he was for some years one of the team of people who took it in turns to compose the Times crosswords. I had to be prepared to turn my hand to anything and really be a general dogsbody. One of my duties was to be an assistant cub mistress. Akela, my boss, was another middle-aged spinster, who was a difficult woman to please, and who lacked a sympathetic touch when dealing with the young. I found it difficult to be loyal to her sometimes, but I think I learnt a lot during that first term, in particular, in handling tricky situations and learning to bite my tongue.

As time went on, I found myself taking on more and more responsibility. I ran the library, and trained the school choir. I was asked to give certain somewhat backward children special coaching. I also decided to join an adult choir, as I very much enjoyed singing. At the end of that first Christmas term, we gave a performance of Handel's *Messiah* in the parish church. I found it an exhilarating experience to stand shoulder to shoulder with my fellow singers and sing my heart out.

I was back home again for Christmas itself. This was always a festive occasion of course, but funnily enough, we never had a Christmas tree, but we did have our usual 26lb Norfolk turkey. We all loved cold turkey, and a bird of this size meant there was plenty left over to cut into, but it was quite a juggling act to get it cooked. We had an old kitchen range, but the oven was not very big, and the bird had to be strung up from the top corner and stand on end in a baking tray. We more often than not used to make our Christmas presents, and everything was practical, useful and of a modest cost of a few pence. I remember one year, when I was younger, asking Mother for an advance of pocket money to buy her present. It was 1d for a box of matches! One year we had a fall of snow and celebrated a white Christmas by sitting outside in glorious sun eating Weetabix spread with strawberry jam and cream!

In the following summer of 1946, it was decided to organize a cub camp in Scotland. It was quite a major undertaking, as Akela and I were to take forty-five young boys on this camp. The plan was for three Rover or senior scouts to go up ahead of us, and to set up the camp on a farm between Langholm and Hawick in the Lowlands. We then brought the boys from Cromer to Scotland by train. It was a long journey for all of us. I thought it would never end! A bus had been hired to meet us at the station and take us to our camping site where the three scouts had done Trojan work in making preparations and getting in stores. There were several bell tents for the boys and the scouts, while Akela and I had a small tent each. We were in a field of long grass, on a slope which ran down to an icy cold burn, in which we did all our washing morning and evening. We cooked all our meals over a camp fire and milk was fetched from a nearby farm. The scouts' brief was to help at meal times and when we were in camp, otherwise they were free to follow their own pursuits. I am afraid that very early on Akela had upset these older boys, so there was a bit of tension where they were concerned, not helped, I may add, by the scouts bringing me a mug of early morning tea and pointedly not doing the same for Akela. One of the most difficult tasks was getting the boys out of their sleeping bags in the morning, and down to the burn to wash in the ice cold water. Looking back on it, I don't blame them. I didn't like it much myself. The three scouts supervised the fire and cooking breakfast in billy cans. I am sure these young boys benefitted enormously from such camps, especially coming so soon after the war, when such activities had been very restricted. One little boy was a little bit weepy, but I always found that the cure was to keep the boys as busy as possible. In all my teaching life in boarding schools, I have only ever come across one boy who was incurably homesick.

My First Job

Our days were filled with energetic expeditions up mountains, long walks in the countryside, while from time to time a bus was hired to take us further afield. We took the boys to a tweed mill near Langholm, and we had a day out in Edinburgh. It was almost impossible so soon after the war to buy film for one's camera. The only way round this was to buy a camera which was supplied with one reel of film. As I hadn't got a camera anyway, I invested in a little instamatic, and used the film very sparingly. This cost me the princely sum of £3. As well as these expeditions, we also did routine cub work when the boys did their various proficiency badges. We had camp fire sing-songs in the evening and an open church service on Sunday. The weather was never allowed to interfere with what we had planned to do, and we were not lucky on several occasions. I remember on one or two wet days, that very uncomfortable feeling of clammy damp clothing which we were unable to dry, but we survived.

This camp had taken up ten days or so of my summer holiday, but shortly after I got home again, I had an invitation to go and stay with Aunt Kathleen in Dorset. She had a nice old house in Beaminster now, and again I took my bicycle and explored the surrounding countryside. During this visit we were invited to a drinks party given by an old friend of my aunt, and among a collection of some fairly elderly guests were a few young naval officers who were stationed not far away. This was to be my first meeting with one of them called Robert to whom I was later to become engaged. He was tall and very fair and definitely handsome. I think I was smitten at that first meeting and I was soon to learn that the feeling was mutual, when he asked me out a few days later, after which we started to write to each other, and our love blossomed. I had the feeling that Aunt Kathleen felt personally responsible for pulling off this coup. As she never drank alcohol, I couldn't imagine her going to a drinks party so I have since often wondered if the whole meeting was a set-up.

I should mention here that my two aunts were both Christian Scientists. They never seemed to have any illnesses, or if they did, they kept very quiet about it and certainly never called a medical doctor. Years later in the 1960s, Aunt Armorel was ill with pneumonia and refused drugs which would have helped her, and she didn't live to tell the tale. I was often taken to a Christian Science Church, and given articles to read on the subject. Neither of the aunts like trapping mice for instance, and Armorel in particular used to have an elaborate method of catching them in empty cocoa tins. She would then take them outside well away from her boundary and let them go to plague someone else! Being vegetarian, even the cat had to conform to a diet which didn't offend. I remember Kathleen once leaving a cat with Mother to look after, and it ate raw peas, nuts, sultanas and pulses.

The following winter of 1946–1947, was a phenomenally cold one. The school had no central heating, and by the January term when the really cold weather and snow arrived, we really did suffer. There was no question of closing the school, and we were expected to carry on as usual. We all put on layers and layers of warm clothing, and topped the lot with an overcoat. We wore gloves or mittens and those who had them, donned fur-lined boots. It made writing difficult being so muffled up, but there was no alternative. The temperatures were so low that part of the sea off-shore froze over. I have never seen that happen since. Nowadays it is unthinkable that we should have had to endure such conditions, but I suppose we were tougher then and more used to the rigours of the winter without proper heating. I think too that the war had accustomed us to hard times, and to keeping a stiff upper lip. It was all what Mother would have called 'character forming'.

By the spring of 1947, A. K., my faithful mentor, felt that I should start thinking of a move into another job. I had cut my teeth, gained some useful experience and would have completed two years in this post, so I wrote to Truman and Knightly, the scholastic agents, to see what they had on their books. There seemed to be a lot of attractive posts on offer, so I thought that by the beginning of the summer term, I should see the Headmistress and hand in my notice. She generously wrote me a good reference, and I left at the end of term, having already lined up four interviews. Such was my confidence I had no doubt that I would land one of those jobs!

Chapter II

Within Sight of Windsor

I HAD DECIDED ON A BOYS PREPARATORY SCHOOL as I thought that there would be less bickering in the staff room with a preponderance of male teachers, and in the course of two weeks, I had four interviews in London, usually in a West End hotel. On each occasion I was interviewed by the headmaster. Only one of them invited me down to see his school, but all of them offered me a job. The school I did go to see was near Camberley and I was amused to see that the boys all had pet tortoises. These were marked with their owners initials painted on their shells, and they were tethered with a cord threaded through a hole drilled in the side of shell and anchored to a very long hedge. The reason I eventually turned down this job was the fact that there were two joint headmasters. I felt that this might present problems. As A. K. had so wisely told me to do, I said I would like to think about it and would let them know. I then sat down and had a big think and considered all the pros and cons. I finally settled for a school in a small village between Slough and Windsor. I liked the idea of being near enough to London to be able to go up from time to time. The headmaster was very musical and put on a light opera every year. There were lovely spacious grounds and the school had a good reputation scholastically.

September was upon me in no time, as I made preparations for my venture into pastures new. My parents were always interested in what I was doing but they were only too glad for A. K. and Mr Llanmorris, who was also a headmaster, to do the advising, being much better qualified to do so. Off I went by train again with my two-wheeled steed, my ever-present companion. I was given a very nice bed-sitting room at the top of the Edwardian house, with a lovely view across to Windsor Castle, and I soon settled in with the few possessions I had brought with me, mostly books and my painting things. The school was not large and there were three masters and the head, as well as me. There was a very jolly middle-aged matron, and the headmaster's wife ran the domestic side of things. My brief this time was to look after the youngest form in all subjects, and to teach English to the older boys.

Needless to say I was roped in to help on the musical side, but I liked that. The first year I was there we produced Gilbert and Sullivan's *Trial by Jury*. I found myself rewriting the score for the treble voices and then training the chorus. Towards the time of the actual performance I spent many hours painting scenery. It was all great fun, made the more so by the enthusiasm of the boys. When I was off duty I would go out on my bicycle exploring, and some of the parents were very good to me and I would be asked out to supper. One worked very long hours because, unlike today, the boys didn't have endless exeats and long half-terms. They came in at the beginning of term, had a Friday to Monday evening half-term, and nothing else until the end of term. There were a few day boys, and occasionally parents came to watch their sons playing in a match, otherwise we were a very self-contained unit. At the end of term I used to take a party of boys up to London on the school train, where they were met and collected by their parents.

In the spring of 1948 my much-loved Grandmother died. It was very sudden and consequently unexpected, in spite of her age of eighty-four. In fact I had recently been over to stay for a weekend with her and she had given me a lovely crushed strawberry-coloured tricot coat and skirt, the first I had ever owned. Pa, who by now had completely retired, rang me up at the school to break the news to me. He asked me if I could get a few days off and go over to Ripley to help him to sort out her possessions and this was arranged and I made my way over there. We found that she had been a great hoarder. Remember those housekeeping books from before the Great War? All our Christmas and birthday cards and letters of many years had been kept, including a little homemade card of yellow paper with a cut-out of a duck stuck on it, with the words 'Good luk' written in a childish hand at the bottom. Also among her papers I came across my father's divorce papers from his first marriage. He then told me about his first wife and a little bit about what had happened.

The death of Grannie meant that my father inherited some money and some very nice pieces of antique furniture and those Chinese incense burners, which then stood in our garden until they were sold. Some of the money went towards paying a local builder to make some alterations to our Norfolk home, including putting in a much needed inside lavatory.

Following fairly soon after my Grandmother's death, a great tragedy befell me. This was the death, in a road accident in Germany where he was stationed, of the young naval officer I had met through Aunt Kathleen in Dorset. We had become engaged unofficially while he was on leave, but had decided to wait until his next leave for him to meet my parents, and to do everything properly, I having already met his parents. This disaster happened two weeks before my twenty-first birthday. I couldn't bring myself to tell my parents immediately. I felt completely crushed, and couldn't bear to talk to anyone about it, but I knew my life had to go on. I was at home for the Easter holidays and my birthday. There was no special partying for the occasion, but Pa opened a bottle of very old claret which he had kept when he inherited his step-father's cellar. It was a rich honey colour and tasted wonderful. He also gave me a lovely diamond and ruby pendant which had belonged to Grannie, and which had come down from her family. I was very touched by this generous gift, but in spite of these celebrations, I nursed a heavy heart. I thought long and hard that I must tell my parents about the death of Robert as it seemed right that I should do so, though I dreaded having to talk about it, and neither did I want my sisters to know and so to be constantly questioned about the tragedy. Being a large busy family it was incredibly difficult to find a suitable moment when I could talk without interruption, and finally I told Pa first and Mother later. They were both a great support to me, and Pa wrote me a long letter of comfort and understanding when I was back at school for the summer term.

During my time at this school, on the advice of A. K. and Llanmorris père, I did a correspondence course to start getting myself some teaching qualifications. It was hard work doing all this studying as well as my school duties, and it meant working in the holidays as well. The plan was that when I had that qualification under my belt, I should do a course at the College of Preceptors and sit an examination at the end. So I worked my way through all this, including a trip, organized by the College of Preceptors in the summer holidays, to the south of

France, to stay with a French family in Toulon. This was my first journey abroad. I went by train from Victoria Station, changed trains in Paris from the Gare du Nord to the Gare de Lyon, and then on what seemed like an endless journey through the night, sitting upright – no money for such luxuries as a sleeper – until I saw the dawn breaking and felt the hot sun of the south of France through the glass of the carriage window. We arrived shortly before lunch time and, impressively, the train was only two minutes late after all those hours journeying. I was met by my French hosts, who were a middle-aged couple who spoke not a word of English, which of course was the idea. I struggled along with my schoolgirl French, getting more confident as the days went by.

The other members of the party who were also on the course were being hosted by different French families. In the morning we all gathered at the Lycée, for three hours of classes in French. Then we were either taken out to a restaurant for a lengthy lunch, which went on until about three o'clock, or we went back to our respective digs for a bite, before being taken out on an expedition in and around Toulon. At the weekends and on about one day a week, I was taken further afield along the south coast, where I remember bathing off the coast at Hyères, and going up into the mountains of Provence to Aix-les-Bains. On that journey I saw my first golden eagle. I was enchanted by Provence and would love to go again, though sometimes memories are best; one can be so disillusioned and a lovely dream is shattered. Another visit was to the old town of Arles, where we went to the colosseum and saw a bullfight. There were huge crowds in the stadium, and everyone got very excited and there was a carnival feel to the whole scene, which was very picturesque with the brilliant colours and pageantry of the occasion. I was a bit apprehensive about it all as it was certainly not to my taste, and seemed a very one-sided affair, but I sat through it, glad that I had done so and feeling more able to argue against such a sport, if the subject ever came up in the future. I had been told by an Englishman that a Spanish bullfight was pure artistry whereas a French one was pure butchery. I can't think that I would have liked a Spanish one any better.

The time was approaching for my return from the south of France. I was to break my journey in Paris, where Armorel had arranged to meet me, so that we could have a few days staying with a friend of hers who lived near the centre of the city. The idea I think was to educate me further! I remember my bedroom in the friend's house in particular. It was on the first floor and had French windows leading on to a tiny balcony, while the room itself was very feminine with white flounces on the curtains and the bedcover. The large square pillows were edged in masses of lace and the duvet was voluptuously inviting. My breakfast arrived on a tray and consisted of a very large cup of coffee together with croissants, brioches and apricot jam. But the days with Armorel were typically energetic and interesting. We walked everywhere and saw many of the famous landmarks such as Notre Dame, the Tuileries and gardens and we took a boat trip on the Seine. We ate inexpensively during the day and it was also typical of Armorel's generosity that she wouldn't allow me to pay for anything.

Back at school, life went busily on. A Frenchman had joined the staff. He was a very jolly little man who had a lovely sense of humour. He told me a story of how when he first came to England in the 1930s, he was invited to a rather grand house party. In the afternoon some of the house guests gathered to play croquet. he was paired off with a fairly formidable woman and they started to play. His English was rather limited and when his partner successfully put her ball through one of the hoops, he congratulated her by saying 'You lucky bitch!' thinking that that was the feminine of 'You lucky dog.' He didn't discover for some years what an awful faux pas he had made. I rather doubt if anyone would have been very pleased to have been called the latter either. Another amusing little incident which happened to me was when the mother of one of my day pupils came to see me, and asked if I would mind making sure that her son had only a small helping of mince when it was served at lunch. Apparently he so disliked it, he had been shovelling it into his trouser pocket, and she, poor woman, was faced with a cleaning up task on 'mince for lunch' days.

I frequently spent my half-term with Aunt Armorel in her house in Nottingham, and Johnny Llanmorris used to come down and fetch me on his motor bike, a Matchless 750. This intrigued the boys no end. They were sure he was my boy friend. They couldn't have been further from the truth. I had known the family nearly all my life, and he was like a big brother to me. We used to tease Armorel for what we called her Garrett Hatcheries, i.e. her matchmaking schemes. Whether she had any designs for me, I am not sure, but looking back, I think she probably had. I spent many a happy trip on the pillion of that bike. Johnny taught me much about architecture, photography, music and many other subjects that interested him, and we did a lot of exploring together. He was a great companion. It was at about this time that Armorel came down to see me and taught me to ride this same motorbike in Windsor Great Park. I managed that all right, but found it nearly impossible to hold the machine upright when I was standing beside it, because it was so heavy.

While staying in Nottingham, Aunt Armorel's coal was always delivered by horse and dray. The old coalman, who wore an old leather waistcoat and cap, both shiny with age, was quite a character. He would tip the coal, by the sackful, down a chute into her coal cellar, and when the delivery had been made, he would come to the back door to say he had finished. When Armorel asked him how much she owed him, he would say 'I'll have to ask me hoss.' This meant he had to go down to the street and count the empty bags he had thrown on the horse's flanks!

When the summer holidays of 1949 came, I went home to Norfolk and started to plan a bicycle trip across England and Wales, to the Llanmorrises who were living on the west coast, south of Barmouth. They had once again asked me to go and stay. I started to plan my journey with Pa's help. I wanted to wend my way taking in castles, interesting churches, and other places which I had always wanted to visit. The only restriction my parents put on me was to insist that I joined the YWCA so that I could stay at their hostels *en route*, and that I should send them a postcard every morning before I set off on the next leg of my trip. Pa put my bicycle in the boot of the car and took me to Downham Market, to set me on my way, as the first fifteen miles were pretty flat and uninteresting.

I took nine days to do this trip. Some days were easier than others, partly depending on the hills and how much I had to walk. At no time did I feel threatened. I don't think I would like a daughter of mine to do such a journey alone today, but it really was very different fifty years ago. The hostels varied enormously from lovely country houses to part of a ruined castle where one had to self-cater and hike across a field to a farm for milk. I had a lovely time looking at churches and cathedrals, and visiting Stratford upon Avon and the interesting town of Ludlow in Shropshire. I sketched and took photographs with my little camera, it being easier now to get film for it. My last day took me from Abermule to the coast, some sixty miles, which was quite a long hop, but was even more so, as I had to do a lot of walking, pushing my bicycle up the hills of Wales. I arrived hot and tired but feeling pleased with my achievement. I was given a great welcome and slept well that night.

Meg and Johnny Llanmorris arrived, as did the youngest son plus girl friend, and we lost no time in climbing Cader Idris, going to Abergynolwyn and Llanfihangel-y-pennant, walking up the course of the River Dysnynni; how those lovely lilting Welsh names come back to me. Johnny and I also went down a disused gold mine near Dolgellau. One day we walked twenty miles, which was most likely the longest walk I had ever done. I thought my legs would never function again after that!

The Llanmorris's house was a stone's throw from the sea, and one could look out to the island of Bardsey. They always had a pair of binoculars at the ready and we watched birds and small boats at sea from their sitting room window. I remember Mr Llanmorris telling me that on Bardsey there lived a sheep farmer whose son had never come to the mainland until he was grown up, consequently he had never seen a car or train. I wonder if anyone lives on Bardsey now. It used to be a bird watcher's paradise.

I started my third year at the school near Windsor, and that winter term we did a production of *The Pirates of Penzance,* and I seemed well-bedded down into the routine of school life, but as time went on and the new year dawned, I began to feel that I needed a complete change. I think this was engendered by the sadnesses I had had in the previous year. The death of my fiancé had certainly unsettled me. I had completed the programme of studies I had set myself, and I began to think in terms of finding a job abroad, and seeing a bit of the world while earning my living. I sounded out A. K. and Mr Llanmorris who both encouraged me to do just that. In the late spring I lined up to my headmaster and told him what I wanted to do. He made all sorts of noises about how sad he would be to see me go, but he was very generous in allowing me time off in the summer term to go for interviews, and gave me a glowing reference.

Again I decided to go Truman and Knightly to see what they had to offer. I picked out three potential jobs. One was a large girls' school in Santiago, Chile, another a girls' school in Kenya, and the third a co-educational private school in Nicosia, Cyprus. I had interviews for these posts in London, and surprisingly, I was offered all three posts. I followed the same tactics as before, and went away to think carefully what to do. Owing to my experience in Cromer, I preferred not to be in an entirely girls' school and those two posts were for a three year contract, while the Cyprus one was for two years. I thought it safer to go for the latter. My fare would be paid and I would live in and my salary was £200 per annum all found. When term ended I was given an affectionate farewell and another chapter of my life was coming to an end.

In the summer holidays of 1950, I was invited to join Armorel, Johnny and Meg Llanmorris on a trip to Scotland. The plan was to go north up the west coast and to try and get to Cape Wrath, the north western tip of the mainland. From there to go along the north coast and then come south again. We all met up at the Llanmorris's house on the west Wales coast. Armorel had an Austin 7 then, and we had to travel pretty light to get everything in including a tent and four adults! It was all a bit of a squeeze. We planned to sleep 'rough', although the tent would sleep two people if need be. We took some provisions with us, but generally speaking our kit was pretty basic.

The first day it poured and poured with rain. We got as far as the Lake District, exploring in a limited sort of way because of the foul weather. We couldn't find anywhere acceptably dry to spend the night, such as an old barn, so we decided to sit up and sleep in the car. Don't forget this was an Austin 7 so we none of us did more than doze fitfully, leaning against each other for a prop for our heads. We were mighty glad to see the dawn and glad too that the roof had not leaked. After a cold breakfast, and having stretched our legs, we set off on the next part of our journey. This took us to Hadrian's Wall and we walked along a section of it, and we went to Lanercost Priory and Birdoswald, both of which we looked at with interest. By nightfall the weather was really no better, and so we decided to treat ourselves to the luxury of a B&B. We had not intended to do this, but we all felt so ragged after the night before, that we succumbed. After that we stuck to our resolution.

Sometimes two slept in the car and two in the tent. If it was a specially fine night, we all four slept under the stars. We always made a camp fire in the evening and sat round it while we cooked our meal on it. Armorel was very knowledgeable about edible and poisonous fungi, and under her aegis we collected all sorts of queer looking mushrooms which she then fried up and we ate them on rather smokey bits of toast. I must confess that, although some of them looked fairly unappetizing, they tasted delicious. None of us ever had any ill-effects. On the shores of Loch Awe I slept in a ditch which filled with water in the middle of the night! Near Ullapool we found an empty railwayman's hut which had been abandoned. This was luxury indeed and we piled in to prepare ourselves for a really comfortable night. Unfortunately, we hadn't noticed that it was standing on very uneven ground and at quite an angle, and we kept sliding down to one end in the course of the night. If the door hadn't shut firmly, I think we would have shot out in our sleep. Another find for the night, right up in Sutherland, was a funny little stone croft. Empty and somewhat dilapidated, the roof was intact and there was a little fireplace with a pile of peat blocks to burn. We made a fire which nearly smoked us out, but we were able to boil some water and make ourselves a meal; to a certain extent we lived off the land by gathering wild fruit and anything else vegetarian which presented itself, and this supplemented the simple supplies we bought *en route*. Outside the croft there were lovely views to compensate somewhat for the primitive conditions inside. We slept in sleeping bags on the floor beside the smouldering peat fire.

The whole trip was enormous fun in spite of our wet start. We all got on well together and Armorel was always an interesting person to be with. We bird-watched, walked and climbed, explored ruined castles, and on the north coast near Tongue, we bathed in the nude in the icy cold but fantastically clear and quite deep water, diving from rocks poking up out of the sea. I remember particularly the many cormorants we saw on that stretch of coast. Sadly, we never got to Cape Wrath because the ferry went only once a week and we had missed it by a day. It was certainly an education for me as it was my first trip so far north into Scotland. Some fifty years later, my husband and I had a holiday in Scotland, following much the same route, though in a comfortable car and staying in civilized B&Bs. As we went further and further north, I thought how little changed it all was from my first visit. I thought the roads were better, but it was still unspoilt, wild and beautiful and with remarkably little traffic.

Chapter III

Cyprus

FTER THIS TRIP I went back to Norfolk to be with my family and to prepare for my overseas journey and new job. The first thing I did was to buy myself a large strong trunk and plan very carefully with endless lists what I should put in it. My passage had been booked on a Lloyds Triestino boat sailing from Venice to Limassol in Cyprus. I left my family in Norfolk, knowing that my parents understood why I was going off like this. I travelled from home by train to London, and then across London to Victoria Station where I caught the boat train to Paris. On arrival there, I had to get myself and my trunk across Paris to the Gare de Lyon. In spite of my French being quite good by now, I found it very difficult to understand the accent of the Parisian porters. Waiting for the night train from Paris, I felt the buzz of excitement as the platform filled with fellow travellers and I found myself looking forward to the unknown ahead of me. Again I sat up all night, trying to sleep, with the aid of a pillow I had hired from the cabin steward. The journey seemed to go on for ever. We crossed from France into Switzerland at Geneva and then through the Alps by the Simplon Tunnel and into Italy at Domodossola. At each of the frontiers the train screeched to a standstill, and, amidst much shouting on the platforms, the passport control people were taken on the train. They worked their way down the coaches checking our passports and health documents. When we were cleared, the journey was resumed and we made our way across the flat plain of northern Italy and finally to Venice. We had been on this train from Paris for seventeen hours.

We arrived in the late afternoon, and from the station I had to get myself to the Lloyds Triestino offices to pick up my ticket. I managed to get hold of a porter who got me and my trunk to a gondola which took me on the canals to a point near the offices. Looking back on it all, I can't think how I managed the language, but somehow it all worked out. After getting my ticket, and dealing with porters I didn't understand, I managed to get taken out to the boat. I had to be on board by the evening as we were due to sail at 11 o'clock that night but I decided to go to the boat earlier as I didn't much fancy wandering round Venice being ogled by the Italian men, which I had noticed happening after my arrival in the city.

On board I had the cabin to myself as the other berth was empty, which pleased me. Being an Italian boat, we were served lots of very Italian food. This meant there was a lot of pasta on the menu, which I didn't mind, except that they dyed the spaghetti either a lurid lime green, or a violet colour. I suppose this was meant to make it more attractive to present and eat! When we were out at sea none of this mattered very much because I became rather ill. At first I thought I was feeling seasick, but this was soon dispelled when I started to run a high temperature. I felt ghastly. The ship's doctor saw me and it was thought that I had contracted 'flu, as there had been a bit of an epidemic in England before I left. To cap it all, we ran into very rough weather, so much so that a steward put a net up on my berth to stop me being thrown out. The voyage took a week in those days, and by the time we arrived off the Cyprus coast I was feeling no better, in fact I felt like dying.

On arrival outside Limassol, we lay off-shore as the Cyprus harbours were not deep enough to have boats come alongside. It was normal for the passengers and their luggage to be brought the last few hundred yards by lighter, but because of my fever, a yellow flag was run up and no one was allowed to land. The immigration and health people came on board, and after two hours delay and much discussion, the passengers were allowed off. Finally I was given permission to land and I dragged myself up, and went ashore too. My future employer had come down from Nicosia to meet me, and she must have wondered what she was letting herself in for. I endured the long car journey to Nicosia and on arrival was promptly put to bed and a doctor was called. Two days later, officials from the immigration and health department came to check on me, but, by this time I was beginning to feel a little better, so I think they were satisfied that I hadn't brought some unheard-of disease to the island. It was not an auspicious start to my two year contract.

Cyprus proved to be a very interesting and pleasant place to live. It was still very colonial then and the climate was a lovely dry heat. There were many congenial people to get to know and I enjoyed the work and the play. The school where I taught had been a private house, and was built of warm honey-coloured stone round a central courtyard. It was very attractive with bougainvilia, plumbago, jasmine and other such exotica growing up the pillars round the courtyard. In the grounds were citrus trees, and I remember well my first taste of a ripe orange picked and eaten from the tree. It was nectar indeed and tasted so different from the ones I had had in England, which had ripened in the hold of a ship. The school was co-educational and the pupils were largely children of service families stationed on the island, as well as a few children of local business men. There were about twelve boarders and I had accommodation in the boarding house about half a mile from the school.

This establishment was run by a charming woman whose husband was an archaeologist and lived there too. There was a Turkish Cypriot cook in residence who was somewhat unpredictable and hot-headed. On one occasion, I was sitting at the head of one of the two tables in the dining room, with my back to the kitchen door, when he burst in, grabbed me from behind and put his hands round my neck. He tried to pull me backwards off my chair. It was a horrid moment until he was pulled off me and led away. Anyway that was the end of his job as a cook, and to this day, I have never liked sitting with my back to a door. We never knew what had sparked off this hot-headed display.

In that same house, later on we had another lively incident which played itself out one evening. The Collings and I were sitting listening to the Beethoven Violin Concerto, when I noticed what looked like a torch moving about in the room next door, which was divided from us by doors with frosted glass in them. It was a hot evening and all the windows were open. I guessed, correctly as it turned out, that we had a cat-burglar next door. I signalled to Harry who was nearest to me, and he cottoned on to what I was trying to tell him. Silently we arranged that on the signal 'Go' he would leap up and fling the glass door open. Meanwhile, I was to leave the room and go round to the verandah where the intruder must have made his entry. I reached the verandah as the burglar jumped out of the window, pursued by Harry. I saw a glint of steel in the intruder's hand and then heard the clatter on the ground as the knife he threw at me missed and skidded along the verandah floor. The burglar jumped over the wall into the garden and made off, hotly pursued by both of us. We tore down the road outside and could hear him panting, but we finally lost him in a dried up river bed. Back we came to the house to phone the police. As we walked in, the third movement of the concerto was just starting and Elizabeth looked up from her mending and said 'What on earth are you two doing!' It was quite an anticlimax. When the police arrived we gave them the knife and the burglar's shoes which he had left behind, and we also discovered that he had snapped off a stand tap which stood some eighteen inches high in the garden. I should think it must have injured him, but he was never caught. Fortunately we had stopped him in his tracks and nothing was missing, in spite of there being cameras and money about.

Early on, I joined a choral society. We concentrated mainly on oratorios, such as Handel's *Messiah*, Haydn's *Creation*, Mendelssohn's *Elijah* and the great Bach *Passions*, to name but a few. I was lucky on one of our performances to be chosen to sing the solo soprano part. I also joined a drama group, and the first play I was involved in was *A Midsummer Night's Dream*, playing Hermia. We gave public perform- ances and it was all great fun. In the winter months, I joined a large group of people who did weekly Scottish country dancing. As well as the expatriate population, there were a lot of army and air force personnel on the island, so as a young woman – I was twenty-three when I went out there – I had a lot of parties to go to and plenty of willing escorts! There were Regimental dances, which were dressy affairs, as well as other social gatherings. Another activity I took part in, in the summer months, was to join a small group of amateur climbers. This was run by an Air Commodore who was stationed on the island. We did a certain amount of rock climbing in the Kyrenia Mountains. I remember being terrified the first time I did anything like this. There was always a splendid picnic laid on at the end of a stiff climb, with a wonderful view from the top to go with it.

Through Harry Collings, I became very interested in archaeology. He was doing a survey of the island, and when there was time from all my many interests and activities, I would sometimes go out with him to some of the digs which were in progress. As I could draw, I was asked to do very detailed scale drawings of the artefacts which had been dug up, for the Cyprus Museum, where the objects would eventually be displayed or stored. Often these items would be only part of a whole object, but it all had to be recorded in the minutest detail. I remember drawing a rusty dagger which had been found; it had to be minutely measured and every little indent had to be recorded. Another thing I did sometimes, was to try to piece together shards, which were pieces of broken pottery, which had been found. The whole island was a treasure trove for the keen archaeologist.

Looking back on my time in Cyprus, I can't think how I had time to do all these things as well as hold down a busy job, but I suppose at that age one didn't mind burning the candle at both ends. I played tennis, but as it was rather hot during the day, I used to get up early and play at the English Club soon after six in the morning, and then go back for a shower and breakfast, before starting my teaching. We worked until early in the afternoon, so one had time to rest in the heat of the day. I remember on one occasion being asked to take the youngest form for Scripture because a colleague was ill. I read the children a simple story from the New Testament and then gave them all a piece of drawing paper to illustrate the story. Imagine my amusement when one little boy showed me his interpretation, which was a picture of a bowler-hatted gent in the desert, carrying a suitcase with the letters J. C. on the side of it!

My teaching colleagues were all English except for one Turkish woman. Another member of staff who was particularly kind to me early on in my time there, was an elderly woman called Mrs Millington Drake. She lived with her husband near Myrtou, some distance from Nicosia, where they had a very quaint house which was built into a rock on a hillside, so it was rather like a cave. They had lived in Cyprus for many years, and their house was full of things they had collected locally over the years. To some she was a rather formidable woman, but she took me under her wing and said very firmly that she would call me 'Bill', why I cannot think, as it was nothing like my real name, but she was not the sort of person one argued with! Again the families of my pupils were very kind to me, and I was frequently asked out for a day at the beach or some other outing at the weekend to explore another corner of the island. Of course, I often met them again when I went to one of my many rehearsals or to the club in the evening.

During the winter holidays, many of us went up to the Troodos Mountains to ski. It was always said that in Cyprus one could ski in the morning and bathe in the sea in the afternoon. The journey up to the mountains meant a fairly long drive of some hours, which became a very twisty, hair-pin bendy sort of road as one got up into the mountains. The first part of this journey was in the warm lowlands and through little villages. As the road started to climb, the villages changed their character. There were lots of fruit and almond trees, which by March were in blossom, grouped round each village. The first time I went was with my employer. Margie was always very kind to me, and was very anxious that I should be made to feel welcome, as I was so far from my home and family, and she took a lot of trouble to settle me in. In early March I was up there skiing again, but very unfortunately, I had a very nasty fall and smashed up my knee. The skiing was not very easy as there were a lot of trees and there were not really any recognizable ski runs. I was brought down off the mountain and driven back in agony to Nicosia. After a medical examination, I had X-rays, which revealed a badly torn cartilage. I went into a private clinic and had the cartilage removed. I remember thinking that I had never had such awful pain ever before in my life. The other thing that worried me considerably was paying for all this. I don't know if people had medical insurance in those days, but I certainly did not. When I finally came out of hospital, I was on crutches for quite a long time, learning how to walk all over again. It always seems strange to me now to hear how quickly people get over such operations, when I think back to the very different way these injuries were treated nearly fifty years ago. I felt even more anxious not to let Margie down, and hobbled back into the classroom as soon as I was able to.

Little did I know that worse was to come. I was beginning to get back into my stride, when I had a letter from Mother giving me the devastating news that Father had died very suddenly and unexpectedly. I was completely bowled over and numbed by the news. I simply couldn't take it in. I think that when one is young, until one parent dies, one somehow thinks they are immortal. It had just never occurred to me that this might happen. Once again Margie was kindness itself and she gave me some time off. There was an English Archdeacon out there whose children I taught, and he came to see me, which helped a little. With Margie's co-operation, I made plans to see out the summer term and to then come home for three months' summer vacation to be with Mother, before returning to Cyprus for my final year. I made arrangements for a bank loan to do this, as I had already had an advance of salary to pay for my operation and hospital stay. I booked my passage home and finished the term teaching, still hobbling about on a walking stick. As I had time to reflect on all these happenings, I felt so glad that I had told Pa of my personal tragedy and my reasons for going abroad, but also sad that I had lost a father to whom I had grown closer as I grew to adulthood.

As the date of my departure drew near, I packed and put my travel documents in order. My passage was booked and I was ready to go. The day before I was due to sail, guess what? I went down with appendicitis! Everything had to be cancelled, and Mother telegraphed. I could only begin to imagine her disappointment. To make matters worse there was a delay in getting hold of a surgeon, and my appendix burst and I became rather ill with blood poisoning. All this delayed my recovery and made me very weak. Another thing which upset me a lot at this time was that I received a parcel from England. It was a book which dear Pa had posted to me, surface mail, for my birthday.

After three weeks my surgeon allowed me to rebook my passage, this time it was via Genoa, provided I could find someone who was going on the same boat, who would look after me, and I was lucky to find two friends who were going to England who were willing to do this. The first port of call was Piraeus, the port for Athens. We

8. The Corinth Canal showing its almost sheer sides.

then had an interesting and slow sail through the incredibly narrow Corinth Canal. I had been through this strait on my way out to Cyprus but because of my illness I hadn't been able to see it. The boat only just fitted in between the sides and went very slowly to avoid causing erosion to the banks, and one felt one could almost put out one's hand and touch the steep sides of the canal. I was told that Commandos trained on these walls during the war. I noticed that there were fig trees growing out of the rock on either side of us. After we left the Corinth Canal, we looked back and could see what looked like a ship sailing across the land. It was in fact another boat in the canal.

As we were making for Genoa, we sailed round the toe of Italy, through the straits of Messina and up the west coast of Italy *en route* for Naples, our next destination. Our journey was interrupted because the island of Stromboli was ablaze with a highly active volcano. It was evening and the mountain was spewing out red hot rocks and sparks, and the whole sky was alight. The Captain of our boat said that he was going to sail right round the island so that we could see this awe-inspiring sight. It is the only time I have ever seen anything like this and we gathered on deck to watch the firework display! When we got to Naples my companions and I had a few hours ashore before we sailed on to Genoa, and then on by train across the continent. When we were going through customs in Genoa, I remember seeing large families of Cypriots sitting with all their luggage done up in huge bundles, or packed in large Ali Baba-style straw baskets. They also had considerable quantities of Cyprus brandy with them. I was told by someone who purported to know such things, that these travellers would fill one bottle with cold tea made to match the colour of the brandy, then if the Customs questioned them, they would say 'Oh it is only cold tea for the journey,' and offer the official a sample sip from the doctored bottle!

By the time I got home I had lost the best part of six weeks of the precious twelve I had originally. But it was better than nothing, and I was with Mother to give her some comfort and support. Pa had died of a thrombosis. He was only 63, which was no age really. I stayed at home for the whole of the vacation and when the time came to leave to go back to Cyprus, I found it incredibly difficult to say goodbye, especially to Mother who had so much responsibility to bear alone, including the youngest two daughters, Mary and Fanny, who were still at school.

The journey back to Cyprus was uneventful thank goodness, as I felt I had had more than my share of drama by now. When we got to Piraeus we had a few hours in port, and many of the passengers took the opportunity to go to Athens to see the Acropolis and the Parthenon. Of course I went too. I was enormously impressed by the ruins, especially their massive size and the wonderful position on which they were sited. Although I was nothing more than a tourist, I also felt I was quite a seasoned traveller. On arrival back in Cyprus, I got back into the routine of life as quickly as I could, and felt I must try to look forward and make the most of my remaining time on the island. At the weekends, I often had an invitation to go off on a journey of exploration of the island. There were visits to Hilarion castle, a fairy-tale ruin in the Kyrenia Mountains, and further afield were the castles of Buffavento and Kantara. In the spring these lovely places had a wonderful display of wild flowers; I remember particularly the little cyclamen carpeting the ground at Kantara, and lower down the mountain small wild dark browny-red tulips. Whenever we picnicked in the countryside, we often had locally grown oranges to eat. It was customary to leave the peel beside the track for the goats to eat during their wanderings. At first I found this quite hard to do, having been brought up to take my litter home with me! Another pastime I tried was sailing, off the north coast near Kyrenia. I must confess this was not my favourite occupation as I often felt a bit queasy. I found that bathing in the sea was enjoyable in the hot weather, but the water was never really warm.

Another experience I had for the first time in my life at about this time was to feel an earthquake, or perhaps I should say a fairly severe tremor. I was awoken in the night by a rumbling sound and felt a funny sensation. On putting on the light I watched my dressing table stool gently slide across the polished floor. I don't think I really even then fully understood what was happening, but when I sat up in bed I felt very giddy and rather sick. I rushed to the wash basin and was very sick, and was still there when someone else in the house got up and came to see if I was all right, and it was she who told me what was happening. It was all over in a very short time, but I can only think that, bad sailor that I am, my stomach didn't like the rocking sensation!

I tried to keep up my drawing and painting, and, as I had to pay off my bank loan, I decided to do a set of pen and ink drawings of Famagusta to help towards doing this. There were a lot of interesting ruined churches and other ancient buildings there, and, as I had been invited to have an exhibition of some of my work, I hoped to be able to sell some pictures and improve my financial situation. I made several trips down there and eventually completed a portfolio of drawings. I was very surprised and delighted to sell all my pictures at the exhibition. I had obviously found a hole in the market. Another opportunity came my way after this, and this was to illustrate a book written by a Greek doctor who had served in the British Army during the war. The book was printed privately and I was required to do a lot of small pen and ink illustrations, and to check his English grammar and spelling. Life was certainly full of variety, and it all helped to improve my finances.

During this second year, I decided to have a go at taking my advanced driving test. This, and my ordinary driving licence, would be valid in England as Cyprus was a British Colony. Looking back on this, I am amazed at the confidence of youth. Margie was very good and I was able to use her old Morris almost whenever I liked, and I never made any practice runs, but went off and took the test without batting an eyelid. I think it was quite a stiff test. I had to drive along some horrific routes and negotiate rough mountain roads which I didn't know, but I emerged triumphant which was a relief.

Another interesting trip I did was to go east from Kyrenia and up to the pan-handle of the island. This area was called the Karpass. The country was quite different there. Once one had left the mountains, the land flattened out and there were wide sandy beaches with a sort of marram grass growing in the sand, and there were cattle grazing on the shore. It was a strange sight. There were a lot of goats on the island, and we often had goat meat to eat. I found it quite palatable in taste but tiresome to cut and eat because it had a lot of gristle and sinew running through it. We also got used to seeing the servants running out with buckets in the rainy season, to collect snails. These were cooked as a delicacy and served with butter. I found them a little bit like a kidney, but rather chewy and rubbery. I went to the ancient ruins of Salamis and when walking through the ruins found a long snake skin which had been cast by its owner. It was nearly three feet long so I was glad not to have met its occupant. Not far from Salamis,

9. Cattle on the shore of the Karpass.

I went to St Barnabas's Monastery. Here were three very elderly monks, who looked very alike and were reputed to be brothers. They were Greek Orthodox and wore long black robes and round black head-dresses. They had long white beards, and although we could not communicate by language, they were very hospitable and jolly. As was the normal custom they showed us round their church and then, very pointedly, stood round the offertory box. We took the hint!

As I was a Cub Mistress I thought I should arrange a cub camp for a few days. After discussion with Margie, I went ahead with the arrangements. About fifteen boys wanted to come and I had the help of a senior Girl Guide and two Boy Scouts. We camped in some eucalyptus woods some miles from Nicosia at a place called Athalassa. We did all the usual things, putting the boys through their tests, camp fires, sing-songs, map reading and some simple orienteering. It was hard work and good fun, and I was lucky to have some excellent support from the older members of our party. When we returned from this camp, we heard on the wireless the sad news of the death of the King, George VI, on 6 February 1952. Little did I know then that I would see his daughter crowned in Westminster Abbey the following year.

During my last year I met a young Army officer at a dance, and we fell madly in love. We saw a lot of each other in the ensuing weeks and spent as much time as we could together. He was a few years older than me, good-looking, at least I thought so, and we had a lot in common and shared many of the same likes and dislikes. We both came from the same social background which perhaps mattered more then than it does now. Everything seemed perfect, except that hanging over us was the fact that at some time he might move at very short notice to Suez. Trouble was brewing there and later two thousand paratroops were moved to the island. They lived in an enormous tented camp waiting for the summons to come. After some months of bliss, the dreaded call came in the middle of the night. I had a hasty phone call and he, and all the others, were away. We wrote faithfully to each other for the remaining months of my time in Cyprus. The sequel to this part of my story was to be played out after my return to England.

It was in the Easter holidays that Elizabeth Collings asked me if I would like to go on a trip round the island with her. I was very glad of this diversion to help lift my spirits, and I thought it would be very interesting. I had seen quite a lot of the island already but not always with someone who knew far more than I did about the ancient sites which we were to see. Elizabeth was very keen on archaeology and took an active interest in Harry's work, and was very knowledgeable too. Harry was going to be away in Greece and we would have the use of a borrowed lorry. The plan was for me to drive the lorry, and we would stay in the guest rooms of monasteries, or failing that, in little pensions in the villages. We took quite a lot of provisions with us. The weather was normally quite nicely warm by April, and although we had to be prepared, we didn't expect much rain as most of the rainfall was in the winter months.

We set off laden to the gunwales with a tent in case of emergency, and, most important of all, several bottles of three star Cyprus brandy, not for our consumption, I hasten to add, but to have by us as gifts. This was especially relevant when we stayed in the guest rooms of monasteries. These rooms were free but it was customary to make such a gift as well as putting a suitable contribution in their church alms box. We took some provisions with us, but bought bread, olives and cheese for our lunch daily. Of course we had cameras, note books and I had my sketching things with me. As it turned out though I didn't do much of this as we seemed to be on the move so much.

We set off from Nicosia going north along the familiar road to Kyrenia on the north coast. This road took us through the pass over the mountains behind Kyrenia, and right under the castle of St Hilarion. On either side of the road in this part of the island were acres of olives trees, and especially nearer the coast tall narrow cypress grew in and around the villages. In Kyrenia we turned westwards along the coast road to the village of Lapithos. Here we stopped and watched a potter making terracotta pots of every conceivable shape and size. There were rows and rows of them standing in the sun to dry. The whole village seemed to be involved in the industry of pot making, and the sides of the road were lined with hundreds of them. In all the surrounding area, and in fact all over the island, donkeys were used extensively by the local Cypriots. Very close to Lapithos and right on the coast we looked at the ancient remains of Lambousa. They date from the eighth century BC. I found myself becoming quite blasé about these and other ruins as there was so much that was so old on the island.

Our journey continued on to the west through Myrtou, where Mrs Drake and her husband had now retired to their 'cave' dwelling, Morphou where we looked at Ayios Monastery, and on to the ancient and once most famous city of Soli. It was supposed to have been named after the philosopher Solon. It had been a capital of one of the nine kingdoms around 600 BC. but had reached the peak of its glory much later in Roman times. There was a fine Roman amphitheatre complete with the actors' entrance. We saw what seemed, to my inexperienced eye, extensive and unrecognizable ruins. Many of the stones from these and other sites had been taken by the villagers over the centuries for their own building. It was ever thus I fear.

From Soli we went on to the great ruins of the palace of Vouni and the surrounding remains high on a hill with wonderful views. I felt as though I was standing on the top of the ancient world. The ruined palace was spectacular and was like a platform on the summit, and one could look across to the south coast of Turkey on a fine day. I can't begin to touch on the history of this place, but I felt truly humbled to think of the sophistication of the way of life here as long ago as 500 BC. They had baths, a hot water system, and deep wells to supply these.

On leaving Vouni, we cut south to go to Kykko monastery where we drove on a very rough but metalled road. The abbot of Kykko at that time was Makarios who was later to become the famous political figure Archbishop Makarios. We visited a number of monasteries including one called Ayios Theophilous which was miles off the beaten

10. One of the monastries we stayed in showing the abbot in his Greek Orthodox robes.

track, and high up in the mountains. As we got up into these mountains, which were heavily wooded with pine trees, the road got rougher and rougher, and more and more twisty as we climbed. There were steep hair-pin bends and alarming drops on the edge of the not very wide road. I dreaded the thought of another vehicle coming down from the top. Fortunately this didn't happen, but the situation was not helped by the fact of the so-called road surface having large loose stone chips on it, and when we could see the monastery high above us and had a few more bends to negotiate, we hit a problem. I turned on a very steep right bend, got round more or less but the tyres slipped on the shale and started sliding backwards. I tried to hold the vehicle with the brakes but was still slipping nearer and nearer to the edge. Elizabeth leapt out of the cab and tried to put a stone behind the back wheels. We came to rest about a yard from the precipice behind us. I tried again to go forward without avail and so lost some of my valuable three feet. I was becoming increasingly alarmed, when we heard a lot of shouting, and looking up, we saw eight or ten monks in their long robes, coming helter-skelter down the steep slope from the monastery above. They had seen what was happening and mercifully reacted quickly. They heaved big stones behind the wheels, and then one of them signalled me to get out of the lorry. He took my place while the remainder put their shoulders to the back of the vehicle. Amidst much shouting and effort the lorry roared away in a cloud of dust the last few hundred yards to the top, with the monk at the wheel as though he had been doing it all his life. The monks were covered in dust and cheered and laughed as we walked up with them to join their companion. There was much shaking of hands and thanks on our part, as we gave them a much earned bottle of brandy. I felt quite limp and weak at the knees and could have done with some myself!

We were shown to the guest wing of the monastery, which were rooms down one side of a courtyard. They were sparsely furnished with an iron bed and clean linen, with a wash-hand stand in the corner together with a bottle of drinking water. We were asked what time we would like to eat, and then we flopped on our beds to rest and wait, glad of the respite. We heard the chicken which was to make our supper, being caught and killed. The meal duly arrived with a bottle of red wine and was served on a little table in our room which was lighted at dusk by candles. We slept well that night. In the morning we were served a simple breakfast and then we were shown round their church by one of the monks. After this was the familiar routine of the alms box at the end of our tour, which was fair enough. We had been made very welcome and their hospitality had been heartening. It was thoughtful of the monks to see us down round the first few hair pin bends, but after that we were on our own, and we started the next leg of our tour without any further drama.

We made our way back on the road to the north coast. In this area near Lefka we were surrounded by orange groves, this being one of the principal citrus growing regions of the island. As we went west the road hugged the coast and we kept an eye open for an excuse to stop and look at remains and churches. We spent another night at a monastery and much the same routine took place. We noticed there seldom seemed to be anyone else staying at the monasteries. Nearly fifty years ago there was nothing like the tourist industry there is today, and in the early fifties Europe was still recovering from the war. We eventually found ourselves in Paphos. From here we visited the Baths of Aphrodite, the fascinating Tombs of the Kings, and the sights within the town including the castle. It was here in Paphos that I tasted my first mouthful of squid. There was in fact, a lot of lovely fish to be had in the restaurants in this part of the island. I remember having delicious red mullet, which I enjoyed apart from all those little bones! We stayed a night in a simple little place which called itself an hotel. It was clean and inexpensive which was all we wanted. At times I felt somewhat satiated with the looking at ruins, but I wouldn't have missed this trip for anything. Looking back I wish I had taken more photographs. When we got as far as Lefkara, we saw women making lace. It was the centre of the Cyprus lace-making industry, and outside every village house were women working away at what I would have called tatting. This was lace-making on pins. They were very skilled and produced some lovely work and I bought a set of table mats which I still have after nearly fifty years. The Greek Cypriots also did very attractive cross-stitch embroidery on the front of blouses. We were told of a Greek shirtmaker who had a little shop in Nicosia, who had a sex change and subsequently sold embroidered blouses in his/her shop!

As we made our way along the south of the island, we visited Curium and then Kolossi Castle. This was a square block like a tall keep, and was built by the Knights of St John of Jerusalem. It was framed by those same tall narrow cypress trees which we had seen so often before. We passed close to the spectacular monastery of Stavrovouni built on the top of a high pinnacle of a hill, looking like an eagle's eyrie, and

11. Kolossi Castle.

had a wonderful view from the top. We didn't go right up to it, but admired it from afar. By the time we had completed our journey along the south coast and round the corner to Famagusta we had done quite a mileage. Famagusta was an interesting town; as I have already mentioned it had at least nine ruined churches all quite close to each other. The other great attraction was lovely clean sandy beaches, though sadly I understand a lot of this has been spoiled more recently by the building of hotels for the tourist trade, alongside and almost on these lovely stretches of smooth yellow sand. Of course we went to nearby Salamis and walked in the steps of St Paul and St Barnabas whose monastery was also nearby. Remember the three brothers early on in my story. We continued north up the pan-handle of the island and saw all the places and things I had noted on a previous trip. The cattle were still grazing on the beaches! We saw and visited many other churches, castles and ruins which I tried to read about each evening. When we finally got back to Nicosia, I considered myself very lucky to have had the opportunity to have seen so much.

It was now time to start my last term which would complete my two year contract. Looking back I had had a number of set-backs and sadnesses. As well as my accident, I had rheumatic fever too. In spite of all these happenings, I hoped that Margie felt that I had served her well. She certainly gave me a glowing reference and we parted the best of friends at the end of the term in June. I had payed off all my debts, and had even managed to save a little money. My passage home was paid for by Margie as part of the contract, and I said a fond farewell to the island where I had been both happy and sad. It was somewhat ironic that I had left England to cure a broken heart, and on leaving Cyprus two years later, my heart was now with an absentee boyfriend in the Canal Zone.

Chapter IV

Westminster Abbey

I LEFT CYPRUS IN EARLY JULY 1952, and again had the opportunity to see some of the ruins of ancient Athens *en route* for Genoa. This time we sailed in close to the island of Capri as we went up the west coast of Italy. I looked at everything with interest but all the time inside me were mixed feelings of having left Jeremy behind in the Canal Zone and the sense that I was going further away from him, as well as harbouring an excited anticipation of going home and seeing my family. I had been away ten months, the longest ever away from home. Mother met me on the platform of our tiny little station and we both felt quietly emotional at being reunited.

After spending some time at home catching up on the family news, and giving a Mother a hand where she needed it, I went off to stay with the two aunts in turn. Armorel was still in Nottingham, and Kathleen who was now married to Ernst was also living in a village in the same county. I saw some of the Llanmorris family, Meg and Johnny in particular and the parents. They all gave me a great welcome and I felt grateful to have such loving and loyal friends. They were really my extended family.

My next urgent priority was to get myself a job for the September term. I certainly couldn't afford not to earn. I felt that Truman and Knightly had served me well in the past, and so I put myself on their books again and asked them to let me know what posts they had vacant. I was anxious to get something fixed up before the summer term was over in the English schools. They duly sent me several possibilities, and when I looked at them, I saw what appeared to be a particularly interesting job being offered at the Westminster Abbey Choir School. I decided that I wanted that post and I wasn't, for the time being anyway, going to apply for any other interviews. Usually for these interviews one's expenses were paid which was a relief. I had managed to save a little money from my Cyprus experience, but I was not all that flush.

I travelled up to London by train and met the Headmaster at the school. The post offered was to live in, and to teach French and Geography to all four forms and to be in charge of the youngest form and teach them most subjects. I would have to be prepared to take Art classes weekly. This was because, although there was an Art master in the form of a professional and quite well-known Royal Academician, he was frequently unable to come owing to his many other commitments. The salary was £300 per annum all found. The post was offered to me there and then and I accepted. The pay may seem a pittance now, but to me it was riches. I would be living in a highly desirable and pleasant part of London, within the precincts of the Abbey, and in the quietude of Dean's Yard.

I hurried back to Norfolk to tell Mother the news of my future job. While there I decided to spend a little of my savings on buying myself an antique bureau. Mother and I went off to King's Lynn and poked about among the antique shops until I found one that I liked and which suited my pocket. It was a Queen Anne bureau made in oak with the original brass handles and was in very good order. It cost me £25! Somehow we managed to get it home in the car. I was as pleased as Punch to own my first piece of furniture and lost no time in moving into it.

As September arrived, I put my mind to getting myself ready for my new way of life. I was still writing to Jeremy and he to me. We missed each other dreadfully and had no idea when we would be able to see each other again. I told Mother all about him, and of course marriage was in my mind for the future. Patti was now married and had a small daughter. She lived not far from Mother so she saw a certain amount of her. Beth was a driver in the WAAF so she had left home. Mary was to go to Exeter University and Fanny was in her last year at school.

The Choir School always went back for the September term in time to sing at the Battle of Britain Service. It was one of the many big services which took place during the year. Among others were the Judges Service at the beginning of one of the Law Sessions, the Maundy Service when the Sovereign dispensed the Royal Maundy to selected pensioners, and the Order of the Bath Service in Henry VII's Chapel.

The latter two services were the only regular ones which were attended by the Sovereign. For the Judges Service, all the chairs in the nave were removed to make a huge sort of reception area for the bewigged gentlemen to muster. This always annoyed Sir William McKie the Organist and Master of the Choristers as, while they were waiting, they would smoke and chat loudly forgetting that they were in a place of worship. To bring them to heel, he would play the most almighty chord on the organ, with all stops pulled out I shouldn't wonder. They would on this 'command' stub out their cigarettes on the floor of all places and shuffle into position to process forward for the service.

The school itself was a long, tall, narrow Victorian building on five floors which included a basement and a top floor where there was a play area for the boys. The Headmaster and his wife had their own house next door and I had a bed-sitting room over part of this house. I and a junior master were the only members of the teaching staff who lived in, but the Matron, Assistant Matron and the Housekeeper were also resident. The remaining teaching staff including the music teachers came in daily or weekly. One of the masters was the son of Kathleen Harrison the actress, and she used to come occasionally to school functions.

There were thirty-six boys in the school and they were all choristers, unlike many other cathedrals who had a preparatory school of which some pupils were choristers. A full choir, in my day, was twenty-two boys. Sometimes the top twenty-two sang and always Sunday Evensong was sung by the bottom twenty-two. This meant that the middle boys were always the hardest worked. They were all intensely musical of course, having been hand picked at a voice trial which they had to pass at the age of eight, before entering the school. They all had to play at least one musical instrument. At the three-day voice trials which took place once or twice a year according to how many places had to be filled, Sir William McKie tested the boys on the musical side and I meanwhile put the boys through a simple test in the three Rs. This was necessary to make sure that any chosen candidate was intelligent enough to be able to cope with the very heavy work load which they would face. They entered the school the term they were nine and left between thirteen and fourteen. If a boy's voice broke before he was due to leave he became a non-singing chorister, which sounded a bit of a contradiction! The choristers regularly sang ten services a week, and before each of these they had up to an hour's practice in the Song School, just off the cloisters. It is interesting to note here that the chorister who produced the sweet singing voice which was suitable for filling the Abbey, often came from a boy who was not large in stature, while those at St Paul's Cathedral who needed a more hooting tone to fill that building, were much larger boys generally. This had the effect of our nearly always being beaten on the football field, as they were more powerful altogether, a decided advantage in a tackle.

As well as all this music, the boys had a preparatory school curriculum, when lessons had to be fitted in round the music programme. They played football and cricket on the green in the middle of Dean's Yard, and more serious games and matches at Vincent Square. Every boy had to do an hour's music practice daily on his chosen instrument. Sometimes when they had a few hours free, I would take them to relax, to the garden of Lambeth Palace, the London residence of the Archbishop of Canterbury, at that time Dr Fisher. There was a nice rough semi-wooded area at the bottom of this large garden and here I ran a cub pack and we used to be allowed to light small fires, and hold our pack meetings in these pleasant surroundings. I often took my sketch pad and paints and did botanical studies of flowers growing in the garden. Apart from the background noise of traffic outside, one would never guess that one was in the centre of London. Very occasionally Dr Fisher would wander down and talk to us.

Christmas and Easter were particularly busy times with lots of extra music to learn. The boys had to be in residence all through Christmas and they did not go off for their Christmas holidays until after the Epiphany services on January 6th. Then they had a ten day break, having had the day off on Boxing Day. The same happened at Easter as they had to sing all the Easter services. When they went over to the Song School before each service, they had to be accompanied by a member of staff in order to protect them from members of the public who sometimes were a little too attentive. Likewise they were collected from the Song School after they had disrobed at the end of the service. Whenever I was on duty, I had a special little pew I sat in where I could watch the choir with an eagle eye. I had what became known as my 'Choir School look' when I was able to control the choir from a distance of some fifteen paces. I remember on one occasion this became very necessary when I saw one of the senior boys processing in for a service with a ball shape and the ends of two knitting needles protruding from his cassock pocket. I fixed him with a beady eye and dared him to bring them out during the sermon. All this had come about because several of the older boys had asked me what they could make for their mothers as Christmas presents. I bought a whole lot of coarse wool and taught them all to knit things like dish cloths, kettle holders and oven cloths. They got absolutely hooked on knitting and couldn't put it down. When I saw this coming into the Abbey, I was horrified in case Sir William McKie should find out. He would have exploded! Sir William was known for his explosions and it was not funny to be on the receiving end of his sometimes fiery outbursts. On one occasion the boys came back from the Song School bursting with amusement because, in his anger over some wrong note, he raged so much that his false teeth flew out of his mouth! One could imagine how this would go down with the boys. Sir William may have been a martinet, but he produced a choir which was the envy of everyone who knew anything about Cathedral choirs, and under this gruff exterior a kind heart beat. He was a confirmed middle-aged bachelor.

At the end of my first term at the Choir School, my predecessor and a friend of hers asked me if I would like to join them for a week's skiing in Zermatt. I jumped at the idea, especially as the friend's father owned a chalet in which we could all stay free, gratis and for nothing. Again I found myself travelling overnight across the continent to Switzerland. The chalet was wonderful being roomy and beautifully warm. The views from the windows on one side were straight out on to the Matterhorn. It was perfect. We were thoroughly spoiled by Alfred who came with the chalet. In fact he was a ski instructor by day, but he would come to the chalet first thing in the morning and stoke the boiler, bring our milk and bread for breakfast, and generally tidy up. In the late afternoon he came again and lighted a roaring fire for us for the evening, cleaned our ski boots and got wood in for the fire. He was a middle-aged jolly sort of man who fussed round us three girls like an old hen. It was a lovely holiday, or as lovely as it could be without Jeremy.

Once the spring term of 1953 dawned the boys had to get down to some very serious work. This was the beginning of the preparation for the Coronation the following June. There was much music to be learned, some traditional such as Handel's *Zadok the Priest* with which they were already familiar, as well as pieces which were composed specially for the occasion. One of these was William Walton's *Te Deum.* The boys struggled a bit with this composition. Firstly many of them didn't much like it, and I think like much modern music of a classical nature, it needed to be listened to over and over again, and as one began to become more and more familiar with it, so it grew on one. They were told that they had three weeks in which to learn it, and that they couldn't go home for the holidays after Easter until it was learnt. Of course they did it, and the composer came down to hear them sing it and was amazed at their mastery of the work.

Within the Abbey there was much preparation going on. Stands had to be built as there would be seven thousand people attending the service on June 2nd. The annexe at the West Door had to be erected, and armies of technicians were preparing the lighting and sound for filming and broadcasting. Lavatories had to be built in, as some people would be in the Abbey for many hours. One day during the preparations four men in white coats arrived and asked one of the vergers where the carpet near the High Altar was, as they had come to take it for dry cleaning. They rolled it up and walked off with it. It was an audacious theft. I never heard if it was ever recovered. The Duke of Norfolk, as Earl Marshal, was in charge of all the ceremonial in the Abbey, and the Duchess stood in for the Queen at the rehearsals. I often went up to the Muniment Room in the Abbey to watch some of the rehearsals, and on one occasion I was there when the Queen came to watch her under-study going through her paces. The Muniment Room had a little balcony high up in the corner of one of the transepts from which one could look down on all the activity in the choir and chancel.

A regular visitor to the Choir School was Field Marshal The Viscount Montgomery of Alamein, or Monty as everyone knew him. He used to come to the Abbey services quite often, calling it his parish church, and rather adopted the Choir School. It was he who gave a medal on a ribbon which was always worn by the Senior Chorister when robed. He gave the choristers a Christmas party every year, and took a genuine interest in the boys, though he could be a little tactless to say the least. We had a boy who had very difficult wiry hair which simply would not lie down and behave itself and was an ongoing embarrassment to its owner. Every time Monty came to the school, he would say, 'You boy, what's your name boy, get your hair cut.' Anyway Monty used the Choir School quite a lot during the run up to the Coronation, as he was required to attend some of the rehearsals. When it came to his dressing up in his garter robes he was in his element. One day he came to lunch wearing his dress uniform. We were having salad for lunch and he stuck his knife into a tomato which exploded down the front of his uniform. He said 'Look at that, it went off like a bomb.' If he said it once he said it half a dozen times. Another rather amusing incident was the time that he rang up and the call was taken by a member of the domestic staff who had not been at the Choir School for very long. Monty announced himself as 'Field Marshal The Viscount Montgomery here,' to which she replied in broad Cockney 'Oh yeah, Buckingham Palace 'ere!' He was not amused.

Back in the Choir School as the Coronation drew nearer, the Headmaster called the staff together and offered us all seats in stands outside the Abbey, with the exception of one master who was to escort the probationers, or youngest members of the choir, into the Triforium for the service. The original idea was that any one of these boys would be ready to go down to the main choir should one of those boys be ill or for some reason be unable to sing. This was totally unpractical as the Abbey was so packed it would have been an impossible feat to achieve. All the staff except me accepted their seats with gratitude. I politely declined as I had other plans. I wrote to a distant cousin of mine whom I didn't know very well, to see if he, as a peer, could get me in the Abbey. Although he said he would have liked to have helped me he couldn't do so. So that was that. My next plan was to approach Guy, the master who was to look after the probationers. I asked him if he would like some help with his little party of boys. He, being the nice man that he was, enthusiastically agreed. As the great day approached there was more and more activity in Dean's Yard. It was the 'back door' into the cloisters and the Abbey and there were many comings and goings. The Coronation coach was parked there one day, which naturally caused much excitement. Some of the boys got into the habit of having cameras at the ready, for there was often an unexpected windfall of a shot, including the Queen herself on one occasion.

When Coronation Day dawned, we were all up very early. I dressed in my finery. This consisted of a dress I had worn at a garden party, and a hat of course. Over the top of all this I wore a lightweight coat, which was merely for the purpose of covering up my dress, while I got out of the Choir School. I joined Guy and the probationers, he leading the way and I bringing up the rear. We had to enter the Abbey by a very roundabout route. As we went through each little door we were checked. Each time I smiled sweetly and we went on to tackle the next check point. We went up narrow stairways, round little corners until I had quite lost my sense of direction. After going through six checks, we arrived in the Triforium where we were to sit. We had a marvellous view of everything. Being so high up we could see over the organ loft and into the choir. Behind us was a long open space the size of a cricket pitch, where we could walk about and stretch our legs. The only other people up there were the Queen's scholars from Westminster School, who were to shout the 'Vivats.' We had the use of some lavatories which had been specially built up there. We entered the Abbey at 7 a.m. and came out at 3.40 p.m. It might seem a very long time, but there was so much to watch that the time seemed to fly by. We watched the guests arriving, and opposite us was a block of senior Naval Officers in uniform with their medals glistening and their gold braid adding highlights of colour to their dark uniforms. Many of the ladies wore long dresses, tiaras and sparkling jewellery. Like us, many of them had sandwiches to sustain them. Up in the Triforium we were just under some pretty powerful lights, which were pointing down on to the nave, so that when we were standing up and looking over the rail, it was very warm indeed. Whenever the young choristers took their eyes off what was going on, I said 'Watch this, every minute of it, you may never see such a sight again in your life.'

Members of the Royal Family processed in as well as other dignitaries. In fact everyone was a dignitary that day! As 11 a.m. approached, one felt the excitement all round the Abbey. There was a hush of anticipation, as we waited for the Queen and her entourage. And then an anticlimax when seven maids with seven mops appeared, or rather an army of women in white coats and pushing carpet sweepers materialized from nowhere, to sweep the carpet in readiness for Her Majesty. When they had disappeared, there were a few more minutes to wait and then the procession started. There was a fanfare from the trumpeters in the organ loft and the Queen moved slowly along the nave from the West Door. As she passed the men bowed and the ladies curtsied. For a few moments she was out of sight as she went under the organ loft and into the choir, when, for us up in the gods, we saw her again as she took her place beyond the choir. The music, which we all knew very well by now, still thrilled us, and the solemnity of the occasion was something I would remember to the end of my life.

When the time neared for us to leave the Abbey, we could all honestly say that we were oblivious to the passage of time. As it was a case of first in, last out, we didn't leave the Abbey until 3.40 p.m. The whole day was a triumph of organization. That evening the Dean of Westminster, Dr Don, who had a leading role to play during the Coronation Service, came over to the Choir School to join us for staff supper. He sat down at the table and after saying Grace, he put his hands on the table and said, 'Well Headmaster, I had 7000 people in my Abbey today.' At which the Headmaster said 'No Mr Dean, 7001.' By this time I had told him that I had been determined to get into the Abbey, and that I had achieved this ambition. I added that I had thought it would be better that he didn't know what I was planning to do, but he had guessed when I turned down the offer of a seat outside Dean's Yard weeks ago.

The day after the Coronation, the boys had a well-earned day off. I took most of them down to Lambeth Palace. When we got down there, we had just gone through the main gate when Dr Fisher appeared. The boys all crowded round him and some of them said 'Sir, Sir you made a mistake in the service!' They knew the service backwards after so many months of rehearsals. He was not in the least put out and said that he had to cover up a small mistake the Queen had made. He loyally would not say what that mistake had been. The boys were full of chagrin that they had missed that one!

Another important happening which took place in January 1953, though perhaps it was slightly eclipsed later by the Coronation preparations, was the launching of the £1,000,000 Abbey Restoration Appeal by Sir Winston Churchill. The restoration was to be a 10 year programme, but in fact it was to go on for much longer than that. Certainly Coronation year was a good year to bring the need to the attention of the public.

After all this excitement it was quite difficult to get back into the daily routine again but the choristers' work had to go on. One of my many duties was to supervise the boys' daily music practice. They had to do an hour's practice a day and this had to be fitted in between their school work and their Abbey duties, so sometimes it meant getting a boy out of bed early to do this before breakfast, and woe betide any boy who forgot or skipped his stint. There was a row of practice rooms and we had six to eight pianos on the go at any one time. On the whole the boys were very good. Being so musical I think it was not such a chore as in some schools. Some of the boys used to compose in their spare time. They had a good library and there was a snooker table in the older boys' common room and I came to rather enjoy having matches with them. Another one of my responsibilities after I had been there for a few terms, was to take the football team to matches with other preparatory schools. There was a school minibus which I was entrusted with and it was always a treat to get out into the countryside after life in London. One of the schools we went to used to ask some of us down towards Christmas time to collect holly and greenery to decorate the school. Then everyone would help to make the school look festive.

In those days we had dreadful smog in the winters. They were real pea soupers and taking the boys across Dean's Yard to the Song School was quite a responsibility. I used to make them hold hands in a long chain and counted heads carefully on arrival. This may sound unnec-essarily cautious to us nowadays, but some readers may remember what these days were like in London in the 1950s. Talking of counting heads reminds me of another amusing instance which happened to me. I had taken the boys down to Vincent Square to play a football match, and we were a little on the late side getting back. Soon after leaving Vincent Square, I was aware that one or two boys were trying to say something to me, but I told them to be quiet and get moving. On arrival back at the school, I found that I had two strange boys in tow. They had been trying to tell me that they didn't belong to my party, but I, in my impatience, had scooped them up and told them to stop arguing. I was not allowed to forget that in a hurry. The choristers came from various backgrounds, and for some it was a big change to live away from home for the first time. In all my years teaching, I had only once come across a boy who was seriously homesick. One or two might have a little weep on the doorstep when saying goodbye to their parents, but if they could have seen their sons ten minutes after they had left, they would have been reassured.

Opposite the Choir School in Dean's Yard, was Westminster School.

We saw a little bit of them and one or two of the masters. One of these masters had what one might now call a vintage car, which was parked in the Yard. One night, unbeknown to its owner, some boys from the public school dismantled it and carried it, piece by piece, to an empty room in the school, and then put it all together again. The first thing that happened the next morning was that the car was reported missing presumed stolen. Then as time ticked by the truth came out. History doesn't relate the conclusion for the guilty parties, but I thought it rather ingenious. Other residents in the Yard were the Headmaster of Westminster School, some canons, and next door to the Choir School lived the Precentor. His name was The Reverend Cyril Damms. He and his wife used to ask me round to supper occasionally. I remember that when he sent out his Christmas cards he always signed them, 'from the whole Damm family'! At the far end of the Yard was Church House where synods and other important ecclesiastical meetings took place. We often saw gaitered bishops in all their finery, walking past the school. During the year there was occasionally a special wedding at which the choristers were required to sing. One of these during my time was the wedding of Viscount Althorp to the Honourable Frances Roche, later to become the parents of Diana, Princess of Wales.

By the summer of 1954, I had a letter from an old colleague from Cromer days, the very same Cub Mistress with whom I had gone to Scotland all those years before, asking me if I would like to join her with my present pack. She was taking her boys from Norfolk to a camp based in a village in Herefordshire. I was somewhat taken aback as we had not always seen eye to eye, and I hesitated in taking up this invitation, On reflection, I thought it would be enjoyed by the boys and I stipulated that I should be in complete charge of my group. I had about fifteen boys and we travelled down by train to Hereford, and then by bus out to Kingstone where we were to sleep in the village school, and arrangements had been made for someone to open up the school kitchens every evening, to cook us a hot meal. Again we had three Rover scouts to help. We were lucky in having glorious weather for the whole week. We did some pretty long walks, to Kilpeck church, the abbey at Abbeydore going cross country through fields and along small tracks to other places of interest. We hired a coach to take the whole party to Hereford to see the Cathedral and the black and white house in High Town. I think they all enjoyed themselves, but I am sorry to say that the friction among the adults repeated itself, but I weathered it all and hoped that the younger members of the party had not noticed too much.

After this I went home to Norfolk. Mother was enlarging her farming activities really to make ends meet. She had also turned part of the house into a self-contained flat which she let out to an RAF family. All this helped but she was still very hard up, and so I wrote to the Army Paymaster General to see if something could be done about increasing her widow's pension, which had been reduced because my father had commuted his pension years ago. The powers that be were very good about this and were willing to help. To do this they required a copy of her birth certificate. Here was an unexpected stumbling block. Mother was, and always had been, very cagey about her age. I pointed out to her that I couldn't go to Somerset House to get a copy unless I knew which year she had been born. She finally divulged the dreaded secret and practically made me swear on the Bible that I wouldn't tell any one, and when she died I was to make sure that her age was not announced in the paper 'for the village to see' as she put it.

All this time Jeremy and I were writing to each other. He was finally coming home and was to be stationed in the north of England, so I didn't know how much I was going to see of him, but at least we were in the same country. I still had a little time left of my holiday, and so I went off to Wales to stay with the Llanmorrises for a week, knowing that some of the younger members of the family would be there. Back in Norfolk at the beginning of September I counted up my pennies, and decided to see if I could find a second-hand car within my means. I answered an advertisement for a little Morris 8 tourer. A local farmer whom my mother knew said he would go with me to look at it, and make sure I was not being sold a pup. I was grateful for this as I didn't know the first thing about cars really. It was a two seater with a little space behind the front seats and a canvas roof. It was given the thumbs up by our friendly farmer and I bought it for the princely sum of £90. Now I had my independence, which was great. Off I went back to London for the autumn term, with no parking worries as I knew I could have a parking permit to keep it in Dean's Yard.

As the monies from the Abbey Appeal started coming in, so the restoration started in the Abbey. This meant that there was considerable disruption as time went by but the services went on as usual, and the workman had to stop during the services, and move to another area. It obviously prolonged the time a job took. There was scaffolding, platforms and ladders everywhere. For some of the workers in some of the more remote areas of the roof, for instance, it took as much as ten minutes for them to come down for their coffee breaks. The dreaded death watch beetle was discovered in some of the timbers, and so a lot of oak had to be taken out and replaced, though some of it was quite sound. The Clerk of the Works asked me if I would like a bookcase made from some of the uncontaminated wood. I gratefully accepted and he arranged this. I still have that bookcase.

On another occasion, the Dean came over to the Choir School and said 'I want to touch the roof of my Abbey before I die, who would like to come with me?' I hastily said 'I would.' He smiled and said 'I thought you would,' so off we went. When we got into the Abbey we asked the foreman which part of the roof we should go for. It was decided that the best route up was to make for the North Transept. We climbed many ladders, and walked along many platforms as we got higher and higher. One certainly had to have a good head for heights because we were a long way up by the time we reached the top. Having reached our goal, we each stood on a long plank and with paint brushes in hand, we painted some gold leaf on one of the bosses. We had made our mark and our contribution to destiny!

One Sunday, I was invited by Sir William to join him in the organ loft for Mattins. He also had up there the Senior Chorister who was not singing that day because of a cold. The organ loft was very much Sir William's domain and he used to often have one or two friends or guests up there. Being a cigarette smoker he didn't like going too long without a smoke, so during the sermon he would go down and out of the Abbey and have a little puff in the cloisters. As he left that day, he said to me 'Play the "Amens" if I am not back in time.' I was horrified and thoroughly on edge all through the sermon. I was thankful that the chorister was there and I conferred with him about which manual I should play on if it came to that, the correct stops having been pulled out. Anyway he gave me Dutch courage. Sir William, I may add, was not back in time, and, as I did the necessary with my heart in my mouth, I heard his step on the stairs up to the organ loft. After that I was not so keen to go up there for a service in case I was landed in the same situation again.

Another big surprise which happened during this period, was Sir William's engagement to be married. We were all thunderstruck. He had certainly played his cards very close to his chest. His wife-to-be was a Canadian by the name of Mrs Phyllis Birks. She was a charming woman and if anyone could soften Sir William she could. Sir William walked with a more spritely step these days, and blossomed forth in to a large brand new car, a Humber Hawk! The boys were agog by all this.

The next happening of great moment to me was my reunion with Jeremy, when he came up to London to see me. We had a lovely evening together and just talked and talked and caught up on all our news, but he said it would not be easy for him to come down from the north very often, but we continued to write every week. I was hardly ever free at the weekends to travel up to see him. It was all very frustrating. Perhaps I was naive, but I never smelt a rat, but how I was to be disillusioned. I eventually had a long letter from him saying that he had been married all the time that I had known him. I was horrified, mortified, hurt that he hadn't been honest with me. He talked of divorce and marriage to me. I was having none of this, and though I was broken-hearted, I could see no future in such a plan, besides I was not going to break up a marriage especially when there was a child involved. It would never have worked and I might have been the next victim. This decision may seem strange to some, but in my family anyway, there was a code of behaviour which we had all been brought up to respect. When I was next at home I told Mother the whole story and she said that she had always thought there was something wrong as the affair had gone on so long with no mention of marriage. How right she was. I think with hindsight my owning a car brought all this to a head, as Jeremy was probably alarmed that I might drive north to see him and the cat would have been out of the bag. With this devastating experience behind me, I threw myself more whole-heartedly into my work at the school. It has never been in my nature to brood and feel sorry for myself but it was nevertheless a bitter pill to swallow.

Visitors often dropped in to the Choir School from time to time, and one of them was an Anglican Franciscan monk. He was always very good value with a fund of amusing stories to tell. I remember one night at staff supper he told the story of a big reception at Windsor Castle where a major-domo introduced a Canon and Mrs Venables, as The

Venerable and Mrs Cannibals! Another visitor was one of the Canons from the Abbey. He always had a kipper for supper, regardless of what we were all having because he loved kippers and could never have them at home because of the smell of their cooking permeating the rarefied air of Little Cloister where he lived. Monty continued his interest in the school, and this led to his inviting a few boys down to his home, Issington Mill, in Hampshire, from time to time. This consisted of going to tea and I would drive these boys down there, and after the first time, I learnt to take my newspaper to wile away the time, because never once was I asked in, or even offered a cup of tea. I really don't know how he thought they arrived. When they emerged, the boys had been given a jolly good tea and been shown round his campaign caravan which he had in his garden. They piled in the minibus and back we went to London. I had never even had a glimpse of the great man!

Life went on for the next year. Occasionally I managed to free myself for the odd day off on a Saturday, and on one of these occasions, I had an invitation to go down to see a cousin I had, who lived in Kent. Although I didn't know it at the time, he had a scheme afoot. He had planned also to invite another cousin of his down for a weekend on a different occasion and to give him my telephone number. Anslow was in the Army and working at the time in the War Office, in what became a very busy branch a few months later when the Suez crisis finally broke. He carried my telephone number in his pocket for nine months, and then at the height of the crisis, when he had been eating and sleeping in his office, he got so fed up he decided to take a few hours off, and ring up this female. I knew of him because we were both on the same family tree. Our mothers and aunts had known each other as children, and we had mutual cousins, through our grandparents. We met for the first time over dinner at his club. After that we saw more and more of each other. I was very cautious because of what had happened the year before, and I summed him up as an equally cautious type. Imagine my surprise when he proposed within three weeks. Before I met him, I had been considering taking a post in a school in Canada at the end of the following summer; escaping from a broken heart again I suppose! Some of the choristers from St George's Cathedral, Kingston, Ontario came over to join us at the Abbey Choir School for a spell. I found myself teaching these boys and their work was way behind our boys. The headmaster said that he would recommend me to the post in Canada. But after Anslow came on the scene and his subsequent proposal, I was in a bit of a whirl. I came to love Anslow deeply as I had never experienced before, and I accepted him. This meant cancelling all my plans to go abroad.

We decided that we would not announce our engagement until we had done the rounds of the families. We had a weekend in Norfolk, and then I was taken down to Wiltshire for an inspection by his family. His father was a retired Army officer, and through his mother Anslow came from a long line of British officers in the Indian Army. Everyone was delighted, my mother especially, I think, because she had known of the traumas I had been through over the years. Next, we had to get down to some serious planning. Anslow's tour of duty at the War Office was coming to the end at the beginning of March. This meant that we wanted to get married in the middle of a term, which was not at all convenient for the Headmaster. The Dean gave permission for us to be married in the Abbey, and he said that he would like to marry us, but could not do so during Lent. We both saw the Headmaster and put the whole problem to him. I had served him well for nearly five years and with pressure from the Dean and other staff who wanted to help, he gave his blessing to releasing me.

There followed a time of much preparation for the great day, which was fixed for Shrove Tuesday, 5 March 1957. I didn't want to put any financial burden on Mother, and paid for the wedding myself. I could not have done this without the generosity and the help from the Dean and Chapter, for they paid for the printing of the service sheets, and the flowers in the Abbey, as a wedding present. The wedding itself was to take place in St Faith's Chapel, one of the side chapels. Only Royalty are married at the High Altar. This in itself presented a problem as it only held ninety people, and we had to ask all the Abbey clergy, who would be robed on either side and just below the altar, as well as members of the Chapter Office. Dr Peasgood, or Ossie Peasgood as he was known, who was the Sub-Organist, would play the organ. He was a very fine musician, and a very jovial figure. He was a complete opposite in character to Sir William. We were to have the Abbey choir, and among the music we chose were two of the Coronation anthems to be sung while we signed the register and the Dean, Dr Don composed a special prayer to bless the wedding ring. To overcome the difficulties of numbers, half the guests were asked to the reception only. I hope we did not offend anyone.

All through this activity we were wined and dined by many of our friends as well as my following through my regular teaching schedule. I had to fit in visits to the dressmaker who was making my dress, an ivory silk brocade with a pattern of small sprays of flowers in the same colour on it, and I was lent a tiara and a family lace veil. We were also very privileged to be allowed to have our reception in Jerusalem Chamber, which is an historic room just off Little Dean's Yard where the Abbey appeal was launched by Winston Churchill. Our reception was the first function to be held there since it was restored. This lovely room was said to get its name from the fact that Henry IV had always wanted to go on a pilgrimage to Jerusalem. He was taken ill in the Abbey one day, and was taken into this room, where he said 'Where am I?' The reply was 'In Jerusalem Sire,' and he died with his wish fulfilled. It is a nice story, but I cannot vouch for its authenticity. I had to use the Abbey caterers, but they were very accommodating over the cost. Mrs Don offered the Deanery for me to change into my going away outfit. Sir William and Lady McKie hosted a lunch party for Mother and three of my sisters; they had had the difficult decision to decide who was to stay behind in Norfolk to look after the growing number of children.

On my wedding day, believe it or not, I worked up to 11 o'clock in the morning. The Headmaster was having his pound of flesh! It was a military wedding and all the serving officers were in uniform. I carried an ivory-covered prayer book and a little posy of lily of the valley. Anslow's and my cousin gave me away and the Dean gave an address at the service. A brother officer of Anslow was his best man, and Johnny Llanmorris, as my proxy brother, did the honours at the reception. Officers from Anslow's regiment furnished a Guard of Honour. It was truly a day to remember.

Part IV
The Grand Tour 1957–1972

Chapter I

Honeymoon, Germany and Carlisle

FTER OUR WEDDING IN WESTMINSTER ABBEY, we had a night at an hotel in London before going down to Cheltenham. Anslow wanted to show me Cheltenham College where he had been at school, and we both wanted a few days of peace and quiet, after the hectic run up to our wedding. We had had many wonderfully generous presents which had been packed into our heavy luggage and were *en route* to Germany, except for a box of sherry glasses which the Colonel of the Regiment had brought under his arm to the wedding. These, with Anslow's uniform and sword which he had to have for the wedding, had to be carted round with us. We had both sold our cars and we were pretty broke financially when everything had been paid for. I remember I only had £15 in the bank! After Cheltenham we came back to London and prepared to catch the train to Austria, where we were to have a skiing holiday. When we got to Victoria Station, we discovered to our horror that the tour company had unexpectedly changed the date of departure and we had 24 hours on our hands. We had changed into our skiing outfits and hadn't got the face to go to Anslow's club, so we asked the taxi driver to take us to a suitable inexpensive hotel near Victoria Station. We found ourselves in what one might describe as a cheap boarding house. It was clean and respectable, but the landlady slopped about in her dressing gown with a cigarette hanging out of the corner of her mouth. We treated the whole episode as a bit of a joke, and were glad when the next day dawned and we could make our getaway.

We travelled across Europe to our destination which was Innsbruck. From there we went by another train to Solden, and on up to Hochsolden, this final bit of our journey we reached by cable car, suitcases and all, including those sherry glasses and the sword. We had a memorable week here when we ski'd and enjoyed the lovely scenery.

I hadn't been on skis since Zermatt so felt a bit wobbly and out of practice. Anslow had done quite a bit of skiing and was far less inhibited. The time came for us to pack and leave these Elysian fields, as we had to go from Austria to Cologne in Germany where we were picking up a new car. From there we were going on to join Anslow's regiment which was stationed in Göttingen, near the East German border. We got ourselves to Innsbruck where we got a mainline train to take us to Cologne. After some hours in this train we reached Ulm in the middle of the night. Here there was much shouting and commotion, and we gathered that we had to move from the back of the train up to the front few coaches in three minutes flat. Out we got with all our luggage and saw to our dismay that the train was more than sixteen coaches long. We had to walk, or rather run, what seemed like miles down the platform in the dark. We kept dropping things, including the sword which clattered noisily on the platform. We ended up with the station master and several porters carrying all our kit and hustling us into the correct portion of the train, while bleary-eyed travellers were popping their heads out of the windows of the sleepers, to see what on earth was going on.

We reached Cologne in the morning, and set about getting to the supplier of our new car. We found a comfortable hotel for the night, and spent some time looking round the city. Anslow treated me to a bottle of real Eau de Cologne. From here we drove to Paderborn where we spent another night, and I, in particular, prepared to be inspected by the regiment. I think everyone was intrigued to see Anslow's new bride, but we were given a warm welcome, and stayed with the commanding officer and his wife for the first night until we had taken over our quarter. The house we had been allotted was a large German requisitioned house on the outskirts of the town. We rattled round in this house for some weeks, until we moved into a smaller and more suitable quarter nearer the barracks.

Göttingen proved to be a lovely place to be. The town itself was a compact university town, and had been virtually untouched by the war. The Germans were very friendly. This, we understood, was because, being so near the East German border and the communist régime which prevailed there, made them realize which side their bread was buttered. We also found that quite a lot of the locals spoke English. We were told that the German spoken there was very pure and without any local accent. Outside the town were extensive beech woods and every weekend the Germans went out en masse to walk in the surrounding countryside. When we explored our immediate surroundings at the weekends, we joined a great many Germans of all ages and all shapes and sizes wearing their lederhosen and woolly hats, and carrying alpenstocks, stepping out as though their life depended on it. We were also not very far from the Harz Mountains where there was a leave camp, and the British families used to go there to ski in the winter. Near Göttingen was the attractive little town of Goslar where another British army regiment were stationed. The camp where we were was fairly self-sufficient for those who wanted it that way. There was a Naafi shop, cinema and various other facilities, though I personally preferred to do my shopping in the town. We had a medical centre and for the more serious needs, we had to go to the Military Hospital in Hanover, some eighty miles away. The battalion kept pigs, from which they made a handsome profit for regimental funds, and grew mushrooms, also for profit, in the dark basement of a barrack block. The barracks once housed a German cavalry regiment, and had been taken over by the British at the end of the war.

During our time in Göttingen, Anslow was asked to represent the CO at a rather formal German army function in the American zone further south. We set off, dressed up for the occasion, and after a longish drive, we arrived to be welcomed by our German hosts. The whole set-up was incredibly formal but what really caught us on the hop, was the fact that the German Officers' Messes were really clubs where they paid for everything then and there in cash. When it came to going in to supper we found that we hadn't brought any money with us. What were we to do? I detached myself from Anslow's side and got myself invited to supper by a German officer who paid for my food, leaving poor Anslow to fend for himself. We somehow got through the evening, but we learnt our lesson, and always had a little money on us after that. Some of the older officers were quite embarrassed by this, because they knew how it used to be before the war, and that they had more recently enjoyed our hospitality in Göttingen.

After a few months, to our delight, I found that I was pregnant. Our firstborn was due in early March. I had to go all the way to Hanover for my check-ups, but the roads were so good that we none of us thought anything of going quite long distances to appointments, cocktail parties and the like. Ma-in-law came out to stay with us, which was lovely. I got on so well with her that her visits were always looked-forward-to events.

By the autumn we were all to move from Göttingen to Berlin. There was much packing and preparation for this as the advance party was to go in October. In the regiment there was a problem soldier whom every officer dreaded having under his command. Things always seemed to go wrong when he was around. He was finally put into the Officers' Mess to be the silver cleaner, but even there he failed as he was genuinely allergic to silver polish! When the move was imminent, Anslow was unfortunate enough to have him in his company. Needless to say there was a crisis. This was because he decided to make some substantially large balsa wood plane models, which he insisted that his long-suffering wife should pack. She had had enough, locked him out of their quarter the night before he was due to go to Berlin with the advance party, and wouldn't let him have his passport! Anslow and I went round to the quarter and pleaded with his wife through the keyhole, to open the door and let the wretched man get his papers, which she finally did with very bad grace.

When the time came for us to leave, we had to be, what is called 'Marched out of our quarter'. This meant that the inventory had to be minutely checked. I was very amused by the wording of some of it. For instance there were listed – Pots chamber, pots coffee, pots tea, and then – Forks dinner, forks dessert, forks garden! I was also amazed to see that the quartermaster's staff counted the brass screws in the bolt on the lavatory door. All the china and glass was put out on the dining room table and everything was tapped with a small china rod to make sure that there were no cracks. Years later a quartermaster told us that he only had to look in the oven, when taking over a house, and if that was clean then he knew that the rest of the house would be all right.

For the journey to Berlin, those of us who were going by car had to travel in convoy from the East German Border at Helmstedt along the corridor, or road which was under the control of the Russians. This journey had to be made within a certain time and there was no getting out to spend pennies or to stretch one's legs. The journey was about 100 miles and one had to be sure that the petrol tank was topped up. There was also a train, and when this was used by the British service personnel, there was always an escort on it.

When we arrived we found that we had been given a very pleasant four-bedroomed house. In those far-off days, we also had a batwoman. She was meant to clean Anslow's uniform, as well as keeping the house in good order. At first we had a funny little German woman called Emmy, who was knee-high to a bee. She looked like another Mrs Tiggy Winkle. She insisted on putting chopped nuts in and on all her cooking including our bacon for breakfast. She lived in, and arranged her bedroom so that she had an altar at which she could pray. She seemed to spend a lot of time on her knees. What we did object to was the fact that she would put our teacloths to soak before washing, with her underwear including her combinations! We never cured her of this habit and she left. Next we had a lovely woman called Klara, who looked after us loyally and well, and after the birth of our daughter, was a tower of strength to me in a quiet unobtrusive way.

One of the regiment's main duties in Berlin was to guard three German prisoners – Schacht who was a financier and politician in Hitler's régime, Schirach, a Nazi who had been a gauleiter in Vienna and responsible for the policy of deporting all Jews, and last but not least Rudolph Hess, who was Deputy Fuehrer and consequently high up in the Nazi hierarchy. The latter had landed in Scotland in 1941 with proposals for a compromise peace treaty. He was captured and treated as a prisoner of war. At the Nuremburg trials after the war, they were all sentenced to imprisonment. Schacht was eventually acquitted, Schirach had to serve twenty years and Hess got a life sentence, which really meant life. They were all confined in Spandau Prison. The four nations who were involved in performing this duty were the British, Russian, French and American. They each did six weeks and then there was a handover, which included a luncheon, to which were invited all those officers who had been involved in the guarding of these prisoners and their wives. When we handed over to the Russians, Anslow and I were to attend such a lunch. I was heavily pregnant when this happened, but I dressed myself up in a suitably smart outfit, which happened to be royal blue with a hat to match, and along we went. Imagine my surprise to find that all the Russian wives were dressed in black and wore absolutely no make-up. I felt a bit like a Jezebel, but nothing daunted, I took my place between two Russian officers, only to find that neither of them spoke anything except their mother tongue. I discovered that if I spoke in French one of them could just about understand, and did a translation to those around us. It was all rather laborious but we got by, though all the time I felt the disapproving looks of the female Russians.

There were quite a lot of social gatherings while we were in Berlin, so there were a lot of parties to go to. It was also possible to arrange a trip into East Berlin. This was in the days before the wall dividing the two communities was put up by the Communists, but we still had to get permission to go over to the east. We went in a coach on a carefully controlled sight-seeing tour, in which we were only shown what the Communists wanted us to see. The coach took us along a wide road which had newly built blocks of buildings on either side, and everything was made to look flourishing and completely recovered from the war, but here and there, down one or two little side streets, one had a glimpse of acres and acres of bomb damage and rubble, which had been left untouched since the damage had been done more than twelve years before. Also in the built up street there were one or two large shop fronts of the state owned shops apparently stuffed with merchandise, but actually no customers in them. It was all a propaganda exercise. We were also allowed to go to the opera over there, which was very good and very inexpensive. Another area, where some British personnel were allowed to go, but not us, one could buy, very reasonably, lovely Meissen china. We managed to ask someone to get us a hand-painted and very decorative plate. Other excursions were to walk in the Grünewald, an area of woodland where it seemed the entire population of west Berlin went at the weekends, and some people sailed on the River Havel, which was more like a large lake. Generally speaking, one was fairly restricted, though, as my pregnancy progressed, I didn't feel much like doing any of these things.

By early March, I went into the Military Hospital not far from our house in Charlottenburg, and gave birth to a lovely daughter whom we called Elizabeth. We thought she was adorable of course. Anslow stayed with me all through the birth, which was quite unusual in those days. When I came home and had got myself into some sort of routine, as I had seen my mother do with all her babies, I put little Lizzie out in her pram in the garden to sleep. The German women who saw this were horrified, and there was a lot of tut tutting. They seemed to go into purdah both before and after a birth, and one never saw German babies outside except in the height of summer. When the warm weather came, one saw the German mothers wheeling their babies in funny prams which were like baskets or cribs made of woven willows on wheels. Maybe they didn't have prams which were solid enough to keep out the cold. Not long after this we had a posting home to England as Anslow was to go and command his regimental depôt in the north of England, so once again we had to pack up and go through the routine of marching out of our quarter.

Travelling, I was soon to discover, was now not so easy with a baby to think of too. We drove to Calais, which was quite a long haul from Berlin, and found a nice little hotel for the night. The next day we flew, car and all, on a Silver City plane to Lydd airport in Kent, from where we made our way to Anslow's parents in Wiltshire.

After a short stay, we made our way to Norfolk to show off our daughter to her other grandmother, and to see the rest of my family, and from there we set off for the north to see what was in store for us in Carlisle. The quarter was about the same size as our Berlin house, and had a nice bit of garden. We were both keen to grow our own vegetables and we duly put it in order and planted it up. We didn't appreciate then that the winters in Cumberland, as it was called then, were quite severe, and we were unable to dig our leek crop, which was frozen solid in the ground for several months! It turned out that we were to have only some nine months in Carlisle before we were to move yet again. We enjoyed our short time there, and explored the countryside; Anslow had invitations to shoots on the Otterburn Moors, and we made a lot of friends. We also thought we would like to start owning some of our own furniture. We had discovered that in the auction houses in the north, one could pick up items very reasonably. We bought a Victorian reproduction of an Elizabethan court cupboard in oak for £18 and antique oak grandfather clock made in Carlisle for the princely sum of £4, and an old mantel clock with a good brass movement for 9/–, this would be about 45p in our present currency. We decided to have Lizzie christened in the Regimental Chapel in Carlisle Cathedral and Bishop Bloomer performed the ceremony. The Bishop and his wife lived in a splendid residence in the county called Rose Castle, and once a year they hosted a lovely ball in the Castle, to which we were invited during our time.

Also during this period it was the time of a lot of the amalgamations of regiments in the Army, which caused the inevitable redundancies.

There were compensations for those who could apply for what became known as a 'golden bowler.' We talked it all over between ourselves in order to decide if it might be wise for Anslow to apply. He felt that as he was starting a family and his future in the Army was rather uncertain, he might be wise to try and fine a niche in the civilian world, which would extend his retirement and make the educating of his children easier. He had interviews for one or two business jobs, and also took a course which culminated in taking the exam of the Chartered Institute of Secretaries. As it turned out, the Army wouldn't let him go, which was quite nice to know, but it did mean that retirement would come earlier than in civilian life, but the decision had really been made for us, and I don't think Anslow really wanted to leave, so that was that.

Because of the amalgamations, the remainder of the regiment, who were still in Berlin, decided to make more of a special occasion of the annual parade which was held to commemorate the Regimental battle honour. Anslow decided it would be a nice idea if everyone at the depôt could be given the chance to take part in this particular weekend of celebration. It took a lot of arranging but finally he chartered a plane to take us all out for three days. I would not be able to take Lizzie with me, and so we had some very good friends who looked after her for those few days. Fortunately she was a very easy accommodating child, and in spite of her being only ten months old, we really had no qualms at leaving her, though I must confess to a lump in my throat when we said goodbye to her.

The next posting when it came was quite a surprise. First of all it was promotion to Lieutenant Colonel and the job was in Lagos, the capital of the British colony of Nigeria on the coast of West Africa. Anslow was to go out on what was called secondment and would be working in the Army Headquarters there. Once again we packed up the house and all our heavy baggage was crated ready for its long journey by sea to Lagos. We did the rounds of family for our farewells, and then Anslow went out a month ahead of me, while I went down to his family in Wiltshire with little Lizzie who was now just over a year old.

Chapter II

West African Experience

WAS SOMEWHAT APPREHENSIVE at the thought of the long journey ahead of me, with Lizzie to look after by myself. Remember too that apart from the little hop over the Channel the year before, this would be the first long air flight I had ever undertaken. We flew from Heathrow first class in a BOAC Stratocruiser. These planes were very comfortable, and as well as having plenty of seat room, there was also a little bar and lounge downstairs to which one could go to have a drink or stretch one's legs. I am afraid I have never been a very good traveller, and this journey was no exception. I felt most unwell, so much so that oxygen was brought on for me when we stopped in Rome. Lizzie was no problem in spite of this, as the cabin staff were enchanted by her, and took her off my hands and looked after her until I felt a little better some hours later. The flight took seventeen hours in those days. I was mighty glad to feel us touching down on arrival in Lagos. What I was not prepared for was the temperature when the plane door was opened. I could not believe it. It was like that whoosh of hot air which hits you on opening the oven door. The temperature was in the nineties and was very humid with it. This was more or less what we were to expect for the whole of our time in Lagos. It was because we were at sea level and nearly on the equator.

Of course dear Anslow was there to meet us on the tarmac. We had been apart only a month, but it seemed an age. We were driven from the airport which was some fifteen miles out of Lagos, to our house which was quite large and was one of the old colonial style residences, with cool verandahs and a nice large compound. At the bottom of the garden, so to speak, were the servants' quarters which were screened from the main house. The garden had what seemed to me to be some very exotic plants. There was an enormous flame tree, which at a certain time of the year had scarlet flowers in huge masses all over it. There was an avocado tree too. It must have been planted some time ago, as these take some time to come to fruition even in that quick growing climate. There were several different kinds of hibiscus, some with long tassels coming out of the centre of the flower, and lots of other exotic tropical flowers and bushes. The staff consisted of a head boy, or steward, a cook and a small boy in the house and a garden boy. The small boy was a grown man but as his name suggested he was the lowest in the servant hierarchy! Among all the families which we knew,

12. Salu our 'small' boy.

none employed women in the house. Some of the servants had rather strange names. They were often called by their native names like our first head boy who was called Buba. Our cook was named Dick, and the small boy was called Salu, whom we had to replace after a few months, with one called Hyacinth; but more of Salu's fall from grace later on in my narrative. We found it somewhat disconcerting to call out 'Hyacinth' and then to be faced with a large black man with tribal markings on his cheeks.

Soon after our arrival, our heavy baggage arrived. I was amused to see the way it was carried from the delivery lorry into the house. Buba and the others balanced everything, however heavy it was, on their heads, and even ran upstairs with large crated trunks carried in this way, without even a hand to steady them. We had taken out quite a lot of kit, as we knew we would have to entertain a certain amount. Later we were very glad we didn't take out a new car, but bought second-hand when we arrived, from someone who was going back to England. This was because we heard of a consignment of brand new cars which had been off-loaded from a ship in Lagos docks, and their windows had been wound down to safeguard them from being broken. Unfortunately through doing this a worse disaster befell them. They stood on the quayside for a time and a ship came in alongside with a cargo of cement. While they were unloading the wind blew and there was cement dust everywhere, including in the grooves of the wound-down windows; the monsoon came, and I leave it to your imagination as to what happened.

Shortly after our arrival, Dick's wife died giving birth to a daughter. This was quite a drama as can be imagined, and I found myself getting involved in trying to help in the management of this small child. Dick had another daughter who was about five years old and she seemed to take on the responsibilities of motherhood, poor little thing. I asked Dick what he was going to call the new baby. He answered 'Oh Scholastica, Madam, because she is very clever'. After a few months had elapsed, I then said I thought perhaps Scholastica should go on to some solid food. Dick was having none of that, and said 'No Madam, when she is six months old, we will give her hot red pepper soup, this will make her strong.' He flexed his muscles to illustrate what he meant. Kill or cure was what I thought. After that I began to think that perhaps I should leave well alone and not try to impose my European ideas on their African culture and in fact she survived this draconian treatment. As for ourselves, we decided to find someone to be a sort of nursemaid for Lizzie as I found the climate fairly trying. We were lucky to find the daughter of a British Army officer, who seemed to fit the bill, and who wanted to earn a bit of money.

The Army Headquarters were not far away, and Anslow had a staff car to take him to and fro. He was also allocated a Land Rover which was being sent out from England. This took months to arrive, in fact he began to wonder if it ever would, when suddenly there it was with 'for Laos' painted on the windscreen. Someone's geography was not very good back in England, and it went all the way to the Far East, before it was tracked down and diverted to its proper destination. I think all things considered, we were lucky to ever see it again.

Our day started early, as Anslow had to be in his office by 8 a.m. Everyone worked until 2 p.m. and then had a late lunch, before having a siesta in the afternoon. By about 4.30 p.m. we roused ourselves and went down to the Mess nearby where there were tennis courts and a squash court. Anslow often played one or the other, while we watched or sat under a fan in the Mess and had a cup of tea or a cool drink. The climate was hot and sticky all the time and there was very little drop in temperature at night. At home we were lucky to have an air-conditioned bedroom and dressing room so the nights were bearable. The other bedrooms had to have mosquito nets over the beds, and we all took a daily dose of the anti-malarial drug Paludrine. Our second bathroom was only used as a bathroom when we had a house guest, otherwise we kept the bath filled with water for use in an emergency. The water supply left a great deal to be desired, and with a small family, it was essential that we had a back-up supply. I remember a time when we had no water whatsoever and had to make tea with soda water! Electricity was also a commodity on which one simply could not rely. Whenever we had a dinner party, we always got the hurricane lanterns primed and at the ready, as we frequently had to use them. We had the airmail *Times* sent out to us daily but it took several days to arrive and so we were never quite up to date with world affairs. We found this paper ideal for wrapping our breakables, when we had to move. Anslow used to bring the local paper home from the office every day. The news was somewhat limited, but we used to be very amused to read the wording of some of the African obituary notices. One of

13. Bush cattle on arrival in Lagos.

these I will always remember; it said 'In loving memory of Chief Owolowa who passed into a state of complete immorality on —'.

When we wanted to go shopping, we had to go a few miles off the mainland on to the island of Lagos which was reached by driving over a long causeway, leading on to a comparatively modern bridge called Carter Bridge. On the way there, we frequently saw herds of the most pitiful looking cattle which had been driven down from the north, on the hoof. They were mere skin and bone, and I suppose it was from such animals that the beef came, which Dick bought in the local market. Once over the bridge, one joined a complete hurly burly of traffic, animals, people and every hazard one could imagine. There were some extraordinary loads being carried on the heads of the Africans, such as double beds, armchairs, in fact anything you might care to name would or could be up there, expertly balanced and leaving the hands free. Even little school children carried their ink bottles and books on their heads. There were large portly Nigerian women with their babies and toddlers on their backs, held there with gaily coloured lengths of material. The women were the business members of the family, and it was usually they who ran the stalls beside the road. There was much hooting of horns and shouting as we tried to clear a way through the seething mass of people, without risking running someone over. It was of course very hot but we had to keep the windows of the car shut, to stop thieving hands from helping themselves or frightening Lizzie. The electricity wires ran down the streets criss-crossing from side to side in a haphazard fashion as they connected up to every little shack. On one occasion when we were driving through this typical scene, we were behind a lorry piled high with a mixed and hazardous load and with several Africans on the top of the whole thing. As it wended its way, it was catching the top of its load on the wires and plucking them like violin strings, and bringing the lot down with plenty of bangs and flashes, as it went. Amidst much screaming, the chaps on the top managed to convey a message to the driver, but not before they had cut off a large area of the town from its electricity supply.

When we reached the town centre, we parked the car and were immediately besieged by hordes of boys who wanted to look after our car. We soon learnt that it was wise to take on one of these boys, because if not, one ran the risk of having the car damaged. We used to choose the biggest and strongest of them, on the assumption that they might control the smaller, disappointed ones by sheer intimidation. It was all worth it for a few pence at the end of the day. The main shop was a big store which sold most of one's needs except food, as long as one didn't have too high an expectation, while the fresh food was bought by the cook, whom I would see at the beginning of each day to arrange our meals. The first time I had to do this, he came home with a live chicken in the bottom of his grass-woven shopping bag and this animal pecked its way around the compound for the rest of the day until the moment for its demise arrived, when Dick dispatched it. At least we knew it was fresh. As we never found the eggs very fresh and appetizing, we decided to buy some chickens and have our own eggs. Anslow, being the handyman that he was, made a run and some nesting boxes, and we were well set up and the envy of our neighbours. One of the items I always bought were pineapples. This was because I liked to choose fruits with a good green top which I would cut off and plant in a little patch which we had cultivated; after some nine months we had a lovely row of flourishing pineapple plants which were throwing up thick stems with new fruits on the top.

The bathing near Lagos was very tricky. The only place which was entirely safe was at a place called Tarquah Bay, and to get there one had to have a boat. The harbour itself had a very dangerous rip tide

14. Lizzie beside a home grown pineapple.

with strong currents, and a sand bar across its entrance. There was a bay off this entrance with a long wall of sand which made it safe from currents and from sharks. We decided, like many of our friends, to have a modest motor boat. We went to a boat builder and had it made to suit us and our pockets. Once we had this mode of transport, we spent many happy visits with Lizzie at the weekends on these golden sands, where we were also able to enjoy a much appreciated breeze. There was also another beach on the other side of the harbour, called Victoria Beach, which we went to once or twice, but Army personnel were forbidden to bathe there as it was very dangerous. Periodically people were taken by sharks or swept out to sea, if they were foolhardy enough to swim there. Anslow ran an Army sailing club within Lagos harbour but even there one had to be very careful, as there were very dangerous tides and currents.

As I said earlier, we did a lot of entertaining, and Dick, with a little supervision, coped pretty well. Running about all over the walls of our rooms were harmless little geckos or lizards, in fact we didn't mind them a bit as they helped to keep down the insects, but at one dinner we gave, an amusing incident took place at the table. One of our guests was a well-endowed woman who wore a dress with what Anslow called an 80% fall-out on the bust line. During dinner, she suddenly started squirming and clutching her bosom, and asked to leave the table. It turned out that a lizard had dropped off the ceiling and straight down her cleavage. When all had been dealt with, she settled down again, only for the same thing to happen all over again, but this time it seemed that the creature had shed its tail in there and it had started wiggling about as it was trapped in her ample bosom! Poor woman, she was so embarrassed! Anslow and I had a good laugh the next day.

Traders used to come to the house with all sorts of wares which they tried to sell us and if anything took our fancy, we would halve the asking price and then start to haggle. It was during one of these sessions that I thought I would buy a crocodile handbag, and the trader asked me if I wanted crocodilly back or crocodilly belly, as he put it. The Nigerians made quite attractive things from horn and carved wood but generally speaking, many of these objects didn't look right in a house in England. Another regular visitor to our verandah was the barber who cut Anslow's hair. A 'visitor' who at one period didn't come although we could have done with him, was the dustbin man. The public services left a great deal to be desired and we were often having battles on various fronts to get things done. Several of the British wives had a bit of a moan about the lack of waste collection, which was no joke, hygiene-wise, in that heat and I said I would go down and see the Minister of Health, following my mother's maxim of always going to the top. I was ushered into Mr Abeola's sanctum, and explained our trouble to him. He said 'Leave it to me.' I took him at his word, reported back to my fellow wives, and we sat down and waited to see what would happen. A few days later, up drove a large Ministerial black limousine driven by a chauffeur in uniform. He knocked at our door and said that on instructions from Mr Abeola he had come to empty my dustbins! These were duly loaded into the boot of the limousine and driven away. Nothing would persuade him to arrange to take anyone else's bins, not necessarily so personally! The other wives wondered what was going on, and, I think, thought that I had arranged this preferential treatment! It could only have happened in Nigeria.

It was at about this time that we heard that there was going to be a total eclipse of the sun. Knowing how superstitious and even primitive some of the uneducated Africans were, we thought we should gather the servants together and try to explain to them what was going to happen, in case they panicked and thought that the world was coming to an end. In spite of this when the event took place there was much wailing and apprehension in the compound as the light disappeared, and then a few minutes later the cries of relief as the sun 'switched' itself on again. Their culture was permeated by voodoo and strange beliefs. I remember on another occasion the panic there was among the servants when a dead white cat was found in the garden. None of them would touch it or bury it, and it fell to Anslow to deal with it. They were just too terrified to have anything to do with it.

We made a number of weekend visits to British Army friends in Abeokuta, Ibadan and to Enugu in the Eastern Province, all places where there were military barracks. It was always a pleasant relief to go 'up-country', because it was marginally cooler than Lagos. Anslow used to go further north to such places as Kaduna, and Zaria where there were battalions of Nigerian troops commanded by British officers. Some civilian expatriates used to go to a real hill station called Jos. I always regretted that we never went there as it was on a quite high plateau by Nigerian standards, and was much cooler; even roses grew there in the gardens. When we were staying near Ibadan, again in a lovely old colonial house, we were having breakfast on the verandah, when to our surprise, a chicken with a wooden leg arrived on the breakfast table to partake of some crumbs. Our host explained that it had had an accident and lost half its leg, so one of his servants carved a new leg complete with all its toes and they had strapped it on to the stump, and the chicken learnt to use its artificial limb.

Later on in that same year, Anslow had a liaison visit to his opposite number in Ghana, so we decided to go en famille, by car. This trip needed careful planning especially as we were taking Lizzie with us. She was about twenty months old by now and running about all over the place, and I was pregnant again. We travelled in Anslow's staff car with an Army driver whose name was Haaga. He was a very pleasant, reliable man to have with us, and he was devoted to Lizzie, and indeed to all of us. Our journey took us west, the road generally hugging the coast. At first we drove on tarmac but the road was not very wide, and frequently we met ramshackle old lorries thundering along towards us giving us precious little quarter. We always gave way to them because they were bigger than us! On the road too were local buses or 'mammy wagons' which looked as though they were made out of flattened out petrol cans. They were always stuffed to bursting with people and had enormous loads on the top, as well as having more passengers clinging on to the outside of the vehicle, and also many equally overloaded mini buses. At times our road degenerated into a dust or laterite road. This caused a huge cloud of red dust to billow up as every vehicle thundered past. This dust got into everything, in spite of having the windows firmly shut. On arrival at our night stop every afternoon, we often had to wash the red dust out of our hair. How we longed for an air-conditioned car.

Our first night on this particular trip was in Cotonou, the capital of the French colony of Dahomey (later to become Benin). What was especially memorable about this place were the flies. They were every-where, so much so that when we sat on a verandah for a drink, under some coconut palms, instead of putting the glass on the table mat, one used the mat to put over one's drink. The little hotel where we stayed was very basic but perfectly adequate. After so many hours in the car, we took Lizzie for a walk on the beach before settling her down for the night. Haaga was given an allowance for the night and he disappeared, and reappeared in time for 'take off' the next morning. Our breakfast of paw-paw and fruit juice was served in the shade of the palm trees, and then we set off on the second leg of our journey.

The second day we left Dahomey, and entered Togoland, another French colony for which the frontier post was a primitive little wooden hut standing under and enormous baobab tree, where the village elders would have sat in days gone by. Anslow had decided to have his uniform jacket with him as, in those days, it sometimes helped to overcome any unnecessary bureaucracy. While we sat in the car in the shade of the overhanging tree, he went into the hut with our passports. After a few minutes, he emerged and came over to the car to ask me my grand-mother's maiden name, and if she had ever been a member of the Communist Party. Apparently this had to be declared on the forms he had to fill in. Fortunately I knew the first answer and guessed at the second and we were waved through. Some years later when we were in Zambia, I told our High Commissioner this story, knowing that he had served in Ghana. His response was 'My goodness, they are not still using those 1910 forms are they?'

On our way to Lomé, the capital of Togoland, we saw fishermen using large circular fishing nets. They stood in their dug-out boats, and very skilfully threw the net in such a way that it landed in a complete circle very gently on the water. As it sank down through the water, so they pulled up a string running round it and trapped the fish in a kind of pocket. I suppose they would see a shoal of fish and cast their nets over them. On arrival in Lomé, we found another little hotel which was called Le Lac. We had been told this was really the only acceptable place to stay. Here the guest rooms were a series of little chalets. Our final day's journeying took us close along the Atlantic coast. The road had somewhat improved as we drove through coconut palm groves and small fishing villages. Leaving Togoland and entering Ghana held no problems. We had to cross the Volta River by ferry. This consisted of a steam boat which had the flat raft-like platform with rails attached to the side of it, and on which we drove the car for the crossing. It was a laboriously slow operation, as the ferry only took about two vehicles at a time, which meant there was a queue both sides of the river, of buses, lorries and cars waiting patiently for their turn to come. After this, we completed our journey without further incident, the road improving as we approached Accra, the capital.

We were staying with Army friends and they made us very welcome. I must say that we were glad to live in a civilized comfortable house after roughing it *en route*. We stayed there several days before returning the way we had come. Our hosts in Accra told us various stories about the prevalence of house burglaries. All their windows were, as were ours in Lagos, covered with a trellis of expanded metal mesh, so that one could open the window without endangering one's possessions. One night they were wakened by a noise, and saw to their amazement, an item of underwear travelling across the room without any apparent means of support, to the window where it was extracted through the hole where the window catch was. What the burglars did was to pole fish with a long stick on to which they hooked the clothing in the room, even putting a razor blade in the end of the stick to deter anyone from grabbing it, in an attempt to save their clothes from disappearing. Anslow and I had a rather disturbed first night, because in the middle of the night, he woke with a shout as something cold and clammy landed on his bare chest. We put the light on and found that a large toad had been enclosed inside the mosquito net when the servants had got the beds ready!

Back in Lagos, we resumed our routine. We had many English friends and we often found ourselves out at the airport saying goodbye or welcoming others who were arriving. On one of these occasions we were waiting to see some friends off, and they were told that there would be a delay before they could take off. The flights to England were always overnight and this was no exception. We waited and waited and finally were told what had caused the delay. When the senior BOAC pilot got into the plane to prepare for take-off, he went through all the checks on his panel of instruments, only to find that the fuel tanks were empty. He radio-ed to those responsible who assured him that X number of gallons had been put into the plane. On closer questioning, it turned out that the mechanic who actually did the job had opened two inspection holes in the wings and emptied the entire fuel requirement for the flight to London into these. Before long, aircraft fuel was oozing out of every rivet in sight. They finally took off two hours late, and the passengers were asked not to smoke on the flight! I think I would have been very anxious as a passenger on the plane in case somebody forgot and lighted up.

My pregnancy progressed without incident. There was a Military

Hospital near Lagos, and it was here in April 1960 that I gave birth to a bouncing boy. There was just one QARANC (Queen Alexandra's Royal Army Nursing Corps) nurse still in this hospital, and there were also still British Army doctors. I say still, because Nigeria was to be given her Independence the following October and many of the jobs were being what was called 'Nigerianized.' Anslow and I were thrilled with the addition to our family and cables were sent off to our respective parents to give them the good news of John's arrival. Six weeks after this happy event, we were due for three months home leave, so we were soon into the preparations for our flight home with two small children this time. It was at this time too that Anslow had the surprising news that he had been made an MBE in the Queen's Birthday Honours list. We had a few friends round for a celebratory drink and a curry lunch.

The plane home was a Britannia and our flight was not without drama. First, soon after leaving Kano, on the edge of the Sahara Desert, we ran into, according to the pilot, about thirteen electric storms. Although we were in a large airliner, we were tossed about like a piece of paper. The luggage was thrown out of the overhead racks, and little John in his carry cot at my feet was sometimes several inches above his bed, as the plane dropped suddenly. I was feeling decidedly sick, and fortunately Lizzie was fast asleep firmly strapped into her seat. It was a frightening experience which seemed to go on for quite a long time. We were due to land in Rome *en route*, but an ominous hole had appeared in the runway and we couldn't land there and were diverted to Naples, where there were absolutely no facilities for small children. We had a long delay there while the air crew who were to take over motored all the way from Rome. When we finally left there, we had an uneventful flight to Heathrow. Then things hotted up again. A stewardess put John's carry cot down on the floor in a corridor and a large woman tripped on the handle and sat down on our son and heir. Anslow was furious with her and got hold of the lapel of her jacket to haul her off, saying 'You are sitting on my son', when the collar of the said jacket came off in his hand. Whereupon the woman's husband started shouting, not at us, but at his wife for causing such a commotion. I was very upset in case John had had his ribs crushed or something, so I refused to move until he had been examined by a doctor. This was seen to immediately and all was well, so we were ushered out of the airport in double quick time. I should think everyone was thankful to see us go.

We took a taxi down to Wiltshire and were reunited with Anslow's family. We did the rounds of relatives, from a furnished flat we had taken on the outskirts of Bishops Stortford. This was in a lovely country house standing in a large acreage of beautiful gardens. The flat was furnished with antique furniture and was roomy and comfortable. We went to Norfolk to see Mother and the rest of my family, and while we were there we had John christened in our little village church. It was a very happy gathering but I couldn't help feeling sad that Pa wasn't there to see it all.

After this period of leave we returned to Nigeria for our second tour. We now had a Barclays Bank employee's wife who came in daily to look after Lizzie, as Jennifer had returned to England. It was at this time that we had a bit of drama in our household. The first thing we knew about it was when the police arrived on our doorstep to arrest Salu, our small boy. When I enquired what it was he was supposed to have done, they said that he had been the prime operator in a series of house burglaries. I asked how they knew it was him, and was told that every house in our road had been burgled in the last few weeks except ours. When faced with this evidence, Salu confessed to all. It seemed that he would not allow anyone to steal from us, and only allowed the lorry they used to be parked in our driveway, in a sort of misguided loyalty to us. Off he was marched and we then found Hyacinth to replace him. Another audacious theft which we heard about at this time, was when the whole of the island of Lagos was plunged into darkness. After copious investigations, it turned out that forty metres of copper electricity cable had been dug up on the causeway and spirited away to be sold!

Later this year, we were asked if we would like to move to Ikoyi, which was a residential area a few miles out of Lagos and still on the island. We jumped at the chance to do this because the area was much nicer than Apapa where we were. The houses were even better, it was quieter and it would be near a little nursery school run by the Corona Society to which we thought we might send Lizzie two mornings a week. The house itself was much larger than our previous one and had an enormous compound and even more exotic plants growing in it. There were very big mango, flame, and frangipani trees, as well as beautifully scented gardenia bushes, stephanotis, bananas, large beds of wonderful canna lilies in all the flame colours, which seemed to bloom all the year round. Growing against the white house were beds of white spider lilies, ginger plants and spectacular leathery crotons, while coral creeper and exotic gloriosa superba lilies climbed up the pillars of the porch. We had a proper lawn which was lovely for the children. A proper lawn in Lagos meant that it was planted with a kind of running grass, each plant being planted individually, and watered copiously when there was water to do so, and as it spread, it joined up and made a solid matt of green which could then be mown.

We had the same sized staff here, having left ours for the next incumbents, while we took over our predecessors' servants. We had an excellent Head Steward who was a Hausa man from the north of the country. They were generally rather taller and their features were more Arabic than their brothers in the other provinces. The native of the south and round Lagos was Yoruba, and in the east of the country were the Ibos. One could often tell what part of the country they came from by their headdress and clothing, and the women could often be identified by the way their hair was plaited in little tiny plaits, in patterns all over their heads, some of the female headdresses being very colourful and attractive. As well as being Head Boy, our steward was

15. Our house in Ikoyi on Lagos Island.

responsible for all the laundry which was done daily on the premises. He would empty the basket and take everything down to be washed in the compound, and when it came back duly ironed at the end of the day, I would check through it to see that none had gone missing, which it had a habit of doing if one was not watchful. One day I found that one of my bras was not in the pile when I checked it. I wondered quite how I was to explain this to the steward. I called him to come and said to him 'where is my, er, um, bodice' indicating with my hands the upper part of my torso. His face lighted up as he said 'Ah, I will go see, Madam.' I then heard him shouting at the top of his voice across the compound, 'Where is Madam's knicker for top?' I was amused at this marvellously descriptive pidgin English. Pidgin English was a language in itself and one had to be careful in one's choice of words when giving instructions, especially on the cooking front. I once told Dick to chop some parsley only to find out that the word 'chop' to him meant 'eat.' On another occasion we were going out, and I told the small boy that the kitchen was not as clean as I would like to see it, and that he was to give it a good scrub up while we were out. The kitchen, I may add, was a basic room, really a concrete square with an electric cooker, table, shelves and a deep china sink. When we returned, I went to see how he had got on, and to inspect his handiwork. The whole place was swimming in water, and the boy was standing bare-footed on the floor in his khaki working clothes looking, perhaps, a bit grey round the gills and saying 'The cooker he bite me Madam!' He had been throwing buckets of water on the walls, electric cooker and all, and then scrubbing everything down with a yard broom. Why he had not been electrocuted we will never know. I should mention here that even in their best whites which the servants changed into for serving at table, they never wore anything on their feet.

Meanwhile everyone was pitched into the excitement of the preparations for Nigeria's Independence in October 1960. There were parades, ceremonies, exhibitions put on by the different provinces, receptions and a large Garden Party given by the Governor-General and Lady Robertson at Government House. Princess Alexandra came out from England to represent the Queen. Anslow and I attended many of these functions. I found it very sad and very moving to see the Union Jack being lowered for the last time. It was all very well done and we wished the Nigerians well for the future.

There was a lot of building going on in Lagos at this time. A very modern residence had been built for the incoming British High Commissioner, Lord Head who arrived on Independence. It was on the waterfront of the infamous harbour. Unfortunately the architect had given this building two large brass doors as the main entrance. In next to no time they became very tarnished in that humid climate, so it was well nigh impossible to keep them looking smart. Inside there was a large open reception area, around part of which was a gallery upstairs, off which were the bedrooms. Lady Head found it tricky when she wanted to move about upstairs in the evening, perhaps in her dressing gown, if her husband was having a meeting downstairs. Further along the waterfront a large and impressive hotel had been built, called the Federal Palace. Until then Lagos had not really had a prestigious hotel of this ilk. There was a ceremonial opening to which everyone who was anyone was invited. Drinks were served on the terrace overlooking the water. Imagine everyone's horror when gazing down at the water, to see a dead animal floating in a sort of eddy under their very eyes. It seemed that due to the currents in the harbour, debris swirled round and collected in this area of the harbour. It was all most unfortunate. To overcome the problem, we understood that they eventually built out a groyne to deflect the rubbish to some other unsuspecting area!

It was during 1961 that the troubles that had been brewing in the Congo became so serious that something had to be done by the outside world. Belgium had given this colony its independence in 1960 but without having built up an infrastructure which would have enabled the inhabitants to self-govern. The result was awful chaos and fighting. This resulted in the United Nations having to step in to try and restore some sort of order. The Nigerians sent a contingent of their Army to the Congo, with British officers commanding, and because of this Anslow accompanied his General on several visits to this unhappy country. Back in Lagos later on, there was a spin off, in that there were what were known as the Lumumba riots. I happened to be driving into Lagos on one of these days, and found myself in the middle of an angry crowd, who were shouting and wielding sticks, turning over cars and throwing smoke bombs. I must admit to being somewhat alarmed, but couldn't turn round and get out of this predicament, so drove on hopefully. I managed to get home in one piece. Some days later, when we got our copy of the airmail *Times*, there was a full account of this happening which made it sound far worse than it seemed. I did not tell Mother that I had been in the thick of it.

Anslow found his visits to the Congo very interesting. He visited a Military Hospital, which was staffed by the Indians, who under the United Nations brief were to run all the medical facilities. The matron of this particular establishment was about four feet tall and solid starch from head to toe. Whenever any of her nurses came into the room, they would say to her 'Permission to speak, Ma'am' and bob a little curtsey. Anslow also went to other hospitals to visit the wounded, as well as the Nigerian units. He was also taken on a wonderful trip in a small Beaver aircraft along part of the River Congo at tree height, to see game. They flew so low that they could see the hippos as they ran along the shore line of the river. It was on this visit that he also had his first ever flight in a helicopter. In that war-torn, chaotic country, it was the most practical way to get from one place to another. Back at home, I kept wondering and worrying how he was faring as there was no way that he could communicate with me.

During what was our final year the newly independent Nigeria was invited to send a contingent back to the Royal Tournament in London. This was the summer of 1961. I was asked to do a drawing of the walls of the ancient city of Kano, in the north of the country, in a design form which could be reproduced as a backcloth to their display at the Royal Tournament. This was accepted but I was very sorry that I never saw the finished Kano Walls in situ, when they were built at Olympia. I had already designed a badge for their new Army which was called The Royal Nigerian Military Forces. This was basically a palm tree with the wreath underneath with their new title and I have often wondered if they still use the badge. Anslow had a lovely gold brooch of this badge made for me.

It was also in 1961 that a plebiscite was held in what had been the British Cameroons, but was by now the North Cameroons and the South Cameroons. The British sent a contingent of Grenadier Guards, and they arrived on HMS *Devonshire* in Lagos for a few days on their way there. We went to a reception on board, and the next day we saw some of the guardsmen off duty at Tarquah Bay, and what a change in their appearance! It was in the days of the winklepicker shoes. Need I say any more? It is amazing what a smart uniform will do for a man.

A sadness which occurred this year was news from Anslow's mother that his father was ill with cancer and that the surgeons had given him three to six months to live. It was a great shock to us, as he had always been so fit and was only in his seventies. Anslow immediately got compassionate leave and went home for a visit to see him. There was little that we could do but pray for him, and try to keep up the spirits of my mother-in-law. I was devoted to both of them, and they had been so welcoming and good to me, but they both understood that we had to see out our time in Nigeria. As it turned out he hung on for fifteen months, confounding the medics.

As the end of our tour approached, there was the usual round of farewell parties. A number of our friends decided to club together and give us a very special evening in the one and only night club in Lagos. Anslow and I had been to it for dinner on more than one occasion and we knew that it was a very nice venue to have a party. It was at the top of a tall building and one had a marvellous view over the whole of Lagos and the harbour. We duly dressed in our evening clothes and set off. As we went into the night club I noticed the wonderful display of flowers which were decorating the room. One of my friends said 'What do you think of the flowers?' I think I should mention here that we never had native flowers from our gardens in our houses, because in that heat they wouldn't have lasted five minutes, so we were all quite used to seeing lovely arrangements of very realistic silk flowers. My reply to this question was how marvellous the artificial flowers are nowadays. I soon realized what an awful faux pas I had committed when I was told that they were all fresh blooms and had been flown in from Holland especially for the occasion, and of course in the air-conditioned room they would last quite well. I felt an absolute idiot.

As the date of our departure drew closer we were getting quite excited about the trip home which we had already organized. It was the middle of the winter in England, and we had three months leave to complete our tour and really nowhere in England where we could stay for as long as that with two small children. Father was amazingly holding his own, and they both urged us to go, and so with his and Anslow's mother's blessing, we decided that we would take our first class air fare in money, which was a privilege open to us, and go south to South Africa for a few weeks, and come home by sea from Cape Town, thinking that we would never have the opportunity again to see something of South Africa. By going tourist class and counting the cost of hiring accommodation in England, if we had gone straight home, we doubted if the whole of our trip cost us anything much. Our heavy baggage was packed up and sent off by sea to our next posting. This was to be Western Command, Chester. We had requested a posting in England, as we felt we should be near Anslow's family at this time.

Chapter III

A South African Holiday

WE FLEW BY PAN AM AIRLINES TO JOHANNESBURG, touching down in Leopoldville, the capital of what had been the Belgian Congo. The plane was packed, and I noted the difference from our first class travel, but with such an adventure before us, it was little matter. We would have guessed that we were on an American plane by the fact that we were served an enormous steak dinner at four in the afternoon! We arrived in Johannesburg late in the evening, and having been warned to do so, we had warm woollens to put on. Johannesburg is 6000ft above sea level, and is decidedly chilly when the sun goes down, added to which we were coming out of a country of high humidity and temperatures. Being south of the equator and December, it was the height of summer in South Africa. We took a taxi to our hotel, bedded the children down, and were not long in following them. They had both been very good, in fact I think I can say that we never had any travelling problems with them. Lizzie was under four and John coming up to eighteen months. They were becoming seasoned travellers.

We planned to stay a few days in Johannesburg. One of the things which I noticed very early on was the segregation of blacks and whites everywhere. The Post Offices for instance had separate queues, as did the bus stops and the actual buses. It was very marked and we were to find out that this was far more noticeable in the Transvaal than down in the Cape. I think too, that we noticed it far more than some, as we had come from a newly independent African country, where things had fortunately moved away from such segregation. While in Johannesburg, we made one or two trips out of the centre of the city. We took the children to the Zoo, and especially enjoyed seeing Indian elephants being used to move tree trunks. Anslow had seen a lot of this when he had served in India, Burma and Ceylon before I met him, but I was fascinated to watch the accuracy and gentleness of these huge creatures as they adjusted a large piece of wood by as little as a few inches to get it in the right position. We also went by train to Pretoria and on arrival made our way to the Union buildings and their magnificent gardens. Pretoria is the administrative capital and the Union Buildings are their Houses of Parliament. There was at that time a lot of to-ing and fro-ing between Pretoria and Cape Town which was the capital of the legislature. It was very hot but not so humid as we had been used to, and the children had little linen sun hats.

Our next move from Johannesburg was to take a train to Durban on the Indian Ocean. This took us east through the Drakensberg Mountains and then we gradually dropped down to Pietermaritzburg and the coastal plain before reaching Durban. Being at sea level again, it was a little more humid. We made our way, this time by taxi, to our seafront hotel. Durban was very much a tourist resort, and this was going to be a bucket and spade holiday for the children. The actual bathing was dangerous here, but the children did no more than paddle in the pools in the sand. There were warnings on the beach and one's attention was drawn to watch out for the red flag flying. There were hefty lifeguards on the beach watching the swimmers intently. I was to find out how efficient they were. I loved swimming in a big sea and the breakers were fantastic. I joined a lot of swimmers enjoying it all as much as I did. Anslow stayed on the beach with the children making sand castles. After about ten minutes of this exhilarating experience, I started to swim for the shore, only to find that I could not make any headway at all. I swam as hard as I could and didn't appear to move forward at all. Being surrounded by swimmers, I was not in the least alarmed, but asked a youth to give me a hand to swim in to the shore. Again nothing happened, but unbeknown to me one of the lifeguards had spotted me, and swam out with powerful strokes and brought me in. Fortunately Anslow hadn't seen all this happen as there were too many people. I did tell him afterwards when the young were not around to be alarmed. I found it a very sobering experience that such a thing could happen among so many people. We did one trip outside Durban. We had some South African friends whom we had met in Nigeria, and they were staying at Umlhanga Rocks a little way off along the coast. Here the bathing really was even more dangerous as there were sharks to contend with and no shark nets as there were in Durban. We were regaled with horrifying stories of people being taken by sharks quite regularly. We contented ourselves with enjoying our friends and taking the children to see some brilliantly coloured macaws in a sort of bird sanctuary.

From Durban we were booked on one of the Union Castle Line ships which sailed weekly round the Cape and home to Southampton. Our plan was to stop off in Cape Town and have a little stay there, before catching another liner to go back to England. Once on board we settled ourselves into our quarters, which in spite of being tourist class were beautifully comfortable. We had two cabins off our own little hallway, so we seemed to have a small suite. There were marvellous facilities on these ships. There were several lounges, bars, shops and a swimming pool. Also there was a super nursery and crèche with qualified nannies to look after the children. Our two couldn't wait to go there after breakfast each morning. There were lots of toys for them to play with and the people looking after them made it a lot of fun for them. It was bliss for Anslow and me. There were special arrangements of times and food for the children's supper, which left us free to enjoy dinner in a relaxed way when they had gone to bed. There was even a babysitting service! During the day we walked on the long decks for exercise and many passengers played various deck games. We used the swimming pool a lot. The boat called at East London and Port Elizabeth. We went ashore at both places, but didn't find East London very inspiring. At Port Elizabeth, we took the children to a snake pit, where a keeper, wearing leather gaiters, was handling poisonous snakes.

It was rather exciting arriving at Cape Town and to see the famous Table Mountain for the first time. It often has what the South Africans call a white tablecloth on it. Sometimes we saw this cloud as a wisp and sometimes as a white fluffy cloud dripping over the sides of the table. Those with an experienced eye were able to tell what the weather was going to be like by these signs. We watched over the side of the ship as she slowly manoeuvred to her berth. Our hotel was a friendly family place and we couldn't have been more comfortable or better placed for going out and about on foot in Cape Town. I thought it was a lovely city, with wonderful shops and good eating places. Near our hotel, which was close to the famous Mount Nelson Hotel, there were beautiful shady gardens for walking and sitting. The thing which I remember particularly about them were the huge banks of brilliant blue hydrangeas in full bloom. They really were spectacular. We were to spend Christmas in Cape Town, and so we enjoyed ourselves doing some Christmas shopping in Stuttafords, the large departmental store in the main street. To our eyes it was Harrods all over again. In Cape Town we noticed another group of coloured people who were what were known as the Cape Coloureds, and were of a different extraction, and there were a set of rules and regulations for them too. Off the main street in Cape Town in some of the side streets were wonderful flower markets, where there were buckets and buckets of the most exotic and highly coloured blooms you could imagine. These stalls were mostly run by the Cape Coloureds.

We took buses out to the seaside resorts and spent a whole day at Kirstenbosch, the beautiful botanical gardens outside Cape Town. The visions which have hung in my mind all these years of that day, were a sea of brilliant blue agapanthus in one place and another of the white variety, and the proteas which were in full bloom and made a spectacular display wherever we looked, and the scene was enhanced by the impressive backdrop of mountains. It was an enormous area and we couldn't hope to see it all. We pushed John round in his little pushchair and Lizzie ran most of the way! We couldn't go to Cape Town without going up Table Mountain of course. This we did in the traditional way by cable car. It is a lovely way to do this because one gets a splendid panoramic view of the city below and the harbour beyond. Once up, we were on a flat plateau. We saw lovely wild flowers, some growing out of huge slabs of rock, I wished I could have identified some of them. It was quite chilly up there in the wind and we were glad of coats and jackets. We sat down on a rock and ate our picnic and took photographs to record that we had been there and we were lucky that day too that there was no tablecloth on the table. Another long excursion we made on foot with the pushchair was to walk from a point where a bus had put us down, up Kloof Nek. This was quite a steep climb up to the east of Table Mountain on to a ridge where again we had a marvellous view from a different angle. It was a very long walk and that day I went through a pair of sandals, and Lizzie spent some time up on Anslow's shoulders. Soon after a jolly Christmas in our hotel, we had to pack up and prepare ourselves for our final voyage home.

Again our ship was one of the Union Castle boats. This time it was the *Pendennis Castle*, their flagship. It was every bit as comfortable as the *Pretoria Castle* we had been on before. The voyage took two weeks in those days though later, these ships did the journey in eleven days. We called at Madeira in the Atlantic, and as the ship lay off-shore we were taken off in a lighter in the same way as that trip to Cyprus some ten years before. The capital of the Portuguese-owned Madeira is Funchal and it was here that we came ashore. The first thing we noticed was that all the town's drains ran down deep culverts in the middle of the roads. Over them were stretched wire netting on which was trained to grow masses of purple bougainvilia, to cover the unsightly scenes underneath. It made a spectacular transformation. For the children's amusement and our comfort, we hired a funny little brightly painted cart with a cover to protect us from the sun and drawn by an ox with a large bell dangling from its neck. In this outfit we were taken on a little tour of the town. Many of the streets were cobbled and not very comfortable to walk on, so we were glad to have done our sightseeing this way. I would like to have bought some embroidered table linen and napkins, and there was lots of this lovely work to choose from, but it was quite expensive and I resisted. Back on board, we found that we had been joined by quite a number of new passengers. As it turned out we hardly saw any of them, because soon after we set sail, we ran into bad weather of a force eight gale and a forty-foot swell. This continued until we were clear of the Bay of Biscay, and within sight of Southampton. Mercifully, as I had been at sea for ten days and had found my sea legs further south, it didn't affect me, but those poor passengers from Funchal took to their beds and didn't reappear until we docked. Before doing so we had rung our parents from the ship to tell them the glad news of our return.

We went straight down to Wiltshire to see Anslow's sick father, who considering his illness, was in remarkably good heart. He was delighted to see his only grandson who was to carry on the family name. We decided to stay in a nearby pub which let out rooms for a while so that we could be with the family. After that we did other family visits including Mother in Norfolk. I remember on this visit that Mother looked at us in horror and said we looked thoroughly ill and should go to the Hospital for Tropical Diseases in Cambridge because we all looked yellow! The sort of tan that one got in Nigeria was not one that made one look bronzed and healthy, and that, as well as the anti-malarial pills, probably did make us look odd, especially in the middle of an English winter. Time was marching on by now and we had to make our way to Chester for Anslow to take up his appointment there. We had ordered a new car and, loaded to the eyebrows, off we set.

Chapter IV

Chester

OUR QUARTER IN CHESTER turned out to be what was known in the army as a hiring. It was half a large old rectory on the Duke of Westminster's estate and about four miles from Chester. Anslow had to drive the few miles through the park of Eaton Hall to get to the Headquarters, where he was to work. We were on the edge of the village of Aldford, and inside the park gates and surrounded by rural scenes. It all looked perfect. We had hardly settled in before word came that Father-in-law was sinking fast. He died at the end of March. I somehow felt that he had hung on until he had seen us home, and then quietly let go. Anslow of course went off to make arrangements, and to discuss with his mother about her future. She came to stay with us for a protracted visit, and we decided to take our house unfurnished in order to house the surplus furniture which was to come our way. A mere six weeks after Father-in-law's death, Anslow's Aunt Vera died. It was very unexpected. She had been badly burned from an electric fire which had set fire to her nightdress. As she was Mother-in-law's only surviving sister, it was a double tragedy for her. Anslow had been very good to Vera for years and she left all her furniture to him and her jewellery to me. We had accumulated some of our own furniture during our short stay in Carlisle and this had arrived from being in store, and we found now with the last unexpected legacy that we had enough to furnish the whole house. Later on in our time in Aldford we bought some more furniture among which were two large antique wardrobes with mirrors on the doors which cost us £3 and £4 each!

Ma-in-law was the easiest of people to have in the house as she was a very undemanding and generous person and took her loss without fuss and self-pity. She adored the children and quickly made up for lost time in getting to know them. I hoped they helped her to adjust to her new way of life. The house was not altogether easy in the way that it had been divided into two. We had the kitchen end and were on three floors, but with only one bedroom on the first floor. There were large cellars which made a lovely workroom for Anslow. We sorted ourselves out and managed as best we could. We had a lovely large walled garden but it was very neglected so there was plenty of work to be done there, and in the roomy old-fashioned greenhouse. Anslow's father had been very keen on bees and we had inherited all his equipment, so he decided to keep bees in the little orchard of our new garden.

Later on during our time in this house, we were entertaining the brother of a well-known MP and he heard that we kept bees. At the dinner table he started to reminisce about an eccentric Brigadier who had been stationed in Chester during the war. This officer lived in the Grosvenor Hotel, and kept a hive of bees in his bedroom. The window was left open about an inch at the bottom to allow the bees to come and go, though history doesn't relate what the maid, who cleaned the room, thought about this arrangement. When we were being told this story we kept quiet and let our guest ramble on, knowing full well that this 'eccentric' Brigadier was Anslow's father. It was a bit mean of us I suppose, but we did finally divulge the truth, at which our friend huffed and puffed a bit and finally said 'Well, I thought it was very enterprising of him'.

We were very lucky to have two excellent batwomen here. They were aunt and niece and old Mrs Broster used to come in twice a week to clean the silver and to do all the ironing. She performed these duties par excellence. We found out that she had been tenth housemaid to the late Duke of Westminster, and her duties in those days had been to look after the ducal linen. Her domain centred round an enormous linen cupboard, which in later years when the army took over the old Eaton Hall as an officer training establishment, became an officer's bedroom! She was full of stories about the old days there. Apparently Eaton Hall and Chatsworth would vie with each other as to who could put up the most house guests. When Winston Churchill went to stay with the old Duke, it was said that he always insisted that any mutton he had should be hung until it tasted distinctly gamey, much to the disgust of his fellow guests. Outside Eaton Hall on the long drive out from the front of the mansion, was a tall obelisk. This was built by the duke of the day in Victorian times, to blot out the sight of Hawarden Castle which was miles away but in a direct line of vision, and the home of William Gladstone whom he couldn't stand. With all her skills, I thought Mrs Broster would be a good person to ask to teach me how to cold water starch Anslow's dress shirts which he wore with his mess kit. She knew exactly how to do this, and I duly learnt, in case I might need this skill if we went abroad again to faraway places. As it turned out I certainly did when we went back to Africa. Her niece came in daily and did all the cleaning. She was devoted to the children and I could always safely leave them with her if need be. By now Ma-in-law had gone to live in a country house hotel in Wiltshire. It was an arrangement which seemed ideal as she did not like housekeeping and all that that entailed.

We led a quietly social life, but nothing too hectic I am glad to say. Aunt Armorel was away in America at this time but Aunt Kathleen paid us a visit, as did other friends from time to time. Anslow enjoyed his work and the people he worked with. He had to go away on the odd conference, and needless to say it was on one of these occasions that the bees swarmed – shades of my father, I thought. I was at a bit of a loss as to what to do, as I didn't know where he kept everything. Nothing daunted, I rang the place where he was, up in Anglesey, and asked to speak to him, not knowing that he was actually in conference. He came to the phone and I explained the predicament, and by my doing all the talking and his answering yes or no, nobody guessed it was a mere domestic problem. I shut the children in the greenhouse which I hoped was bee-proof, and where they could see me, and I tackled taking that swarm. It was a very large and heavy one but with my heart in my mouth and my body well covered I succeeded, and by the evening I had them all in the hive. When Anslow came home the next day it was as though nothing had happened.

While we were abroad we had to discourage the children from having anything to do with dogs, because of the danger of rabies. Consequently they were rather inclined to be nervous of them, which we thought was a pity. After much thought, we decided to get a black labrador bitch whom we called Juno, and she came to us when she was eight weeks old. They all became great companions and the children were very gentle with her and she with them. As she grew, it turned out that she had a lovely soft mouth, so much so that she would go to the larder, stand on her hind legs and very gently take a fresh egg off its tray and carry it back to her bed in her mouth. She was too young for

Anslow to take out shooting, but he did have a few invitations to shoot on the estate shoots. These were very well-organized affairs. The beaters all wore white coats and Tyrolean style hats with a feather in the side. As one might expect there was a very good spread at the shooting lunch.

We had a very severe winter during our second year at Aldford, so much so that the mains water froze in most of the houses in the village. Thanks to Mother, we were the only house to escape this fate. Being well-seasoned in Norfolk winters, she had advised us on the phone, to open the manhole where the mains turncock was, and throw in some fresh steaming manure over the tap. It did the trick. We had nearly six weeks of this weather. The countryside looked lovely but it made getting about hazardous. The River Dee froze so hard that the local Rugby football team skated down the River Dee from Chester.

During our second year in Aldford, Lizzie had her fifth birthday, and so off she went to the very good little village school a few hundred yards down the road. The other big event in our lives in the spring of 1963 was that we had decided to buy a house. The previous year we had tried to buy Aunt Vera's house but had not been able to do so. We felt that we would like to have a base to come back to and we now had quite a bit of furniture and nowhere to put it should we move abroad. We looked all down the border country, and after looking at a number of places, and attending a house auction, we finally found the house of our dreams. It was a largish house built of stone, the earliest part being sixteenth century, and the newest being very early nineteenth century. It was a very solid nice looking house with spacious rooms and a friendly feel about it. I always thought that if it had any ghosts, they would be nice ones! It was structurally sound, but looked pretty decrepit as it had been empty for over a year. Vandals had got in and broken windows and torn out the electric fittings. When it was finally ours, we used to drive down for the weekend every week, to clean, repair, scrape and paint. One often hears people say where they were when the news of President Kennedy's assassination came through. We remember very vividly lying in bed in one of the bedrooms we had finished decorating, listening to the 7 a.m. news on a chilly November morning.

After a year of restoration, the inevitable happened, and we had a posting. Anslow was to be promoted again, and we were to go back to Africa, but this time it was to be to the southern hemisphere, to Northern Rhodesia, who was to get her Independence in the autumn of 1964, and become Zambia. It meant that we had to hand over the rest of the restoration of the house to a builder. We then moved in when Anslow's job finished in Chester, and got the house ready for letting.

There was still quite a lot of work to be done on the house, which we wanted to do ourselves in order to keep the bills down. Outside the so-called garden was a jungle. We cut the grass and kept finding tea-cups and saucers which had been left over from the last village fête which had been held in the garden. I can't think how we did all we did in the time, but I suppose we were all younger and more energetic in those days. I had to do a certain amount of shopping for Northern Rhodesia. I took out several lengths of cotton material to make up into dresses, and I also opened an account with Dickens and Jones in London, which I was to find invaluable later on. We bought a Royal Worcester dinner service for twelve for our entertaining. Last but not least, we decided to take out a Nanny for the children. We put an advertisement in the Times and waited. Very unfortunately this coincided with a postal strike, which made life rather difficult, and by the time this was over, we were a bit pushed for time. However, we made our choice and invited Jessica down to spend a trial weekend with us, which was little enough, but it couldn't be helped. We then fitted in a farewell visit to Norfolk for a few days before going back to organize the final run-down to our departure. The packers came in and packed all our kit, which cleared the air somewhat. Then we let the house fully furnished through the Army and met our tenants, and with some regrets handed our new home over to comparative strangers, asking them to keep reclaimed what we had done in the garden. With fingers crossed we left to spend a night with Ma-in-law in her hotel in Wiltshire, including Juno who was to come with us to Africa.

Chapter V

Zambia

OUR JOURNEY TO NORTHERN RHODESIA was to go from Southampton to Cape Town by sea in one of those lovely Union Castle ships again. This time it was to be the *Edinburgh Castle*. The official route was by sea because Anslow had to have all his kit with him in order to be ready for Independence, which was to be declared five days after our arrival in the country. We left Anslow's mother and Wiltshire with sadness mixed with excitement about the future posting. We drove down to Southampton, leaving Juno in kennels nearby, and booked into a large hotel for the night. The next day we had quite a lot to see to. We checked that our heavy baggage had arrived and was ready to go on board, and we delivered Juno and our new car to the correct places at the correct times. After this we could relax a bit, and concentrate on getting ourselves on board, and meeting up with Jessica the nanny. Having done this, imagine our surprise to see Anslow's mother appear. She had decided on the spur of the moment, so to speak, to get herself down to Southampton and surprise us, which she certainly did. We had about an hour with her before the loudspeaker made it known that all those who were not sailing, had to go ashore. We said our goodbyes again, and then went up on deck to watch as we slipped our berth, and Ma-in-law became a smaller and smaller figure waving in the distance.

Our cabin arrangements were perfect. Again we had a suite of two cabins and a shower, and our own little hall. As we were travelling first class, everything was roomier and more up-market, if I can put it that way, than the Tourist class of our last voyage. It was rather ironic really, that we had decided to go south from Nigeria, to see South Africa, because we thought we would never have the chance again to do such a thing, and here we were, on our way again less than three years later. It seemed that we had Africa written on our file. Jessica had a cabin on the same corridor. Her duties started immediately, and she used to take the children for brisk walks on the deck, supervise their meals and put them to bed. There were the same playrooms on board which they both liked going to, as well as the swimming pool and deck games. For the adults in the evening, there was plenty of entertainment, such as cocktail parties, dancing, cabaret, the cinema, as well as a number of comfortable lounges in which to sit and read.

Our first port of call was Las Palmas, the capital of the island of Gran Canaria, one of the larger of the Canary Islands. These islands are volcanic, and so they were rather bare and rocky, and somewhat treeless. As we had several hours here, we all went ashore to do some modest exploring, and then we sat on a beach while the children played in the water. On board again, when we 'Crossed the Line' or to the uninitiated, the Equator, there were ceremonies for those who had not done this before. One of the crew dressed up as Neptune, and the victims were doused in soap and water, and there was a lot of larking about, but it was all good harmless fun. We had gone through all this on our previous voyage. Our next stop was in the night at Ascension Island in the South Atlantic. Here we were not allowed off, even if it had been at a better time, as the island was a military zone with American and British space stations on it. We merely stopped there to leave them provisions and to take on mail. We were, after all, the Royal Mail Steamer *Edinburgh Castle*.

16. Jamestown, the capital of the island of St Helena, South Atlantic.

Our final stop before Cape Town was the island of St Helena. This was of particular interest to us, as Father-in-law had been in the Boer War, but because he had been too young to be sent to the front, he had been posted to the island to guard Boer prisoners of war. We had in our possession a king ebony wood box which had been carved by a Boer prisoner, who had presented it to Anslow's father. Among the various carvings on the lid were the Arms of Jamestown, the capital of St Helena. The island's other claim to fame was that Napoleon had been imprisoned here, after his escape from Elba. In fact he died on the island. When we arrived, we lay off-shore, and were taken off in lighters. When we first saw the island we could see why. It rose sheer out of the water, with a little narrow slit of a valley between two steep-sided hills, with Jamestown nestling in the bottom and at the water's edge. We landed on a little jetty, and walked towards the stone gateway and entrance to the town. Over this arch to our excitement was the coat of arms we had on our box. We also saw the long flight of steps up one side of the steep valley, which led to where the garrison had been housed and where the Boer prisoners had been kept. The whole setting of the island made us realize why it had been chosen as a suitable place to incarcerate Napoleon.

As we had a whole day on the island we made the most of our time

17. Napoleon's grave on St Helena.

by having a jolly good look round. My first impression was surprise to see so many Cape Coloureds. The women all wore very bright colours, and they seemed to be very happy sort of people. Of course a liner coming in was always a big event and I should think a fair proportion of the population came down to the little harbour to see us. After we had landed, the lighters took parties of the locals for a trip round the outside of the *Edinburgh Castle* as she lay off-shore. We pottered round the main street of Jamestown, and then decided to hire a pony and trap with a driver, to take us on a tour of the island and to see Napoleon's house. There were not many roads on the island so this was not such a big tour as it might sound. We passed Government House, which was a very attractive Georgian-style house in lovely grounds. Sir John Field, the governor, and his wife had been passengers on our ship, returning from a spell of leave in England. It was in the garden of this house that we saw an enormous tortoise, which we were told was alive in Napoleon's day. He certainly looked very old. For the last bit of the way up to Napoleon's house, we had to walk, but there were donkeys which one could hire, so we allowed the children to take turns at having a ride on one of these animals. When we reached the house I was, first of all, enchanted by the garden. It was very attractive and colourful, and beautifully kept. The lawns were odd in that they were very deep and spongy to walk on, rather like walking on grassy heather. There were many colourful flowers growing there, some of which were familiar to us, such as antirrhinums and South African daisies. The house was a Regency-style bungalow, and was really a museum. It was furnished just as it had been in Bonaparte's time. He had died on the island in 1821, and a little way from the house, among some trees in a little glade, was his one-time grave. The ground in this little glade was covered in ivy, and in the middle was an area which had railings round it. His body no longer lies there, as it was taken back to France in 1840, and re-interred in the Hôtel des Invalides in Paris. After seeing all this, we returned to our horse and trap and continued on our circuit back to Jamestown. I noticed in the hedgerows there was a lot of the lantana plant growing. In many countries this is considered a pernicious weed, and is a forbidden plant, though it has a rather attractive flower. I have since seen it feature in plant lists in English catalogues. When we had completed our tour and returned to Jamestown, we felt it had been a fascinating visit, which we were very lucky to make, as our ship was to be the last Union Castle passenger liner to call on the island with mail and provisions. In future they would have smaller boats plying to and fro from Cape Town.

As we were in lovely warm latitudes, on one of the Sundays, for those who wanted it, a marvellous spread was laid out for lunch on the deck and while eating we could watch schools of dolphins playing alongside the ship. We also saw flying fish, their glistening bodies catching the sunlight, as they leapt out of the water. On Sundays, one of the lounges was converted for a church service, and there was a chaplain on board to take Mattins. By now we were nearing Cape Town, and there was an air of bustle and anticipation, as everyone packed and made their arrangements, among which was the business of tipping all the stewards who had looked after us, and not forgetting the faithful lamptrimmer who had tended Juno throughout the voyage. He was going to see to the arrangements for her being taken off the ship in her specially made crate. For the last night on board, one, by tradition never changed for dinner, to enable everyone to complete their packing. It had been a lovely trip, but we still had quite a long journey ahead of us before we reached Lusaka.

When we had berthed, we did not go ashore for a bit, but waited on deck and watched some of the heavy baggage being unloaded. This was taken off by small cranes or derricks, as they were called, in large nets, and were swung out over the water and on to the dockside. We then saw our precious car being unloaded, with great big padded claws which grabbed it, making it look like a little toy vehicle as it swung out over the water. My heart was in my mouth until I saw it arrive the right side up, on dry land! Juno was not allowed to enter Northern Rhodesia by road, and so we had to make arrangements for her to be put on a train, to be looked after on the journey, and to be met by a kennel owner who would keep her until we arrived some days after her and could collect her. I remember we were not very happy about having to do this, but we really didn't have any choice. We had been told what to do and found and tipped someone on the train to care for her, and see that she had water and to feed her regularly. The woman meeting her had already been recommended to us and she also advised us that all would be well on the train, as the South Africans were quite used to doing this.

We then went to the same hotel we had stayed in before, while we prepared ourselves for the long drive from Cape Town to Lusaka. We planned to do this in easy stages so that we could all enjoy it, and soak up the atmosphere. We had to be in Lusaka five days before Independence. Our route took us north east from Cape Town and we stayed the first night in a clean and comfortable but unremarkable motel. The next day we started to cross the Karoo Desert and this was to take us two days. One might imagine that this would be rather a boring bit of driving, but in fact there is about a fortnight in the year when the desert comes alive with the most marvellous display of flowers, and we were lucky indeed to hit this period. The soil was that same red which we had seen in other parts of Africa, the terrain was flat but out of it sometimes there rose a sharp little hill of the same colour. I was reminded of the pictures I had seen of Ayer's Rock in Australia. Our road was a not very wide strip of tarmac with a wide dusty verge on both sides, but everywhere round us were clumps of dimorphotheca or South African daisies, and bright yellow low-growing broom bushes in full bloom, and some blue daisy-like flowers which I think might have been catananche, which closed up in the evening or if the sun went in. We spent a night at Colesberg on the northern edge of the Karoo, and here our accommodation was quite simple, but the great attraction was that the owner of the motel had two little lion cubs which he had found abandoned, and was fostering them. They were enchanting and gambolled about like large puppies, and were not big enough to be a hazard to the children.

Another one of our nights was spent at Louis Trichard. Here we found a proper hotel, in the mountains. It had the most wonderful garden with lovely sub-tropical plants and trees and an amazing view. We always tried to stop for the night during the second part of the afternoon, in order to give the children and ourselves a decent break before bed time, and here we could happily have stayed for several days. Before we got to Bulawayo, in fact it was not far from the border of what was southern Rhodesia in those days, we stopped for some refreshment at a funny little place right out in the bush. It was run by a white South African and from his accent I think he was probably Afrikaans. This meant he was of South African Dutch, or Boer descent. Imagine our surprise this time when a baby giraffe appeared and put its head over a half-neck door and looked in. Whereupon mine host produced a bottle of Castle beer, which it drank with relish, the foam

18. Baby giraffe having his ½ pint of beer, near the Southern Rhodesian border.

frothing out of the sides of its mouth and dropping on the floor. It came every day for its half pint 'fix'. Bulawayo was our next night stop. Here all the roads in the town were wide and lined with flowering jacaranda trees, which were a heavenly blue, or cassia trees, which had a yellow blossom all over them. We used to call them the scrambled egg tree! Bulawayo was a big bustling city, with well-laid out parks and gardens which were immaculately trim and colourful. As one might expect, our hotel was very comfortable and civilized. From there the next day we drove on to the capital, Salisbury, now called Harari. Little did we know then, that this was to be our only visit to this country, but more of that later.

We had taken a week to get this far, and so we were now getting well on in our journey, as our next night would be spent in Lusaka, Northern Rhodesia. We would only be calling it this for a few more days, as it would become Zambia on Independence. Anslow was to take up his appointment as Defence Adviser to the first British High Commissioner. Our main concern on arrival was to make contact with Juno. We found her in excellent condition and very pleased to see us. We were told that she had been well looked after on the train and had arrived clean, and had obviously been well-tended, which was a great relief to us.

As soon as we arrived, we were pitched into the Independence arrangements. Again, as in Nigeria, there were parades, and other large gatherings of Africans who came in to the capital from the rest of the country. This time, Her Royal Highness, the Princess Royal, (Princess Mary) came out to represent the Queen. The main ceremony of Independence took place in a large stadium in the evening so that the Union Jack could come down and the Zambian flag be raised on the dot of midnight. Again I experienced a lump in my throat, at the passing of an era.

Our first house in this new country was a medium-sized bungalow, which we went into temporarily until the house we were to live in was completed. It had a nice big compound, and the usual set-up of servants quarters at the bottom of the garden. Growing in the garden were again the lovely colours of the flame, jacaranda and frangipani trees and lots of different kinds of hibiscus, and the brilliant purple of the bougainvilia which was twining itself up the pillars of the verandah. There were banana trees, which the experts called plantains. I don't know if there is a difference. The High Commission where Anslow had his office, was a newly purpose built building. One of his unexpected duties was to issue birth, marriage and death certificates to British Army personnel, if the need arose!

Jessica was settling in reasonably well, though we did have a bit of a set-back early on. We found that she had her nineteenth birthday coming up, so we decided to arrange a party for her. On the morning of the day in question, she appeared at the breakfast table and promptly burst into tears. We asked her what on earth was the matter. To which she replied 'I am getting so old!' In many ways she was fairly immature, and we did have one or two clashes when she didn't want to babysit for us. As this was one of the main reasons why we took her out it was tricky. We tried to be accommodating over this and other things, and often wished that we had taken out an older woman. We soldiered on with her for a year, allowing her time off to do a secretarial course which she wanted to do, and then by mutual agreement we released her from her contract and she went home.

While we were in this house, we had the good news that Anslow had been awarded the OBE in the New Year Honours List. This was cause for celebration and our friends helped us to congratulate him on his achievement. He was typically modest about this, but nevertheless we felt very proud of him.

Bag and Baggage

When our new house was ready, and had been furnished from England, we moved in. This house was a very modern building with glass windows down to the ground both upstairs and down. It was situated on Independence Avenue, opposite State House where the President, Kenneth Kaunda, lived. Again we had a nice large compound, and during the building of the house, the large trees in the garden had been left, but the rest of the area was very much builders' rubble, so once again we had to set about making a garden from scratch. In many ways this was very rewarding because in such a climate everything grew to maturity remarkably quickly so that, literally, we saw the fruits of our labours. We put in a hibiscus hedge to screen the servants' quarters from the house, and to give them an area for their children to play in. We ordered from a fruit grower in Southern Rhodesia, a selection of citrus fruit trees, and we planted a citrus grove of Seville oranges for marmalade, Washington Navel dessert oranges, grapefruit and some lemon trees, and in our second year we were picking fruit from the trees. We planned a herbaceous border, a bed of roses and lots of flowering shrubs. To do all this work we hired some garden boys. In doing this we came across some very amusing names. We had boys called Lemon, Smart, Pencil, and perhaps best of all Suspender. I suppose their parents had no idea what these names meant, but only thought they sounded agreeable. Often a servant would say that he had a brother and could he have the day off to go and see him. We soon learnt to say 'Same Mother, same Father?' as these servants had endless relatives and 'brothers'. Our cook was called Samson and we had a head boy and small boy also. The floors in this house were polished wood and I was amused to see how the servants polished them. They took a coconut with its outer husk on, and cut it in half, and after using the white flesh and the milk from the middle, it was allowed to dry and then the two halves with their rather bristly brushlike husk were used to good effect, after the polish had been applied.

The house, I have already mentioned, had a lot of glass. When we were lying in bed, we were in full view from anyone in Independence Avenue, so we bought some black paint, and painted the bottom row of window panes! When the beds were delivered and put together, the Africans doing this put in some four-inch screws which stuck out dangerously and were liable to catch one's legs as one went past. We complained, and so they sawed off the offending screw ends. Some

African workmanship left a great deal to be desired. There was a large and pleasant verandah at the back of the house. At the bottom of the steps going down from here we planted a lawn, again in the same way as in Nigeria, with grass plants, and it was to one side of this that we made our rose bed of Queen Elizabeth roses, which we found flowered for ten months of the year.

We also had in the garden a blushing hibiscus bush, called thus because the flowers came out early in the day and were white, but as the temperatures rose and the hours went by so these blooms turned to pink and eventually to a rich red before fading away. I used to go out and pick the flowers early in the morning while they were still white, bring them in and put them in water in the fridge, where they kept their virginal colour. When the evening came and the dinner table was laid, they were brought out into the warmth of the room. There before one's eyes, as dinner progressed the blooms started to 'blush' until by the cheese course they were in their full rich livery. It was always a talking point for those who had not seen this before.

The climate in Zambia was very pleasant. We had three seasons, a hot dry, a hot wet, which was the monsoon which nearly always started at the beginning of November, and a cool which was the winter. In this last season, we were able to grow all the English summer flowers such as antirrhinums, nasturtiums and the like. There was a certain amount of small wildlife in the garden. There were lots of lizards and quite large iguanas with brilliant blue heads, and the amazing chameleons with their extraordinary swivel eyes, running about in the trees. At certain times of the year we had pretty little humming birds which sucked the nectar from certain flowers with their long curved beaks. Lusaka is between 3500 ft and 4000 ft high and so it was always reasonably cool at night, and we certainly didn't suffer from that awful humidity we had in Lagos, nor did we have to take precautions against malaria.

Another peculiarity of this house was that every time that we had a dinner party, we had to put the small boy on duty in the broom cupboard, to hold down the trip switch on the fuse box, so that Samson could get the dinner cooked, otherwise everything switched itself off! Finally, on one famous occasion all the lights in Independence Avenue and in State House went out, and various people who suffered said 'The Defence Adviser is having another dinner party!' Something serious had to be done about this, and we got in yet another electrician, who discovered that our electric cooker, from England, was incorrectly wired.

Lizzie was six and a half years old when we arrived in Zambia, so we had to arrange a school for her. Nearby was a co-educational primary school, which, up to now, had almost entirely white pupils, and all the staff were white. On Independence some African children started to go to such schools, and it was entirely right that they should do so, and it was to this school that we sent Lizzie. John followed her when he became five the following year. His uniform amused us, or rather his hat did. He wore grey shorts and a sky blue shirt and striped tie but on his head he wore a grey felt trilby. He looked adorable. Lizzie's uniform was less remarkable.

We got to know quite a wide circle of friends outside the High Commission. It had always been that the white population had made its money in this country but had gone south to spend it. There were the two big copper companies, Anglo American and the Roan Selection Trust always known as RST and all their expatriate employees. There were white churchmen, doctors, surgeons, solicitors and the judiciary, but all these professions would gradually become 'Africanized'. As this happened, so we got to know some of these Zambians too. We met and made friends with one or two white farmers, who had lovely homesteads a few miles out of Lusaka. At one of these we met a couple who had a citrus farm in the north of the country. They extracted the essential oils from the blossom, and their entire crop went into a few gallon containers to be exported for scent making. I remember seeing these containers, which represented their entire annual income, in the back of their car. The wife was the daughter of Sir Stewart Gore Browne who lived at Ngandu in a splendid country house he had built years before. It was a cross between a manor house and a turreted castle which would not have been out of place on the Rhine in Germany. It commanded a wonderful view, and he ran a patriarchal régime there, in the nicest sense of the word. His servants were well-looked after and the whole set-up was positively feudal. His daughter told us a lovely story of an occasion when he went back to England on a visit, in the course of which he and his mother had an invitation to a Buckingham Palace garden party. Old Lady Gore Browne was getting on a bit, and to put it kindly, her memory sometimes failed her. This was in the days of King George V and Queen Mary, and the Gore

19. John's first day in school uniform.

Brownes were to be presented to the King. After the old lady was introduced, she took out her lorgnette and trained it on the king and said in a fairly booming voice, 'Young man, I know your face but for the life of me, I cannot recall your name!' One can only begin to imagine how her son felt, and how the Royal Family may have dined out on the story.

We had not been in Zambia many months before Ma-in-law came out to stay. We were thrilled that she felt she could make the long journey just like that. One of the things that did bother us a bit before her arrival, was the fact that she hated snakes, and we had three snakes in the garden during the run-up to her visit. We think it was because there had been rain which had flushed them out of holes in the ground, but we decided not to say a word and prayed! After that we never saw another snake during the whole of our time there. Perhaps the power of prayer did the trick! During her visit, we planned a trip to Victoria Falls and Livingstone, near which was a Game Reserve. We stayed in a two bedroomed hut with basic facilities, for two nights. We had asked Jessica if she would like to come with us, but she had been rather lukewarm about it and didn't come. We felt slightly uneasy about leaving her behind but had the help of an English family in the next compound to ours, who promised to look after her, and it did mean she could keep an eye on Juno.

Our first evening in the reserve, we went out in the car to see if we could spot some game. We saw a lot of antelope of different kinds, and in the distance a group of elephants crossing our track, as well as a great many noisy chattering apes. It was difficult to photograph successfully, as we didn't have a telephoto lens, which we learnt was a must for a good record of what we had seen. As time was getting on, we turned to go back to our camp. There was one car ahead of us, and it had pulled up to watch a very large elephant which was under a tree, in long grass about 75 yards off the track. On seeing the front car, he put up his trunk and trumpeted loudly and started to rush forward flapping his ears in what looked like a charge. The car zoomed off in a cloud of dust leaving us to get past the elephant as best we could. The animal turned away and we moved forward. Whereupon he swung round and did the same again. I was terrified but didn't want to alarm the children, but we moved pretty swiftly I can tell you. It was probably a male elephant as the females stay in groups, and the young males after a certain age go off by themselves, and only come back as the father of the herd. We had also been told that they nearly always made a false charge before doing the real thing. This thought in the circumstances, did not make me feel any better. What impressed me about this animal was its great size. They are far larger than the Indian elephant which was all I had seen in zoos, and I could certainly understand the stories I had been told of angry elephants crushing cars.

The next day we went to see the famous Victoria Falls. This was frighteningly impressive, particularly so because the Zambesi was in full spate, and the amount of water roaring over the edge was phenomenal. The noise was deafening and we had to shout to make ourselves heard. On the Rhodesian side of the Falls was a statue of Dr Livingstone. Another thing which surprised us was that there was absolutely nothing to stop one from stepping or falling over the edge and into the raging torrent. We hung on firmly to the children's hands when we were there, especially so when we saw a family with children a little older than ours, who were playing tag too close to the edge, I thought. We had been told that every year there were one or two suicides of desperate souls throwing themselves into the maelstrom. After this we walked in the rainforest which was caused from the drift of the spray from the Falls. The Africans have always called the Falls 'the smoke that thunders.' We got quite damp, but in those temperatures we soon dried off. From here we went over to a large modern hotel which was just nearing completion, on the Southern Rhodesian side. The garden hadn't been finished, but it was going to be lovely. We had a very welcome cold drink and enjoyed the lovely view. There had been virtually no development on the Zambian side and there were only a few huts and a sort of trading post, where traders had their wares spread out on the ground hoping for custom. Anslow's mother bought her grandchildren some carved wooden animals.

Another visit we did during Ma-in-law's stay was to take ourselves off to Kariba. This is a large artificially made lake on the River Zambesi. It had been dammed to form the largest artificial lake ever made at that time, and was to make hydro-electric power from a large and very impressive dam. Along the top of the huge dam was a road link between Zambia and Southern Rhodesia, and when the valley was ready to be flooded, there had been an enormously ambitious project called Operation Noah, to save and relocate as many wild animals as possible. It

20. The author with her children beside the Victoria Falls.

had been a marathon task to do this as well as re-siting villages and giving their inhabitants an alternative means of support by fishing in the newly-formed lake. We saw many birds here including the beautifully named lilac-breasted roller. Anslow's mother thoroughly enjoyed her month with us. Africa was quite new to her, as she and her family had always been in India in the days of the Raj.

Back at home after this trip, we decided to let Juno have a litter. We were really persuaded to do this because a friend had a good pedigree dog. A marriage was arranged and in due course she produced eight bitches and one dog. Lizzie asked if Juno had enough waistcoat buttons to feed them all! The owner of the dog had one of the bitches to breed from, and breeders in Southern Rhodesia were very anxious to improve their rather in-bred stock, so we had no trouble in selling them all. We felt this little commercial project would go some way towards paying for her six months quarantine when we came back to England.

When we had been out in Zambia a year, and Jessica had gone home, we decided to go on a trip to one of the big game reserves in the north east of the country. We were going to make for the Luangwa Valley, which was well known for being full of game. We left Lusaka going east on the Fort Jameson road, and after a while the journey was almost entirely on red laterite roads beside which we often saw very tall kapok trees. We spent one night at a roadside motel and on arrival, we all washed the red dust out of our hair! Fort Jameson was 500 miles due east from Lusaka and very near the border with Malawi, but the next day we left this road and turned northwards up the Luangwa River Valley. We had to cross this wide river on a ferry, which took two cars on a raft with rails down the sides, but unlike the ferry over the Volta, it was very much simpler. On either side of the ferry were two strong rope cables stretching across the river, and standing on the ferry on either side of our car, were two Africans who, with the help of a wooden gadget fixed on the ropes, pulled us across. We were amused to see little African boys with hook and line going backwards and forwards with the ferry, fishing over the side, and when successful hawking their catch to the passengers in the cars! I am afraid we did not respond. When we eventually arrived at the entrance to the reserve, we were booked in. This was because they only allowed, very sensibly, a certain number of cars and passengers in to match the accommodation

21. Crossing the Luangwa River by ferry.

at the six camps there were in those days. We made our way to the first camp which we had already booked. Here we had a chalet with two bedrooms adjoining and fairly basic washing facilities. Our chalet looked out on to a watering hole so that when we had sorted ourselves out, and had a meal cooked for us by the resident staff, we were able to sit on a verandah and watch animals coming down to drink. These were mainly different kinds of antelope. That evening Anslow went out with one of the game wardens for a short time at dusk to see if they could see any more game. I was quite glad to stay with the children as it had been a very long hot day, and I was happy to lie on my bed and read. In the night we heard a lot of rustling and grunting around us. We found out later that the hippos often come out of the water at night to forage on the banks, so it was probably their snuffling we could hear. When we occasionally saw them out on the banks of the river, we noticed they had salmon pink tummies! We were up very early the next morning, because we were all going out in the car with a warden to see if we could see anything of interest. These trips were nearly always in the evening or in the early morning, because so many animals lie up and rest in the heat of the day and one wants to catch them on the move, or when they are gathering at the watering places.

On this occasion we saw quite a number of different antelope such as puku with their large ears and russet brown coats, the graceful impala which leapt amazing heights in the air from a standing position, and the large kudu with their corkscrew upright horns. It was that morning that we had our only sighting of giraffe, and I was surprised anew by their amazing height. We saw a lone spotted hyena slinking along and up to no good I shouldn't wonder. They are not attractive beasts to look at and they really do slink!

After this we went back to the camp for a cooked breakfast of, believe it or not, bacon and eggs, and then we packed up, filled our thermoses and made for another camp. We saw very little game when we were driving like this, but as I have said before, it was probably the wrong time of day, but there were nearly always the little puku and impala on the move. They were often on an open bit of ground grazing in a group and yet ever watchful. The other animals I have always loved seeing were the zebra. They were fat and round and well-fed looking, and in reality in front of one, their markings are spectacular. I understand that they can be rather bad-tempered beasts, and are not averse to a vicious kick or bite if one of their fellows thwarts them. We also saw a few buffalo with their armour-plated heads where the broad horns practically joined on the tops of their heads. We took a photograph of one of them, but they were so well camouflaged that they were difficult to see when we had the film developed.

The next camp we arrived at was rather bigger than the first one, and laid out in a different way. The accommodation was in separate rondavels, or little round thatched buildings. Each one was for two people, and so Lizzie and I went into one and Anslow took John off with him. There were about six of these and another one was the washroom and loos. They were spaced out among some tall trees with a distance of about twenty yards between each of them. This camp was beside the River Luangwa, and, in a lovely position on a sort of platform above the river, was a covered open area where we could sit and watch the river, and our meals were eaten here too. We looked down on a wide stretch of river with what might have been sandy beaches and lagoons, and could see hippos wallowing in the muddy edge of the river. On the sandy edge we saw crocodile basking in the sun, but if they saw anything worth going for, they could move exceedingly quickly. We were the only people staying in this camp at first, though on our third day another family arrived. On talking to them, it turned out that they had got a hole in their petrol tank through going over some particularly rough ground. They were travelling round the reserve with the leak bunged up with soap, which tip we duly made note of, in case it should happen to us!

After a hot supper of meat stew, we didn't enquire what the meat was, and fruit, we sat and watched the river, and before long we saw a group of some ten or so elephant approaching the water. They slowly crossed and went off to find new pastures for their night's feed no doubt. As we were all quite tired after a long drive we all turned in fairly early, in any case we couldn't leave the children alone in the rondavels while we sat up. In the early hours of the morning Lizzie and I were awakened by something big and heavy rubbing itself against our door. As well as this there were a lot of the same gruntings and snufflings we had heard before. I told Lizzie to go to sleep, whereupon she said she wanted to go to the loo. I am afraid that I was not going out of that door and across to the wash room, and told her she would have to wait until dawn.

The next day we were again up early, and after breakfast, we went out in our car with an armed game warden with us. He was an African called Kitu and he knew all the best places for us to go to see a good variety of animals. Because our children were under twelve, they were not supposed to get out of the car and walk, as the adults could, but on one or two occasions, he did allow it. We were at the river again and a herd of elephants with their young were crossing, so we took a child each and very quietly watched, having left the car doors open in case of a quick getaway. They really are the most lovely family creatures. The mothers and aunts were helping the little ones where the water was too deep, by putting their trunks round their little bodies and supporting them until they got to the other side. That day we saw two young elephants shaking a tree to bring down some red prickly husks with nuts in them, and another lone animal was on its hind legs pulling greenery out of a tree. Kitu found a dead fish eagle and we took a photograph of him holding out the wings, to show the nearly 7ft wing span. One of our aims was to see black rhino, and he knew where they might be, so off we went on a very windy dusty track, until we came to a very large herd of buffalo which was spread out in front of us, and blocking our track. He said there were about five hundred

22. Kitu with a dead fish eagle.

of them, and he told us to sound our horn. We had been told that we should never do this, so tooted rather nervously and quietly. Kitu said 'More' and leaned over and did a long vigorous blast. Absolutely nothing would shift them. We remonstrated with the warden, and his reply was that they would never charge unless they had a sick animal among them. We wondered how he could possibly know. Anyway we were not to see the black rhino this time.

The next day followed the same pattern in that Kitu took us out to another area to see what we could see. We drove through a largish area which had been devastated by elephants. The trees were broken and dying, and where there were signs of life, we saw one or two gazelles on their hind legs reaching for the greenery at the top, and on one occasion we saw a small deer-like creature actually up the tree, having walked up the sloping trunk. They were certainly very agile animals. All the time we were driving slowly along on the watch, we could hear and often see various different kinds of monkeys, then suddenly we saw a very large herd of elephant. They were in a large group and not very far from us, but they seemed quite unconcerned by our presence. In the middle of the herd was an enormous animal who was head and shoulders taller than the rest. Kitu told us that he was an old male who might be as much as a hundred years old, but was still with his herd. So often the old males join the young teenager males, when they have been disinherited or driven off by a successor. All this Kitu told us. I couldn't help thinking that this old bull had been born soon after the Prince Consort had died!

As we drove back towards the camp, in the afternoon, we saw our first lion, or rather lioness. She was out hunting, and Kitu said that she probably had young and that other females in the pride would be acting as nursemaids and looking after the cubs. Later on we saw several other females lying down in a group. On several occasions we saw spotted hyena again, and the tell-tale signs of vultures overhead, which meant there had been a kill nearby. The children were fascinated by all that they saw, and in spite of the long hours and the heat, were very good about keeping their little piping voices down. This was to be our last day in the reserve, and on the morrow we were heading back to Lusaka, with lots of film to remind us of our unique holiday.

Once back home we had to think about a replacement for Jessica. We decided to try and find someone locally, and had the good fortune to have a black Rhodesian woman recommended to us. She had been a nanny to a white family, and had very good references, so I interviewed her and liked what I saw. She was middle-aged, neat and tidy, and well-turned out, and spoke very good English. We all came to like her very much, and she was excellent at her job. She stayed with us for the rest of our time in Zambia. Her name was Posted which amused us, especially when she said to service people 'I am Posted!' She joined the rest of the staff who looked after us. I might mention here our garden boy, the one called Smart, who had to water the garden every day at about five o'clock. He did this religiously whether it was dry or wet weather. He would stand in the pouring rain holding an umbrella in one hand and the hose in the other! He seemed incapable of working out that if it was raining he could miss out the watering. Another funny sight which we often saw in the wet season was Africans on bicycles in the pouring rain with large banana leaves held over their heads. As they were wearing only a pair of shorts and it was very warm we wondered why they bothered. Sometimes in the rains one's whole staff downed tools and rushed out with buckets to pick up the fat maggot-like bodies of a hatching of flying ants. They would lose their wings and fall to the ground and make rich pickings for the Africans. We were told that it supplied them with a valuable source of protein in their diet. The Africans out in the bush used to bee keep for the same reason. They would wedge a large piece of curved bark up a tree forming a sort of tunnel, and then introduce something sweet to attract wild bees who would then settle into their new quarters. Later when there was lots of filled honeycomb, they would rake the whole thing down and eat not only the honey, but the young grubs as well.

In November 1965 UDI (Unilateral Declaration of Independence) was declared in Southern Rhodesia by Ian Smith. This had a very real effect on our way of life in neighbouring Zambia. We became very short of petrol, so much so that it was rationed quite severely; at one period we had only four gallons to last us six weeks. As we lived four miles out of the shopping area of Lusaka, I arranged a roster among some of the expatriate wives for the shopping runs. We all acquired bicycles. Food also became short, in that we could never rely on being able to get what we wanted. I had a lock-up store cupboard in the house where I stashed away anything that I was able to buy, but of course in that heat one had to be careful what one stored. Elephant steaks and hippo meat came on to the market, and we tried both, and found them very coarse-grained and tough to eat. I remember the great day when we had saved enough petrol to take the children out to the open air cinema, where we sat in the car to watch the film, and had treats of ice cream and potato crisps!

With UDI came the RAF to Zambia, with their cargo planes to take the Zambian copper out of the country and to bring back petrol on their return run. They also brought out a squadron of fighter planes, ostensibly to guard the airport from attack from the south. Later on these planes were grounded for a short time, because a weaver bird had built its nest in the air-intake of one of them. A message went out saying, 'Inspect for weaver birds nests before take-off'. We were lucky enough to have the chance of a long weekend in Nairobi because one of the transport planes was going up empty for some reason or other. We travelled in the plane with only our seats put in specially, and coming back we shared the vast space behind us with gallons of oil in metal barrels. In Nairobi we stayed in the Norfolk Hotel, and went on a trip in a landrover to see game in a reserve near the city. It was a lovely break for us, though the game reserve was hideously touristy after the beautiful Luangwa Valley. The only other travel which Anslow did outside the country was to Malawi, where he had a liaison visit to his opposite number. I would like to have seen some of that country, as the photographs showed a lush green and pleasant land.

As soon as we realized how UDI was going to restrict us, we made the big decision to build a swimming pool in our garden. First of all a big hole had to be dug and this was where Smart, Lemon and Pencil came into their own. Anslow then took over and in his spare time, he did all the brick work, laying thousands of them, at the weekends and sometimes late at night, when we got back from perhaps a dinner, when he would go and do a few lines! We got a contractor in to put the cement slab in the bottom and to plaster the sides. Two or three nights after this had been done, we were awoken in the night by the sound of an underground train roaring along under the house. We put on the light and looked at each other. We both knew what it was, having experienced earthquake tremors in other parts of the world. It was all over as quickly as it had come, but our main concern was, dare I say it, 'Had the concrete slab in the swimming pool cracked?' We rushed down when it was light, to see that all was well, thank goodness. We were rather puzzled by the whole business, as we weren't in an earthquake zone as far as we knew, but later in the day we heard that it was rock deep in the earth under Lake Kariba, which was settling from the weight of water in the dam. To rectify this, the engineers opened more sluice gates to let out some of the water. We had felt this phenomenon some 120 miles away, which was really quite surprising.

Anslow made a filter in a forty gallon oil drum with graduated washed stone, and with a pump and some clever disguise it all looked most professional. He then set about building a six-foot stone wall down one side of the pool which included a changing room. We landscaped the garden round it all, and had a much envied swimming pool measuring 12ft by 24ft and 4ft 6ins deep. Our house soon became the meeting place of a number of the RAF officers in their off duty time. We used to frequently have a steady stream of as many as a dozen for tea every day. Some of them taught the children to swim and dive. The senior airman was an Air Commodore, and the more junior officers would arrive for tea, rather nervously asking if the Air Commodore was there! We had many official and unofficial visitors to Zambia. While we were there such people as Malcolm Macdonald (son of Ramsey Macdonald), Freddie Laker who was trying to arrange to fly his planes in and out of the country, David Shepherd the artist, to gather material for his paintings of animals, especially elephants, all came. After the Rhodesian troubles started there was a steady flow of politicians and Commonwealth Office people. Another group of people we always put up for the night were the Queen's Messengers. These people were often ex-servicemen, who escorted the diplomatic bags to our Embassies and High Commissions all over the world. When they came to Zambia, as it was such a long-haul flight, they stayed twenty four hours, delivering bags, and taking back others to London.

We had a certain amount of official entertaining to do, and dinner and lunch parties had to be carefully planned after 1965, because of the shortages. I found myself going down to Lusaka to see what I could buy before planning my menu. Also the children's birthday parties when they came round had to be catered for carefully, for the same reasons. On John's sixth birthday, he asked among others, young Julius Kaunda, the President's son, who was in his form at school. Julius had been named after President Kaunda's great friend President Julius Nyerere of Tanzania. Young Julius duly arrived in a large car, clutching a book of fairy stories as a present, which John's children still have to this day.

A few days later, our friend the Air Commodore was posted home, and was replaced by another senior officer who became a great friend of ours. He was very anxious to try and bring his wife out from England for a visit, and to make this possible we offered that they should come and stay with us for a fortnight. She managed to get what was called an indulgence flight on an RAF plane which was coming to Zambia with an empty seat. We took to her immediately and soon discovered that her boys were to go to the same preparatory school as John was destined for, which was a nice coincidence. During David and Jill's stay, we planned a trip to the Kafue Gorge. This meant a journey south to the Kafue River, where it was quite wide and flowing over large boulders in a gorge, making a certain amount of white water. I don't remember seeing much in the way of game, but the scenery was spectacular. It was also a treat for us, as we went in David's Peugeot, and he had a more generous allowance of petrol than we did. On another occasion David took Jill to Kariba, and one of the things which she did was to bring back a large lump of elephant dung. She said she was fascinated to see what sized lumps they did, and believe it or not she took her trophy home to England, and she still had it when we visited them years later. Chacun à son gout! We often wondered what the customs officer said on her arrival at Heathrow!

After a year of the Rhodesian impasse, we began to turn our thoughts to our return to England. Anslow rang me one day from the office and said one word, 'Turkey' to which I replied 'carpets' to indicate that I had understood what he was telling me. It was that our next posting was to Turkey, but we could not say anything about it until it had been cleared on the diplomatic front. We had been in Zambia two and a half years, during which time much had happened around us. We had broken off diplomatic relations with Tanzania, the civil war was still going on in the Congo, we had no diplomatic relations with Rhodesia to the south. In fact it was going to be quite tricky getting out of the country. We also reflected how lucky we had been to have seen so much in our first year, when we had petrol and were free to travel. When the political situation had been particularly delicate, we had taken the precaution of dispatching some of the family silver we had taken out, sending a crate home to England, via Mombasa on the Kenyan coast. It took six months to arrive having sat for three of them on the quayside in the monsoon. But I digress. We found that there was a weekly plane from Lusaka to Livingstone, which then overflew Rhodesia and went on to Johannesburg. We booked ourselves on this flight, while our crated heavy baggage went by train, through Rhodesia to Cape Town, to await our eventual arrival there. Then there was the question of Juno's travel arrangements. She would, of course, have to go into quarantine for six months on arrival in England, and we decided that the kindest way for her to travel would be by air, and she would travel in a special air-conditioned section of the luggage hold. She had to have a special crate made of specified dimensions, and would be met at London Airport by the registered kennels we had chosen for her six months stay. It was awful seeing her off, and we had already decided that we would not take her with us on our next posting abroad. After all she would be getting quite old by then and the stress would not be acceptable. After all the arrangements had been made, we left our African home and set off for a well-earned relaxed rest in South Africa to recover from what had been a difficult last eighteen months.

Chapter VI

Interlude in South Africa and a Year at Home

E ARRIVED IN JOHANNESBURG and stayed for a couple of nights. This was because some friends of ours in one of the copper companies had arranged for us to go down a gold mine. A car was sent to our hotel by the gold mine director and we were driven quite a long way from the city to one of the well-known mines. It was a very interesting experience, and we saw among other things that some of the black workers were chained to the machinery they were working. The foreman who was taking us round told us this was done for their own safety. I remember many years later there being a fuss in England about these same workers being chained like slaves in a chain gang. Whether the explanation given to us was valid we shall never know, but what we do know was that only certain workers on certain machinery were chained in this way. I would like to give their explanation the benefit of the doubt.

When the time came for us to leave Johannesburg, we took a taxi to the railway station, as we were booked onto the famous Blue Train which was to take us the thousand miles to Cape Town. By courtesy of Her Majesty's Government we were travelling first class, and we had a comfortable four-berth carriage. We had a steward to look after us and when we wanted him to do so, he came and made up our beds. It was a great experience for the children, especially to see the huge steam engine pulling our train. For meals we went along to the restaurant car where we had delicious food, which I think we particularly enjoyed after having been on a rather unimaginative and restricted diet in Zambia. To us, South Africa was already feeling like a land flowing with milk and honey. When we were awoken with early tea, we saw that the views had changed completely from rather arid dry scenery to lush green. Near the town of Paarl we travelled through a great peach-growing area, and there were acres and acres of orchards. We were not far from Cape Town by now and on arrival there we felt almost as though we had come home, as it was our third visit to this lovely city. Again we stayed in the same hotel we had been to before, and we had a warm welcome from the proprietor and staff. In fact for some years after they always sent us a Christmas card. We only had two nights there as we had planned to take a coach trip along part of the beautiful Garden Route, going east from Cape Town and most of the time hugging the coast. We set off on what was to be a two day journey to Beacon Island, near Knysna. Our first night was at an hotel at a place called Wilderness. Although we were near the sea, we were advised not to swim, as the bathing was dangerous there. On this first leg of our drive we had seen Cape Agulhas, which is the most southerly point of the continent, and not Cape Town as some may think. We passed turnings to ostrich farms, and if we had been in our own car, I am sure we would have slipped off the main road and gone to have a look.

When we arrived at Beacon Island, we found we were nearly on an island which was joined to the mainland by a small causeway. The only building on this small island was the old Beacon Island Hotel. I say 'old' because I am told that there is now another smarter version of what we knew. The whole place was bliss. There were miles of glorious golden sands only two hundred yards from the hotel. The swimming was great fun because there were great rollers coming in, and provided we swam within certain limits, it was all completely safe. Lizzie and John were now very proficient swimmers and they loved every minute of it all. The beaches were absolutely empty, and we were really able to relax and soak up the sun. We had a wonderful three weeks here, and went to see friends we had been given introductions to. Also we went into the rain forests near Knysna and saw the famous lowrie birds which lived in the trees there. The trees were ironwood, and in Knysna we bought a jar carved in the very hard wood, as its name suggests. We used the hotel taxi for some of our outings and to go into Knysna we took the local bus.

Another interesting trip we did was to go and see the grave of George Rex of Knysna. The story of George Rex is a fascinating one. His father George, as a young Hanoverian prince in London, is said to have fallen in love with a seamstress called Hannah Lightfoot, and he went through a form of marriage with her, and she bore him a son. As time passed Prince George came to the throne as George III, and having married Charlotte of Mecklenburg-Strelitz officially, he had many children. His firstborn by Hannah was brought up in the Royal household among his half-sisters and brothers. As the years went by he, supposedly not knowing of his birth, fell in love with one of the princesses. There was immediately alarm from the Royal parent, and young George was told why this could not be, and he was shipped off to South Africa. He took the surname Rex and started up a dynasty in the area round Knysna. For generations they kept their ancestry a dead secret, in fact it has never been openly acknowledged though many people who have known each generation of this family have remarked on the likeness to the Hanoverians and some of our Royal Family. I have a book by Sanni Meterlerkamp, who was one of the family, who has written the whole story with chapter and verse to bear out what she says. When we were in Knysna there were still descendants of George Rex living in the area. It all makes fascinating reading and leads me to wonder how, if that first marriage had been recognized, the course of history might have been changed.

The end of our three weeks came all too soon, and we had to make our way back to Cape Town. When we were planning this trip I had said 'Wouldn't it be marvellous if the *Windsor Castle* were sailing at the right time for us, so that we could go back to Southampton on this very special ship.' When we looked up the schedule we could hardly believe our luck. It all fitted in beautifully. The *Windsor Castle* was the largest and most luxurious of all the Union Castle line. My theory was that the bigger the ship the less likely I was to be seasick! When we went down to where she was berthed we had to locate our heavy baggage, and make sure that it had arrived and that it would be loaded on the same boat as us. Imagine our surprise to receive a message from the man in charge of the whole of the cargo for the boats, saying he wished to see us. Wondering what on earth it was all about, and hoping that there was nothing wrong, Anslow made his way to this man's office. There he met a jolly man who held out his hand and shook Anslow's warmly, and said he shared the same surname. He had seen ours on the heavy baggage, and as it was an unusual one, he had made himself known to us. When we got to our cabin we found a large box of peaches and a pocket, or net, of oranges had been delivered with the compliments of our namesake. For years after that he also always sent us a Christmas card and put us in touch with two other families of the same name. We had known from a South African diplomat whom we had met on a previous voyage, that we had a genuine family link with a branch of the family who had gone out to this country in the last century, and so we had found some distant cousins.

We had a lovely voyage home. The children were now nearly nine and seven, so were old enough to really enjoy many more of the activities on board. Anslow and I had time to mull over our future posting, and make plans for the next period in our lives. He had promotion again, and was to go to Turkey as Defence Attaché at the British Embassy in Ankara, the capital. Before going out to Turkey he would have to go on a year's language course in London, so we decided to base ourselves in our house on the Welsh borders, and to find a day school for the children for that year. After that they would go to their already chosen boarding schools.

When we finally docked at Southampton, we were met by an old family friend, who took us off to her home for a breather, before we set off for home. Visits to the family followed as soon as we had sorted ourselves out.

That year turned out to be a very busy and varied one. Anslow went off to London every Monday morning and for several days each week he struggled with learning Turkish. Not an easy task for a middle-aged man who did not have a great propensity for languages. He was taught by a Turk who had lived in England for some fifteen years and who read the news in Turkish on the BBC World Service. Turkish is not an easy language for us to learn as it is not like any language one had learnt at school. It has a twenty-nine letter alphabet and, to us, difficult rules over the use of vowels. The Ministry of Defence wanted me to go on a language course too, but it was not possible because of the children, and I knew that I would pick it up when we got out to Turkey, albeit rather ungrammatically.

Back at home we had found a suitable day school for Lizzie and John, and we settled into a routine. At the weekends we continued to work on the garden. Aunt Kathleen, Johnny Llanmorris and other friends came to stay. I always regretted that Mother never came, but for years I had never known her to sleep away from home. With her animals it was very difficult for her to get away. We went over to Norfolk of course, and on these visits she was able to renew her interest in her much travelled grandchildren. Anslow was able to help with handyman jobs, and on one occasion, he put up a new loose box for her latest batch of calves which she was rearing. Whenever we went to stay in the winter months we used to take a trailer with oil lamps and rugs to keep ourselves warm. It continued to be an extraordinarily cold house, and we felt it the more for having been abroad in the sun.

The winter of 1967–68 was very cold and we had quite a lot of snow. I remember only too well struggling with getting the snow chains on the wheels of the car in order to get the children to school. I was terrified of getting a bump on the car! As the time of our departure hove into sight we had to arrange a let for the house, and get the packers in for another big pack of all the kit we needed for Turkey. We had been advised that we should take out a dinner service for thirty, and so I went to the seconds shop of the Royal Worcester Porcelain Factory, and we did it this way and saved a considerable sum of money. I also bought several lengths of dress material as we knew we would be doing a lot of entertaining. The childrens' trunks had to be packed and their uniforms bought. It proved to be an expensive time all round.

We then turned our attention to dear old Juno. She was now nine years old, and as I had mentioned before, there was no question of subjecting her to another period of quarantine at the age of perhaps twelve or thirteen. With heavy hearts, we advertised for a family who had children, who lived in the country, and if possible where she could be used for shooting. After sifting through several unsuitable applicants, we found what we thought would be the ideal. She went off to spend a trial few days with this family, and then we made our decision, and said our goodbyes, knowing that we would never have her back again. If she survived our time away, it was hardly fair on her or her newly adopted family to ask for her back. The children went off to their respective boarding schools a few days later, and after another forty-eight hours during which time we ascertained that the children had settled in happily, we were on our way.

Chapter VII

Turkey – Ancient and Modern

W E SET OFF FOR DOVER FULLY LADEN, the idea being that we would go to Paris and stay for two nights with the Air Attaché there, he being that same Air Commodore we had known in Zambia. We were going to drive to Venice where we would take a boat to Izmir on the west coast of Turkey, and then drive on to our final destination. It was early May 1968 and when we arrived in Paris, there was a lot of unrest among the university students who were out on the streets of the city. After we had had dinner, it was suggested that we should go out on the streets and see what was going on. By the late evening things had got very lively, and the students were out in their thousands, turning over cars and looking very menacing. I was absolutely terrified, and really frightened that in the crush I would lose my footing and be trampled underfoot. Much to my relief after a bit of this, we went back to the flat, and Ian decided that Anslow and I should get out of France as quickly as possible, because he had heard on the grapevine that there might be a general strike, and we would be unable to get fuel for the car. All this was later to be called the Student Uprising of 1968 and we had been in the thick of it. We set off early the next morning, and drove through the debris on the streets of Paris, as we left the city and went south. We decided to make for Switzerland, and to linger for a few days there. We found a lovely little hotel in the mountains. I remember that this hotel's speciality was blue trout, and we had a delicious feast of this lovely fresh fish during our stay. The fish were swimming in a large aquarium in the hotel, and one was invited to choose one's supper on the hoof so to speak. We had already seen the babbling brook from which they had been caught.

We had a deadline to meet, and so tempting as it was, we had to go on after three days in this paradise, in order to get ourselves to Venice to catch our boat. This was Anslow's first visit to this beautiful city, and we had booked into an hotel on the island of Lido. We had two nights here which gave us some time to have a look round at the famous places, and to go to a glass factory, where we saw the amazing skill of the glass blowers. I think the very best time to go to Venice must be the middle of the winter when it is not too crowded. This was May and the visitors were beginning to descend on the city, but nevertheless we enjoyed seeing the cathedral of San Marco, the famous Bridge of Sighs, and window shopping in the beautiful, and expensive, shops in the colonnade round St Mark's Square.

After getting the car and ourselves on board, we set sail. The voyage was uneventful, and the weather kind. It was a lovely time of year to arrive in Turkey. The first thing we saw after we were clear of the port, were young boys selling little baskets of the most wonderful looking cherries, beside the road. We bought some of these tempting fruits, and not having been in Africa for nothing, we had some potassium permanganate mixture in one of our thermoses, and we dunked the cherries in this to sterilize them before eating them, and blowing the pips out of the car window as we bowled along the road to Ankara. The drive was a very long one, and in those days could take as much as nine hours. First we drove through the lush plains of the coastal hinterland, through olive groves and large areas of fig trees; the old name for Izmir was Smyrna and the area is famous for its figs. Gradually the scenery changed as we started to drive on to the higher ground of the Anatolian plateau. The villages were more spaced out and the roads in places, were very long and straight. There was one stretch of road near a place called Eskişehir, which was twenty-six miles without a bend. The roads were tarmac but with a dusty edge where one took refuge when being overtaken. We noticed round the villages the strips of land being worked by men with oxen and very primitive wooden ploughs, the design of which had changed little since Biblical times. Generally speaking it was the men who did the upright jobs with the animals, while the women seemed to do all the bending down jobs, like hoeing and planting. Of course, Turkey is a Muslim country and the men are first in the pecking order.

Every village had its mosque with a graceful minaret standing sentinel beside it. Several times a day came the summons to prayer, which used to be called from the top by the muezzin, but nowadays his voice blares forth with the aid of a loudspeaker, possibly when he is comfortably ensconced down below. Those going to prayer wash their feet, hands and faces before going in, in a special place outside the mosque. I have only once ever seen a Turkish woman in a mosque, and that was in Istanbul, where she was allowed in but was restricted to standing in a certain area only. In many of the mosques there are prayer rugs all over the floors, and often those praying would bring their own rugs. Many prayer rugs have a mihrab, or prayer niche, at one end of the design. I once bought a prayer rug with little hands facing to one end of the rug. As we made our way to Ankara, we saw that when there was a call to prayer from the village mosque, those in the fields would go down on their knees facing towards Mecca, and pray in situ. As we approached the city we noticed that Ankara lay in a bowl of low hills. In the winter months this area lay under a blanket of smog. This was because the Turks burnt lignite, or a very poor quality coal, which was very dusty and when the central heating was on, the chimneys belched out this filthy pollutant, which smelt smoky and sulphurous. There was little wind to shift this from the bowl in which it sat. If one lived down in Ankara, one kept the windows firmly shut throughout this season, otherwise the house got covered in a black film of soot. During our time in the city, the World Health Organisation did a survey and pronounced Ankara one of the dirtiest cities in the world, and living there was the equivalent of being a heavy smoker. This was not very reassuring.

We were thrown in at the deep end on the entertaining front, and we soon met a great many people from many different embassies and Turkish generals in the Army, Navy and Air Force. Soon after our arrival Anslow's predecessor gave three large cocktail parties to introduce us to everyone we should get to know. Anslow said after this that he nearly went home on the next boat! This was because the senior Turkish officers, as they said goodbye to Kenneth, kissed him on both cheeks. This subsequently became quite a joke among the Turks, and when they greeted us they would kiss me on both cheeks twice over saying as they did so 'And two for the General'! We came to like the Turks very much. They took some time to accept one but once this period was over they took us to their hearts and became loyal friends for always. We certainly needed our Turkish language because, although many of the more senior officers spoke English, many of their wives did not. We had one or two amusing incidents over this. Very early on Anslow was introduced to a Turkish general, and he trotted out the greeting which his mentor in London had taught him. The general was highly amused and said 'Good Heavens, whoever taught you to say that. That is a very outdated form of address!'

Our first house was in an area called Güvenevler, and was in the smog. The Embassy rented the property from the wife of the then Turkish Foreign Minister. It had a small garden, which was overlooked by tall flats of four and five floors which were close by. The house itself was adequate, and many in Ankara would have envied us, but it only had three bedrooms and one bathroom, which did not leave us much room to manoeuvre. We took over Anslow's predecessor's servants and they consisted of a cook, a steward, a washerwoman, and an old kapıcı, or sort of caretaker/boilerman. Anslow also had an official car and a driver to go with it. We soon found out that the servants had been taking the former incumbent for a complete ride. His wife was often away in England and they had really largely done what they liked. This came to light when the cook, who had been doing all the shopping, charged us for twenty-four lamb chops, and we had never even had any of them! When I asked the steward to clean the house because it was filthy, he said, 'Hoover Yok' which meant he was not going to use the vacuum that day. The final crunch came, when I discovered this same steward in bed with the washerwoman! We were their sixth tenants, and they had been working in the house for eighteen years. The time had come to cleanse the Augean stables.

We sacked the cook, steward and the washerwoman, and kept the old kapıcı, Ibrahim, who was a nice old boy, and did his job well and without fuss. The driver lasted a bit longer, but finally came to grief when he turned up the worse for drink, having got drunk on methylated spirits. The Koran says that the juice of the grape is forbidden, so perhaps he thought that what he had done was acceptable in his eyes. The staff were amazed at getting the sack, and I think they thought that in a few days I would be pleading with them to return. We were not expected to do any serious entertaining for three months so I was quite prepared to soldier on without them. We were blacked by any potential servants, but we remained tight-lipped and silent and after several weeks we found someone to come in and scrub floors and wash up. What was very amusing, was that at the end of a month, I had a phone call and it was the cook who said 'Please Madam, may we come back?' We wouldn't have had them back for all the tea in China, but the siege was at an end, and we were able to take our pick and restaff the house. I had decided to do the cooking myself, we would hire butlers when we entertained, and we got a woman to come in twice a week to do the laundry, and we took on a full-time steward who would clean, wait at table and wash up. This man was about forty years old and came from near Istanbul. He had never worked in an English house before and was really completely untrained. He couldn't read or write, but the plus points were that he was a strict Muslim and when I trained him I didn't have to undo any bad habits. He proved to be utterly honest and loyal, and although we had some battles with him, we never regretted taking him on. I taught him to eat with a knife and fork instead of his fingers; he learnt to write figures so that he could write down telephone numbers. His name was Hami, and he guarded us and our possessions like a lion.

We had not been in this house for long before we kept hearing scratchings and quite a lot of noise coming from the attic. On close inspection we found that the whole of this part of the house was teeming with rats. Thank goodness they couldn't get into the main part where we lived. We slayed several one evening with a stout stick, but something had to be done about them, especially when we discovered that, when the roof of the house had been raised to increase the headroom in the bedrooms, the builders had not raised the down-pipe for the bathroom, and had left it uncapped in the attic, which meant that all the rats from the sewers of Ankara had access to our loft. Not a pleasant thought.

In due course our heavy baggage arrived, but not, I am sorry to say, intact. One of the boxes had been broken into and we had lost several items, as well as there being breakages. I should perhaps explain here that Turkey is not a rich country and with little foreign exchange, she does not import much in the ways of western goods, so we had taken out a great deal of kit, and anything lost was going to be difficult to replace. For our food stores, over and above what we were able to buy locally, we dealt with a Danish firm in Copenhagen. This sounds rather extraordinary, at least I thought so when I first heard about it, but we had an extensive catalogue, and from this we put in a large order every six months, and it was a great day when the order arrived by an enormous transcontinental pantechnicon and trailer. In the house I had a room about 12ft square shelved from floor to ceiling, and this is where I kept all these commodities under lock and key. For entertaining we imported brandy and whisky in gallon containers, from which we bottled the spirit, before handing it out to be dispensed at a party. This was a far cheaper way of organizing the drink than trying to buy it in Turkey. It was interesting that the sophisticated Turks drank plenty of whisky, as it didn't contain the juice of the grape! A lot of our entertaining was also with other diplomats. It was fascinating meeting so many people from so many different countries. Often when we went to dine with a member of a foreign embassy we enjoyed the food of that country. The time we had dinner with the Nationalist Chinese Ambassador from Taiwan was a case in point. We sat at a large round table set for nine guests; if there had been more, then there would have been a second table, as apparently there is something special about the number nine. The table was covered with the most beautiful embroidered tablecloth and had matching napkins, and in the centre of the table was a large circular turntable on which were placed an amazing number of strange looking dishes of food. I was seated on the Ambassador's right, and the form seemed to be that he took his chopsticks and helped me to pieces of food from all the dishes. There was much wine drinking and toasting each other, and as the dishes were eaten so more came to the table. It seemed as though there were a never-ending supply. It was really difficult to know when to stop, but I found out that when the tea was put on the table it was a sure sign that the meal was coming to an end. The Ambassador wore what might be described as native dress, in that he wore a long robe of coloured embroidered silk. Everyone was very polite and every mouthful of food was a ritual. The whole feel of the dinner was as though we were in another era, and it was all positively feudal. When we went to the Indonesian Ambassador we had, among other things, the most delicious spicy meat on wooden skewers. At the Japanese attaché's house we had very hot food which, with the aid of chopsticks, which were smaller than the Chinese ones, we dipped into little bowls of raw beaten egg which we all had, to cool it down. Our host had been a Kamakaze pilot during the war, but fortunately for him, he had not had to pay the ultimate price.

The time came when we had to start repaying all this hospitality and I made a point of serving good English fare. The question of putting our Turkish to the test came up very early on. We were giving a dinner party for some Turkish generals and their wives. Anslow had prepared in advance some Turkish sentences he could use during the meal to the Turkish women he would have sitting on either side of him, as often the wives did not speak English. During the first course he asked one of the ladies in Turkish if she had been away on holiday this year. Whereupon he had a flood of Turkish back which was quite unintelligible to him, but he did catch the word 'Istanbul'. Knowing that many of the wealthy Turks took their holidays in Istanbul, he replied in his best Turkish, 'Çok Güsel' which means 'How Lovely.' There was a hush across the whole table, and then the husband down my end of the table said to me, 'Do you know what the General has just said? He asked my wife if she had been on holiday and she said that we had NOT gone on holiday this year because her mother had died.' I would like to add that this man became a great friend of ours and was very amused by the faux pas.

We made friends with many of them, some of whose fathers had fought at Gallipoli. They used to say that it was the last of the gentlemen's wars. As they won, perhaps they took a slightly different view of that period in history, but they told us that between battles, the Turks would send drinking water over to the British lines, and we would send them chocolate in return. Every year in the spring we used to go to Gallipoli, where there was held a wreath-laying ceremony, and a band was provided by the Turkish Army. It was attended by the British and the Commonwealth Ambassadors to Turkey, who were from Canada and Australia. This journey took two days from Ankara, and we usually had a stop-over in Istanbul. The whole site was very moving, especially the beautifully kept war graves, and the actual large stone war memorial with thousands of names engraved on it, of those who had fallen in those dreadful battles. The poppy wreaths were sent out from England, and brought to Gallipoli by the representative of the War Graves Commission who lived not too far away.

By the time that the children's summer holidays were upon us, Lizzie and John came out by air, looked after by the SSAFA (Soldiers, Sailors and Airmen's Family Association) Escort service between school and the plane, and then on the plane, much to their chagrin, they were labelled 'minors' and the airline took charge of them. It was very exciting seeing them again, and after they had settled in and got to know a little of our surroundings, we decided to take them off on a few days camping holiday, to a lake some distance from Ankara. This place was called Abant, and was a very picturesque area with lovely walks, but unfortunately no swimming, as there were leeches and other unpleasant things in the lake. We had bought a splendid second-hand tent from the out-going British Naval Attaché. It was far more luxurious than anything we had come across before. It had two bedroom compartments, an eating area, a small kitchen tacked on the back, and two awnings on the outside. With our camp beds and sleeping bags, we were very comfortable. Back in Ankara, there was a lot for the children to do. In the grounds of the British Ambassador's Residence was a swimming pool, and tennis court which we were allowed to use. There were a lot of children out for the holidays for them to get to know, and invitations to picnic parties and other gatherings flowed in.

Our Embassy had an English church and a parson, who had the grand title of Archdeacon of the Aegean, to take the services. In a non-Christian country, this was a necessity for all of us. Many British families were housed in flats, some of these were spacious and very pleasant, even though they lacked a garden. The Embassy was quite large, and there were also other British communities living in Ankara.

Ankara itself is largely a modern concrete city. When Atatürk came to power in the 1920s, he set up his capital a good distance away from Istanbul, or rather Constantinople as it was. Being in a bowl of hills, it was easily defended. He did away with the Arabic script and a lot of Arabic words, as he wanted Turkey to modernize and look to the west. He also said that his people must take surnames, instead of being Mustafa, Kemal, and the like; so some of them took names from the place in which they lived or owned property, as was the case for the veteran politician İnönü, or perhaps from what their forebears had done. I found it easier to remember these names if I translated them in my mind, so that the Foreign Minister, who was called Menemencioğlu, was 'the son of an omelette maker'! We also knew a Colonel 'of a thousand white horses' and a General 'son of a hazel nut.' If I was faced with someone whose name I had forgotten, I would say to them 'do tell me how you pronounce your name so that I can introduce you correctly,' and this ploy worked successfully for several months, until I came completely unstuck when a very Turkish looking lady said 'Phillips' to me. She was the wife of an Australian diplomat!

In our local shops in our part of Ankara, we bought, to bring home eventually, lovely thick Turkish towels, and quite a lot of marble, alabaster and onyx, in the form of table lamps, vases, boxes and jars. I loved the different coloured turned onyx and alabaster eggs which I started collecting. My Turkish lady friends got to know this and used to send me a thank-you present in the form of an egg instead of sending the usual flowers after a dinner invitation. Down in the centre of the city, in an area known as Ulus, I got to know a Turkish rug dealer. I had been given an introduction to him by one of my Turkish friends. He was a funny little man called Rhami Bey, and he had a very modest shop in a rather scruffy street, but inside it was an Aladdin's cave, with piles of lovely rugs. They were mostly Turkish but he did have quite a lot from other countries, such as Iran. He would ring me up when he had a load of rugs in and then I would rush down and have a lovely time going through them, and sometimes buying. The usual bargaining went on, but everything was so reasonably priced that one hardly liked to beat him down too much. On one occasion I was there when a few American women arrived and wanted a particular rug. Rhami Bey wouldn't sell it to them. They kept upping the price, but no, he was adamant, and they went away empty-handed. I asked him why he hadn't taken the opportunity to make a handsome profit, to which he replied that he didn't like Americans. The Turkish people are very proud, and I think they had gone the wrong way about the transaction altogether. I once took the children down there and introduced them to him. He had four daughters and no sons, and consequently he ignored Lizzie and stroked John's hair and kept saying 'Lovely Boy'. I think these were the only words of English that he knew. During my sessions down there, nothing could be hurried, and I used to drink endless glasses of rather sweet green tea. During our four years in Turkey we bought about fifteen rugs of various sizes in various parts of the country, but at no time did we pay more than the equivalent of £10 for any one rug. John saved up his pocket money and bought a very nice Kirşehir rug for £3 from Rhami Bey. On another occasion I bought a rather attractive rug from the Kars area, which is in the north east of Turkey near the Russian border. This rug had been repaired at some time and a small piece of another rug had been inserted to mend the tiny hole. I said to Rhami Bey, 'What a pity that they put that piece in that way round as the pattern runs the other way' to which he replied 'Only Allah makes everything perfect.' I felt duly corrected!

After taking over the everyday shopping, I found myself searching out all manner of interesting food shops. The greengrocers had a marvellous display of seasonal fruits and vegetables. The leeks were sometimes nearly a yard long, and the peaches were enormous, so much so that they did not export them as they were too big to pack into the standard crate. John used to ask me if I would halve a peach with him! There was a little grocer near where we lived, called Ihsan Bey, and I was a frequent customer in his shop. The butter we were able to buy normally was not very nice, some people said that it was made from water buffalo milk, but one day when I was in this shop, Ihsan Bey sidled up to me and said, sotto voce, 'Madam I have some ulbs.' I couldn't think what he meant and asked him to repeat it. As I still didn't understand, he surreptitiously produced a pack of American butter with the weight in lbs written on it, as well as the message which said 'This butter is the gift of the American Government for …' (an aid programme in Turkey). I was sorely tempted. I also had a tame butcher which I used regularly, and again near the house was a Pastahani. This was a shop which sold very sticky cakes and gateaux, Turkish pastries which are very rich and sweet, and for those who like them, the most delicious marrons glacés. I always bought my filo pastry from him, and everything which one purchased was beautifully gift-wrapped, even my mundane pastry. In the holidays, Lizzie and John would come with me to his shop and he always spoiled them by giving them a little gift. He would ask me when they were going back to school in England, because he wanted to give them a present. This would be a box of real Turkish delight or some other Turkish delicacy. Everyone was so kind and generous to all of us. My shopping always took quite a time because at each shop I was always given a little glass of sweet black or green tea, and one couldn't refuse without offending the donor.

Later on in our tour in Turkey, when I was rather ill and had to go back to England for an operation, the owner of the Pastahani wrote me a priceless letter. It was in English, and we thought he must have found a translator who wrote at his dictation. The letter started 'Madame, I am very interested in your health. When are you returning. We are waiting for you.' It was a very touching missive.

Bag and Baggage

At the weekends, Anslow and I tried to get out of Ankara to see a bit of the surrounding country. The Anatolian plateau was perhaps not the most interesting country being flat and rather featureless. Some of the distances to places of interest were somewhat daunting, but we explored quite a lot. Anslow and two British friends used to get up in the middle of the night to go and shoot sand grouse, about four hours from Ankara. I went with them once, and the reason for this night start was because we had to be in the 'hide' before dawn. This consisted of a muddy hole in the ground in which two of us could crouch. It was far from comfortable as I had to keep my head down, so as not to show my white face to the flocks of birds when they started flying in, so I hardly saw anything. It was all soon over, and then we had that long drive back again. The nicest part of this expedition was when we stopped in a little mud-hutted village and bought a big round loaf of freshly-baked, crusty bread. We tore off chunks with our hands and munched our way back to Ankara. I only went once! Another place we went to was called Kızıljahamam. This was a good drive from Ankara, but when we went the first time it was late spring, and everywhere was very green and the wild flowers had to be seen to be believed. The whole area was carpeted with the most wonderful tapestry of every conceivable colour. Up a valley in this area one could find marvellous fossils in the chalk rocks. They were mostly of leaves and insects, but what was so nice when we took the children, was that the fossils were so plentiful, that they couldn't fail to find some. They were equipped with a little hammer so that they could split the layers of rock and expose the fossils. We were amused to hear of a picnic which the new American Air Attaché went on soon after his arrival in the country. He and his wife set off in their new Cadillac and drove into open country a few miles out of the capital. The only thing in sight was a flock of sheep, so they got out of the car and spread out their picnic, when suddenly from nowhere appeared a Turkish sheepdog. Now these animals are not the cosy things you might see in Wales, but they are more like a wolf. They are larger and leaner than an Alsatian, and round their necks they wear an iron collar from which project spikes which are sometimes nearly two inches long. These collars are to protect them from real wolves, which might attack them by going for the throat. This fearsome animal ran at our American friends, who abandoned their picnic in haste and took refuge in their car. Whereupon

23. Walking haystacks! Laden donkeys seen on a hill road near Ankara.

the dog proceeded to attack the outside of their car and to gouge the side with the spikes of the collar. Gloria said to Bill, 'Do something Bill,' to which he is reported as replying 'What can yer do?' We learnt to travel with cigarettes and a tin of biscuits when we were going to places off the beaten track, as they were useful to placate a menacing situation, which could have been the case if a shepherd had appeared when Bill and Gloria were in their predicament.

When Anslow and I went down to Istanbul on official visits, we were privileged to be able to stay in the Ambassador's flat in the Consulate. The building had been built by Sir Charles Barry in the last century when Constantinople was the capital of Turkey. Several acres of land in the middle of the city had been given to the British by the Turks. It had a lovely garden and had been the Embassy before the capital had been set up in Ankara. Also in the grounds was a little church which was used by the British community. The whole place was a marvellous haven from the noisy bustle and congestion of the city outside the compound.

Istanbul was a fascinating place to visit, although the traffic was, and I am sure still is, noisy and horrific. The driving was awful too. This was once explained to us by a Turkish friend, who said that being a Muslim country, Allah would look after you, and if your day came to die so be it, and nothing you did would change that. It was a fatalistic belief. I loved to go down to the bazaars where one could buy just about anything, but one had to be very much on the watch for pickpockets and the like. From our days in Africa, we halved the asking price and then started bargaining. There was also a spice bazaar which was equally interesting, and had every imaginable spice on sale in large open-topped finely woven sacks. The mixture of smells from these exotic powders conjured up dreams of Arabian feasts. I remember going there with a Turkish friend called Neriman. She was the daughter of a Turkish diplomat, and she spoke very good English. When I went out with her, she took a very high-handed attitude to the people in the shops, and if anyone overstepped the mark with me by not treating me with the respect which Neriman thought he should, she would remind him that I was a guest in his country. On another occasion when Anslow was away on an exercise with the Turkish Army, I went to stay with Neriman in her house in Istanbul. She told me a very interesting story, while she showed me a rather worn silk bedcover which she said had been given to her grandmother by the Sultan of Turkey. When I asked her how this came about, she told me that her grandmother had been brought up in the harem of the Sultan's palace. In the last century the Sultan's troops would go over the border to neighbouring Greece and capture fair-haired, blue-eyed girls and bring them back to the palace to be brought up with the Royal children. When these children reached maturity, they were used to introduce the fair colouring and blue eyes into the blood lines of the Royal family. Neriman and her sister Fazilet, whom I also knew, were both dark and very Turkish looking, but their brother and their father, the diplomat, were fair-haired and blue-eyed.

When I first went shopping with Neriman I noticed her making a shopping list but not in modern Turkish but in Arabic. She said it was so much easier and it was her 'shorthand'. She took me to a Turkish bath on one occasion, and I thoroughly enjoyed the pampering I had while I was there. I can almost feel those wonderful warm thick towels, and the strong firm rubbing down I had while wrapped in them.

The family used to live in style in one of the lovely carved wooden palaces on the Bosphorus, but as time went by, they hit hard times, and inflation eroded the little money they had, and the old house had to go. Neriman built herself a modern house on three floors so that she could let off some of it to bring in an income. Fazilet moved to Ankara where her husband worked, but later moved back to Istanbul, and now lives on the Asian side, where properties are less costly. I never met their brother as he went to live in Egypt. We knew many wealthy Turks, and the key to their survival latterly has been the fact that they owned property and could supplement their meagre pensions with the rents from them.

During one of the children's holidays in Turkey, we took them down to Istanbul, and the Turkish Army commander and his wife arranged for us to go to the new Opera House which had recently been rebuilt and opened after a fire had burned down the old one. The night we went, there was a performance of the ballet *The Nutcracker*. It was the most lovely treat for all of us. Everything was done in style and we had the best seats in the house. A chauffeur-driven car was sent to take us from the Consulate. When we arrived at the Opera House there was the General's Aide-de-Camp, who was to sit with us and look after our every need. The Army commander's wife was a very good friend of mine, but I remember her saying to me once, 'Edith, we are like sisters but never forget that we Turks are orientals, and there is a small bridge between us that we will never cross.' By this she meant that the Turks came originally from Mongolia; it has always been understood that they did so well in the war in Korea because of this.

After the Christmas festivities, a large party of us used to go up to a place called Uludağ where there was a hotel and some fairly basic skiing. Lizzie, John and Anslow all ski'd, while I pottered about with one or two other non-skiing friends, as I had never fully enjoyed skiing after that accident in Cyprus. The Turkish ski lift was not very efficient, but nevertheless it was very good fun in spite of the ski runs being unimaginative. On one of these trips, Anslow found that there were some almost wild dogs in a pack at the side of one of the ski runs. When the skiers went past them, they ran out as though to attack. A few days before one of them had attacked a woman who had been walking along wearing a fur coat. It had leapt on her back and torn the coat from her. It was all really rather unpleasant and so Anslow complained to the man working the ski lift. Imagine his surprise when a fellow skier, a Turk, on hearing of his complaint, pulled a loaded revolver out of his pocket and handed it to him, suggesting to him that he took pot shots at these animals as he ski'd past. We thought it far more dangerous to have an armed skier in our midst than the wild dogs. Strangely enough the same General who had arranged our visit to the ballet, arrived the next day for a short holiday, and in the course of conversation, we mentioned all this. Mysteriously the whole pack disappeared in the night. It is sometimes useful to have friends in high places.

After about a year in the old house in Güvenevler, we moved up the hill above the smog, and into a very modern house which had only just been built. It was on three floors, as well as a basement where the servants had their rooms. It had lovely marble floors and was ideal for large scale entertaining, although when it rained we couldn't keep the water out. It seeped through the window frames and no amount of running repairs ever overcame this problem. There were one or two other funny things about this house; when we moved in we found that the electricity meter went round backwards and the shower in the second bathroom leaked like a sieve, and the water came out of the electric light fitting in the entrance hall! There was a small downstairs cloakroom in which the architect had put 'his' and 'hers' wash basins, without allowing enough room for them and so the door wouldn't shut. The cure to this little problem was to carve a half circle out of the door! The kitchen had a hatch into a little service passage which led to the large reception rooms. The first time that we had a dinner party, I told Hami to put the food through the hatch. Before we could stop him, we saw Hami, balancing a dish in one hand, while he tried to climb through the little square from the kitchen! At the top of the house we had a penthouse which had a sitting room, dining room, kitchenette, and another room which I used as a sewing room. We used to retreat up here when we were not entertaining, and we put up a table tennis table for the children. Outside this top floor was a wide verandah on all four sides, and I made a colourful roof garden up there. We had a fantastic view of the city spread out below us.

In spite of this impressive house, which had a little space on one side where I made a garden, the whole building stood high on an empty hill which was strewn with quite large boulders and outcrops of rock, and no provision had been made for a road or drive up to our house. When Özturk, Anslow's new driver, came up every morning to take him to the office, he bumped his way up, as he skirted round the worst of the obstacles. I thought this was not good enough and decided that the time had come to try and persuade the powers that be to do something about it. I found out where the Minister in charge of roads and highways had his office. Down I went to a part of Ankara called Kızılay and entered a large office block. Inside was a wide concrete stairway, and hundreds of people milling about. On the stairs was a queue stretching on up and up, of every conceivable kind of Turk. There were women with scarves over their heads and some covered the lower part of their face when spoken to by a man, grubby little children with their mothers, working men and office workers. The one thing they seemed to have in common was that they all looked as though they had been there for days waiting for their turn to come, for what I didn't know. Anyway I wasn't going to join any queue I'm afraid, and so I went up the stairs past all these hopeless looking beings, until I suddenly saw a door which said 'Müdür' which I knew meant manager. I thought this looked hopeful, and so I tapped smartly on the door and went in, slightly conscious as I did so of a surprised look on the faces of some of those waiting nearby. Imagine my horror on finding myself in the Müdür's private lavatory! Thankfully he was not 'at home' and I hastily withdrew. When I did finally find his office, he was most charming, and in halting Turkish I explained our predicament. He promised to look into the matter, gave me an iced drink from his private fridge, and after exchanging some further niceties, we shook hands and I went on my way. Knowing how slowly the wheels ground in Turkey I didn't hold out much hope of anything happening quickly. On return-ing to the house, I noticed a group of workmen, some distance away on the hill, using dynamite to blast away rock to prepare a site for another house. I went over and persuaded them to come and look at my problem, and in less than an hour and a half, they had cleared the rock and made a tolerable dirt track off the road below the house. They were rewarded with English cigarettes, which I had in my store for entertaining, and everyone was happy. Anslow was duly pleasantly surprised when he came home, and when I told him how it had been done, somewhat horrified.

A lot of Anslow's work involved travelling within the country, and on many of these occasions I was able to go with him, and in the course of our four years we covered a lot of ground. When he visited Turkish Army units, he had one or two interesting experiences such as the time he went to a regiment of commandos, who were on an exercise and living off the land. He arrived in time to join them for lunch. A good-sized fire had been built and lighted, while the troops had foraged round in the area to see what they could find to cook. Some of them came back with a tortoise and the poor creature was thrown alive on to the burning wood and cooked in its shell. After a suitable lapse of time, it was taken off the heat and handed to Anslow with a fork. It was rather like being in an Arab country, and the honoured guest having to eat the sheep's eye. He had to decide which of the holes he should go into with his fork to start his meal, with everyone standing round and watching him. After this visit he was saying his goodbyes, when some of the soldiers arrived back with a live snake which followed the same fate as the tortoise. Anslow didn't delay to partake of this delicacy.

Another such journey took us to the south west to the village of Bodrum, the former Halicarnassus, where the castle was once occupied by the Knights Hospitallers of St John of Jerusalem. Here also was the site of one of the Seven Wonders of the Ancient World. This was the Tomb of King Mausolus (from which comes the word mausoleum), built in the IV century BC. I very much wanted to see if I could see any of the remains, and after a lot of asking and strange directions, Anslow and I found ourselves in a little garden of a peasant's house on a hillside, and among the long grass and midst a broken down wall, we could see some lengths of whitish/grey marble lying broken and half covered by undergrowth. In one or two places were the vestiges of one slab on top of another, and with a lot of imagination one could see the beginnings of the steps at the base of the mausoleum.

While we were driving in this area, we went through a village which had a number of rugs hanging up outside a little mud house. This was too much to resist, and we stopped and looked at them. As I have said before, these things cannot be hurried and after quite a chat with the owner, he invited us to his house, where we were given a glass of the inevitable tea, and introduced to his family. All the females in the household had a hand in the making of these rugs. They had their own sheep, dyed the wool with such things as walnut stain and onion skins, and lovely terracotta earth colours. After seeing all this, boiled sweets were then handed round and we got down to the serious business of bargaining and buying. We spent two hours altogether in this village, having bought the only new rug we have, for the equivalent of £8.

After leaving Bodrum and then Marmaris, we hugged the coast going east, we found the road deteriorating into a track and finally in places it was extremely stony and had been blasted out of the rock to make a sort of rough stretch just wide enough for a vehicle. There was a sheer drop down to the sea on the passenger side, and in places when I dared to look, I saw the remains of old lorries which hadn't made it. It was positively unnerving. We were in a long wheel base Land Rover, otherwise we could not have progressed at all. We had to cross several rivers and Anslow drove while I got out and rolled up my trouser legs and waded across to show him where to drive through the water. On this bit of coast, we went to what became my favourite ancient amphitheatre at Kaş. Many of the theatres on the coast were backing on to the sea, but here one sat looking out over the beautiful blue Mediterranean. Turkey is teeming with ancient Roman and Greek ruins, as well as several places mentioned in the New Testament. Many of these ruins have been tumbled over by earthquakes, and the pillars lie like a house of cards spread out on the ground. At Finike we looked at the Lycian tombs, believed to be IV century BC carved out of the living rock high above the town, while on the water front we watched fishermen mending their orange-coloured nets. Further on, when we had been travelling for some hours on this perilous road, we came to a small flat area where we could park the vehicle and rest for a bit. We got out, stretched our legs and spread a rug on the ground and flopped down to have a short respite. Hardly had we done this before we found ourselves surrounded by the most fearsome looking shepherds with their dogs and a few sheep. We knew that we shouldn't stay there and quickly got out the cigarettes and biscuits and handed them round. We then got in and started up the engine, said our farewells and went on our way. We had to get to Antalya before dusk as we never drove at night in Turkey, because of the unlit hazards on the roads, besides which we had friends in the Gendarmerie who would set out and look for us if we hadn't turned up by 5.00 p.m. We slept in Antalya that night, and I could still feel the juddering of the steering wheel in my arms for some hours after we hit the hay.

The next stretch of coast, going east, was where we took the children when we camped in the holidays. The beaches were sandy and generally clean, and the mocamps, as they were called, had showers, places to cook and fridges, if one wanted them. They were often run by the petrol companies and were excellent. These sites nearly always had the flags of several nations displayed at the entrance and I often made it my job on arrival, to get the Union Jack hung the right way up! We liked a place called Side particularly, where there was also a simple and pleasant motel almost on the beach, and we camped in an olive grove belonging to them. On one occasion when we were staying on the south coast, the half-shaft broke on the Land Rover. We made enquiries about who could repair it and we were told that Mustafa in Manavgat would do it. Anslow went off driving very slowly leaving me with Lizzie and John. Some hours later we heard the sound of a motor bike and then saw it approach along the sand. There was Anslow on the pillion being brought back by Mustafa, who then went back to his repairs. When we had word that the vehicle was ready two days later, we set off in a taxi to Manavgat to find the garage, which turned out to be a hut, or perhaps by a stretch of the imagination, a garage. Mustafa spoke good English and had been on an engineering course in Birmingham. In chatting to him, it turned out that he was a keen fisherman and, to our intense surprise, he produced the latest Hardy's catalogue from one of his dusty little drawers at the back of the shed. He then invited us to his house in a nearby village. Here he had beehives, a little vegetable garden and various chickens and ducks scratching around a mud brick house with a thatched roof. We were ushered inside and immediately Lizzie and I were syphoned off, into a separate room with a number of women, while John and Anslow were entertained by Mustafa. We had glasses of tea sitting on yastıks on the floor. These were coarsely woven coloured bags stuffed with straw and made into large pillows to sit on. There were rugs on the floor, and the conversation, on our part, was in halting Turkish. Mustafa became a firm friend and on another visit to the south he took us all trout fishing, and on this occasion John caught his first fish.

The last section of the coast to the east ran up to the border with Syria. Anslow had to go and see someone there once, and so we made the trip south from Ankara through Konya where we saw the Dancing Dervishes. These were a religious sect who were sometimes known as the Whirling Dervishes because they worked themselves up into a trance-like frenzy as they performed their dancing ritual, dressed in white robes and wielding fearsome looking knives as they twirled themselves round and round for hours on end until they collapsed with exhaustion. From Konya we drove over the Taurus mountains and dropped down to the south coast and then turning left travelled some hours east to the town of Antakya, the biblical Antioch. Here there is supposed to be an underground tunnel going through to Syria and through which the Christians could escape persecution from either side. The thing which attracted my attention most in the modern town was that outside all the houses in the streets were ordinary wooden chairs, and hanging over the backs of all of them were long lengths of pasta of all sizes drying in the hot sun. I also saw a signpost saying 'Halep 52 kms'. This was the Turkish name for that magical place Aleppo, to which I had always wanted to go. I suggested to Anslow that I took a bus over for a few hours while he was busy with his job, but he wisely, I suppose, said that should the border close when I was in Syria, there would be a real drama, and so it was a case of 'near and yet so far.' We stayed in a funny little place which called itself an hotel, but to compensate for its simplicity, we had a dish of the famous Iskenderun prawns from the nearby bay of that name. Later on in our tour in Turkey, I had a compensation for not being able to go to Syria, when our Ambassador and his wife went to Damascus and brought me back a beautiful dress length of midnight blue Damascus silk. As we were so far from Ankara, it was difficult to send letters to the children on these trips, and the local posts were impossibly slow and unreliable, so a picture postcard had to suffice, but back in Ankara our letters went regularly in the diplomatic bag back to London and were then forwarded to them from there.

Among our many Turkish friends was a Professor and his wife who had the use of a summer holiday place up on the Black Sea coast, owned by the University of Ankara. They used to have large numbers of people for the weekend, and we were lucky enough to be included on more than one occasion. The country round Akçakoca was quite different from many of the parts of Turkey which we had come to know. Admittedly we went in the late spring the first time and so everything was lush and green, in fact one might have been in parts of England. There were shallow babbling streams with little wooden bridges over them, and small Turkish boys fishing with a worm on a hook, surrounded by large deciduous trees. Also in this area were acres and acres of hazelnut groves, from which the nuts were harvested commercially, and exported. I understood that at that time, and perhaps they still do,

Cadburys imported the nuts for their chocolate from them. We went for lovely walks along the coast to a ruined castle where bay trees and other sweet smelling herbs grew out of the ruins. The turf under our feet was springy and there were many wild flowers. The Black Sea is called so because the sand on the shore is a dull grey-black and coarse, and not at all like the golden sands of the south coast. Storms and mists blow up very quickly on this coast and the sea can be treacherous. It is interesting that there are two Turkish words for black, one for an ordinary black and *kara* for a threatening or horrid sort of black; the Black Sea is called Kara Deniz. A few brave souls bathed there, but were wise enough not to go out very far because of its reputation.

Anslow had to go to Izmir from time to time, and I accompanied him. We explored ancient sites when he was free to come with me, and on one occasion, with the help of our Guide Bleu, we searched out a place off the beaten track. We found a large area of complete chaos, which had been devastated by an earthquake in ancient times. As we picked our way among the ruins we saw two boys with blond hair playing ball together. As we approached we realized that they were talking Greek to each other. We spoke to them in Turkish and asked them why they were speaking Greek, and they said that they always did at home in their village, which was nearby and on the coast. This we found very interesting because it seemed as though they were descended from a Greek family, most of whom Atatürk drove off the mainland in the 1920s. As he did not get them off the Turkish islands close to the coast of the mainland, this has been a constant irritation to the Turks to have the Greeks now owning islands which used to belong to them. On this trip we visited the small peninsular of Çeşme, where we bought the most delicious fat black olives. Neriman had told me that when one buys black olives one must put them in a saucepan with a mixture of olive oil and water, just enough to cover them, bring them to the simmer, then take them off the heat, and leave to cool in the liquor. Then put them in a bottle and use when needed. It is a marvellous way of plumping up slightly shrivelled olives. In this part of the Çeşme we came across an elderly man looking after a little patch of land in which he was growing the most enormous lettuces I have ever seen. They were like monster cos lettuces (we weren't very far from the island of Kos as a matter of fact), and he called them Marram lettuces. He very generously cut one and gave it to us; we wondered how on earth we would eat it all as there was enough to feed an army.

On one of the children's holidays we went to Kuşadası where we camped, so that we could go and look at Ephesus on the west coast, and further to the north to Troy. On one of these trips west we took a detour to take in Lake Eğridir and Isparta. On the lake we stayed at a little auberge which served the most delicious freshly caught crayfish. An enormous dish was brought to the table with the crayfish swimming in butter. As we made our way through this feast, the innkeeper brought more and tipped them on to the emptying dish. We made absolute pigs of ourselves. When we left here the next morning we drove to the far side of the lake and saw that it was white with salt deposits. Back on our original road our journey to the coast took us to another extraordinary place called Pamukkale. Here there are great bowls of lime deposits filled with very warm water. They have formed naturally from water falling from a mountain over a cliff in tiny streams and over the years these great white bowls, like an orchestra's giant kettledrums, have been formed. One could bathe in them and there was a motel to stay in beside them. There are the extensive ruins of Hierapolis destroyed by an earthquake in AD 17 nearby, and which we explored in the cooler evening.

24. Natural warm springs near Pamukkale, West Turkey.

The valley running out to the coast from Pamukkale was full of fig trees, and little boys stood by the wayside with baskets made of grass fronds filled with delicious fresh figs which we bought. We did our customary dunking in the thermos and enjoyed them to the full.

Ephesus was fascinating and there was much to see there, including nearby the scant remains of another of the Seven Wonders, which was the Temple of Artemis. We spent a day at Ephesus exploring the extensive ruins. During the four years we had in Turkey there were digs going on, and more was being discovered all the time. We used to go into Kuşadası village to shop for our daily needs, and I remember enormous piles of water melons on sale for the thirsty passer-by. They were a very welcome reviver on a hot day. On one of our visits to this area, we were invited to a Turkish doctor's summer holiday place on the coast. As always they were very hospitable and couldn't do enough for us, and for us it was an interesting insight into how a Turkish family lived.

The time came to pack up and move towards Troy which I, person-ally, found rather a disappointment. This was because it was so difficult to sort it all out in one's mind, as there were different parts and levels built at different times. What was very evident was the remains of Schliemann's trench. He was a German archaeologist who, controver-sially, dug on this site in the second half of the last century and removed treasure from the country, much to the annoyance of the Turks. We were highly amused at Troy to see outside the entrance to the site, an enterprising Turk who had a pile of logs for sale with a notice saying 'Part of the original horse of Troy!' Round the back of his little hut he had an assistant with a saw and further supplies to replenish the pile at the front.

From Troy we were making our way to Istanbul, and visited Bursa *en route*. This is a fine and interesting city which was once the capital of the Ottoman Empire. It has rather special spa water which is piped into the bedrooms of the main hotel in which we stayed. It is also the centre of the silk industry of Turkey. We were making for the little town of Yalova which was where we would get the ferry across a bit of the Sea of Marmara and so shorten our journey to Istanbul. When we got near the ferry, we joined quite a long queue of vehicles, and as we moved slowly forward, we noticed we were outside a butcher's shop, in the window of which were hanging up five or six whole lamb carcasses.

We then did a sort of double take because suspended beside the lambs, was a fox hanging from his heels and with his overcoat on. We were amazed, and later asked a Turkish friend of ours, who was not surprised and said that they certainly ate fox in certain areas of Turkey. I tried to imagine what the flesh would taste like, as the fox is a carnivore and I think the meat might have been fairly strong flavoured.

When we got to Istanbul, we stayed for a few nights, again camping, but this time we were in the garden of what had once been the summer residence of the British Ambassador. The residence was no more but the garden was a lovely haven in the hurly burly of Istanbul. We took the children for a boat trip up the Bosphorus to the entrance to the Black Sea. On the way back we had a delicious lunch at a waterside restaurant where we had fresh prawns and salad, followed by lovely fresh fruits for which Turkey is so famous, sitting under umbrellas on decking which had been built out over the water. During this visit we went to the Topkapı Palace, which was the old residence of the Sultans. Here there was the most amazing collection of valuable porcelain and jewels and much else. We also visited the Dolmabahçe Palace which was built in the last century, and to which the Sultan of the day moved from the Topkapı. This stood impressively right on the Bosphorus, on the European side, and in Atatürk's day became the Presidential Palace, and was where he died.

There is much else that we saw on our many visits to Istanbul, for instance the great mosques and the Galata Tower looking out over the Golden Horn, the bustling ferries which took us across the Bosphorus to the Asian side. Remember we were there when they were just thinking about putting a bridge across this busy waterway. On the Asian side, we took Lizzie and John to Scutari, which was the Army headquarters, but housed in part of it was the hospital in which Florence Nightingale worked and where we saw her famous lamp. But all good holidays have to come to an end, and we had to make our way back to Ankara, which was a drive of some six hours, though some Turks used to do it in three and a half, which made us shudder! Then it was off to UK and school again, while we settled down to another busy spell doing our duty.

Chapter VIII

An Excursion to Iran

N 1970, ANSLOW HAD TO GO AND VISIT his opposite number in
Teheran, the capital of Iran. This was going to be a long trip,
because we were meeting an American colleague in Isfahan who was
going to take us down to southern Iran, and we were also going to
prepare the ground for our Ambassador and his wife to follow in our
footsteps at a later date.

We were driving ourselves in our own car, and the whole journey
needed a lot of careful planning. Ankara is not much more than a
third of the way across Turkey, and going east one was travelling
into less populated and wilder country altogether. The roads would
vary and although we were going in June, the winter ends late in
eastern Turkey. Because of this we decided to go to Sivas where
we spent our first night, and then cut off up to the north coast and
on to Trabzon (Rose Macauley's Towers of Trebizond). After a long
and tedious journey, it was a welcome sight to see the coast and
the Black Sea lapping its shores. This part was rather attractive and
I remember, in particular, the sight of the cherry trees in full bloom
in the valleys near Trabzon. The town itself is very ancient, and
we saw ruins of the ancient world as well as the remains of the
Byzantine period. Our hotel was adequate and the food passable.
Thankfully I think we had fairly strong stomachs after our years in
Africa. We always travelled with a bath plug in Turkey, or in fact,
in any Muslim country, when we were out of the main cities. This
is because they consider it dirty to wash in used water such as we
do by having a bath and sitting in it, and so they always wash in
running water, and we certainly used our plug here.

From Trabzon we made our way to Erzurum where Anslow had
Turkish Army contacts he wanted to see. Some ten miles out of this
town, we were stopped by a uniformed soldier who demanded some

money from us before he would allow us to go on, whereupon Anslow drew himself up and told the soldier who he was, and that he was on his way to see the Army Commander in the town. The soldier blanched visibly, slammed to attention and saluted, and provided us with an escort in the shape of another soldier on a motor bike to lead us to our hotel in Erzurum. I expect he had been making a nice bit of pocket money on the side, and probably quaked in his shoes for the next twenty-four hours in case he was court-marshalled. We said nothing, as we thought he had already had quite a scare. What I had noticed as we travelled east, and in particular in Erzurum, was that some of the people had oriental eyes, the women and children having bright rosy weather-beaten cheeks and dark plaited hair. To my inexperienced eyes they had a Tibetan look about them.

The next stretch was wide open country, and we had the feeling we were fairly high up. In fact we certainly were, being well over 3000ft and more in places. The countryside was just turning green with the beginnings of spring. There were scattered flocks of sheep being tended by shepherds wearing enormous thick woollen felt capes with very wide shoulders and the whole garment coming right down to the ground almost like a tent. Apparently they were wind-proof and kept out much of the snow and other bad weather experienced in the winter, because the wool was oily. There were some wild flowers heralding the approach of spring, but what attracted our attention was, in the distance to our left, a magnificent mountain, with a distinctive cap of snow on the upper part of it. This was the famous Mount Ararat, which lies on the Turkish Russian border. I was thrilled to think that I had actually seen this Biblical landmark, and thought of those many attempts by various expeditions to find Noah's ark. Because it was on the Russian border, during our time in Turkey special permission had to be obtained before one could go into this area.

We entered Iran and our first stop was in Tabriz, famous for its carpets. What I noticed markedly was that the women all wore the chowdah, which was a black garment which they wore to cover their bodies when out and about. Out in the country they quickly covered the lower part of their faces when men approached. Women in out of the way places covered their faces in Turkey but seldom wholly as here. When we reached Teheran, we were to stay with the Military Attaché, who had a lovely house and garden. After our long and

25. Shepherds in their winter 'coats' in Eastern Turkey.

26. Mount Ararat, Eastern Turkey.

sometimes dusty drive, it was bliss to be civilized again, and to soak
in a hot bath and sleep in a comfortable bed.

The next day while Anslow was on duty, I was collected by an Iranian
friend we had got to know while we were in Ankara. She and her military
husband were back in Teheran and she was to take me shopping. Mimi
was a cousin of the Shah, and was a highly educated and sophisticated
woman. She certainly didn't wear the chowdah then, though after the
overthrow of the Shah years later it would have been a different story.
She had a chauffeur driven car and we went to several fashionable shops,
and she insisted on buying me a length of silk to make an evening dress.
We bought John a silk cravat and Lizzie a silk scarf. She then took me
to the crown jewellers and said she wanted to give me a present. This
was getting embarrassing and I remonstrated, but to no avail. She was
rather like Neriman in that she was not the sort of person one argued
with, besides which she would have been very offended.

In the jewellers, she took command, and they obviously knew who
she was, because everyone fussed round her, and the underlings were
sent scurrying while the manager served her personally. I had no idea
what she was planning and watched every move with interest and
fascination. She said 'Bring me turquoises', whereupon a velvet cloth

was spread over the top of one of the glass counters, and minions brought little drawers full of the pale blue-green opaque stones, which were tipped out on to the velvet surface. Mimi said again 'Bring more' and then, when there were some hundreds of these stones in varying sizes heaped on the counter, she started to sort through them with very nimble fingers. After she had rejected quite a lot, and I suppose there were about a hundred left, she indicated to someone to take away the surplus. She repeated the sorting and gradually reduced the pile to about ten. She then studied these, put her finger on one and said 'Wrap that one'. While the wrapping went on, tiny cups of very strong black coffee were brought to us; this was served with some water which one was supposed to add in a dash to settle the coffee grounds. Mimi told the manager to put the purchase on her account; I assumed that was what was happening when a ledger was brought out and an item entered, because she paid nothing at the time. When we were in the car again she gave me the present. It was very generous and I treasure this expression of her friendship to this day. When I got back to England, I took this turquoise to Carringtons in Regent Street, as I wanted them to make it into a ring to match some earrings I had inherited from my grandmother. When they saw it they asked me where on earth I had got it from. I told them the story briefly and they said that, had they been giving it marks out of ten, they would have awarded it nine, so Mimi knew what she was doing.

That evening Anslow and I were to go dinner with her and her husband in their house, and I took the customary bunch of flowers as a small gift of appreciation to her. As one had come to expect on these occasions, the party tended to divide into male and female groups, but as it was a buffet style meal, I was able to move around and meet more than those sitting immediately beside me.

The next day, Anslow and I were taken out to lunch by an English business man who had connections with our government, and who wanted to talk to Anslow. He took us to a very smart Russian restaurant, and there we had the most wonderful meal of blinis and oodles of real Iranian caviar. This came from sturgeon which were caught in the Caspian Sea to the north of Teheran. Blinis are rather like small pancakes about 4 inches in diameter, and they came to the table, hot and piled high, with butter oozing out of them. The caviar was served in a large glass bowl sitting on a bowl of ice, and the whole was served with wedges of lemon.

We had been invited to spend a few days up on the Caspian Sea with our Iranian friends, but sadly our schedule was already arranged and we had to refuse. The wealthy families had summer houses there, as it was a bit cooler than Teheran and places further south in the height of the summer. It certainly would have been an interesting thing to do, but the last afternoon we had in the city was spent being taken round part of the Shah's palace. This was arranged by Mimi. Everything was very opulent as one might expect. One of the things which caught my attention was that in the reception rooms, on little ornate tables, were bowls of small uncut diamond, ruby and sapphire chippings put there as a sort of decoration.

The next day, having replenished our thermoses and filled our cool box with sustenance, we said our goodbyes and set off for the city of Isfahan. We found the driving in Teheran worse than in Turkey, because it was horrifically fast. We were really glad to get out of the city and on to a clear road. It was beginning to get fairly hot, and as we went south this was going to increase. The first place of any size which we went through was Qom. It was from here that we saw beside the road south the domes of the old water system which still supplies the villages it passes through. When Alexander the Great came down through Persia conquering as he went, these systems watered his armies, as did others we saw in parts of Turkey. When we reached Isfahan, we went to a lovely hotel which had been converted from a

27. *Our hotel, at one time a caravanserai, in Isfahan, Iran.*

caravanserai. It was built round a courtyard, in the centre of which was an attractive garden with roses growing in the beds and fountains playing in the centre. It was all deliciously inviting to hot and dusty travellers. On the ground floor round the courtyard there were tall arches through which were reception rooms. Upstairs, all round this square ran a wide covered verandah open to the gardens below, and on the inner side of which were tall arched doors all the way down each side of the courtyard, leading into high-ceilinged roomy bedrooms with a welcome overhead fan. We were to meet our American friend after dinner, and so we did, to discuss the plan for the next leg of our journey, which was to go to Shiraz, stopping off at the ancient site of Persepolis about 40kms short of the town.

We set off early in the morning to try and get some of the drive done before it got too hot. We were now heading for an area not much short of the Persian Gulf, and it was very hot. Very unfortunately, Anslow had woken up that morning with a temperature and was not feeling much like baking in the sun and looking at ruins. We had plenty of cold drinks with us, and when we got to Persepolis, we parked the car in the shade of a tree and left him as comfortable as possible, while Bill and I went to see the impressive ruins. They were very extensive and it was very, very hot, so perhaps we didn't do them justice, and I was anxious not to leave Anslow for too long, but suffice it to say that we spent nearly an hour there, taking photographs and seeing the most interesting parts. We then set off for the last bit of our journey to Shiraz, and found our hotel. Anslow went straight to bed, lying under a welcome fan, with lots of cold drink to sustain him. I bathed and lay on my bed to recover, and as the sun lowered in the sky I went down and joined Bill for dinner.

Next morning, Anslow was a little better, but with the long journey back in two days time it seemed wise for him to stay in the peace and quiet of the hotel, while Bill took me round Shiraz. One of the things which Anslow and I had promised ourselves we would do, was to buy a rug. This responsibility now fell to me, but I was in good hands with Bill to guide me as he had a number of contacts in the town. Shiraz was the birthplace of the Persian poets S'adi in 1184 and Hafiz in 1300. They wrote of the nightingales and the roses of Shiraz, and I was anxious to try and find a rug which depicted these symbols. We had agreed a rough estimate of what we would be willing to pay, so off we

28. *The author completing the purchase of the Shiraz rug outside the elephant stables in Shiraz, Southern Iran.*

went to start our search. First Bill took me to the souk or bazaar and made contact with his Iranian friend. We went to a great many shops and saw a great many rugs, but somehow they were none of them quite what I thought we wanted. Everyone was very patient with me, and finally after drawing another blank, our mentor said 'we will go to the elephant garages'. We got in the car and set off for another area of the town, to where there were indeed huge elephant stables. They had very tall arched doors and when they were opened, lo and behold, they were packed with piles and piles of every kind of carpet one could imagine. They were all of varying ages, and as we found in Turkey when buying old rugs, we were told that they were eighty years old, so it was all a bit of a guessing game. I looked at silk rugs with small fussy patterns, larger nomadic rugs with geometric designs, and some which were positively garish, but suddenly there appeared a hearth rug about 6ft by 4ft, with a lovely soft rose red background and among the geometric patterns were roses and nightingales. Some of the latter admittedly had six and seven legs, and were strange looking songbirds, but it was the rug for us. Glasses of refreshment were produced to revive our flagging spirits, and the business of bargaining started. I finally paid the equivalent of £8 for my prize. I was confident that Anslow would be pleased, and like it as much as I did.

Mercifully Anslow was feeling much better, as I didn't much relish having to do all the driving ahead of us. The next day we said our farewells to Bill who had been so kind, and we did our journey in reverse, staying in the same places as before. Back in Isfahan, we visited the ancient polo ground and bought an inlaid box to remind us of a memorable visit to this interesting old country with so much history behind it.

At the Iran/Turkish border, it looked as though there would be a long wait. There were literally hundreds of vehicles waiting to clear customs and enter Turkey; they were mostly large container lorries and some of them had been there for days. Gradually we realized that they were allowing private cars through and by nudging our way forward, and easing ourselves into little gaps, with the added help of our cigarettes which we had at the ready, after about two hours we got through. Anslow was quite keen to try to take the central route through Turkey, rather than go north to the Black Sea coast. He wanted to find out if the road, which was 3000ft–40000ft high in places, would be clear of the winter's snow and motorable.

Early on after we crossed the border we came to Lake Van and the town of Van, which had been an Armenian stronghold. The whole area had had a chequered history, and had even been occupied by the Russians as late as 1917. Another claim to fame that Lake Van had, was its swimming cats. These animals apparently, and unusually for cats, swim quite naturally. I knew a Turkish woman in Ankara who had one of them; it had blue eyes and an off-white coat and rather long pointed ears with long whiskery hairs at the tip of them. When we were in Ankara, two English women came out every year and travelled to Van to collect some of these cats and take them back to England, for breeding purposes I presume. They were certainly much sought after. We decided to spend the night in the town as the next day might be a long and difficult one, and also after our delay at the frontier time was getting on.

The next day after some hours driving we had to go over a high pass. When we were nearly through we came across a complete blockage of heavy container lorries, probably some of them had come from as far afield as India and Afghanistan, stuck in melting snow and a quagmire of mud. Everything had come to a standstill. We managed to get round one or two, but eventually like them we had to stop. By now we had wrapped ourselves up in warm clothing, as it was bitterly cold. Every now and then we ran the engine to keep the inside of the car warm. Fortunately we were carrying a certain amount of spare petrol in cans; one had to on such trips. After a long wait of some hours, I desperately wanted to spend a penny. This was decidedly awkward as there were lorry drivers wandering about and absolutely no privacy for the only woman among all these people. Finally, when I couldn't hang on any longer, I took my courage in my hands and crouched down under one of those huge lorries and hoped that no one would peer underneath. After a while, one of the drivers, who had a shovel, used it to good advantage, and dug us out and with a lot of pushing and shouting from his comrades, we skidded our way round the last obstacles and left the quagmire behind us, with the cheers of our saviours ringing in our ears. We were on our way.

We were late getting to Erzurum and mighty glad to hit the hay. Anslow seemed fully recovered and we both slept well. Our final night at Sivas was uneventful, except that as we were looking round the town

29. Woman spinning cotton, near Myra, Southern Turkey.

we came across a little rug shop. Never able to resist such a sight, we went in and after the usual rug-buying routine, chose a top-embroidered kilim. A kilim is different from a rug because it is woven and not knotted and tufted. This one was particularly nice because besides being pleasant colours, the embroidery added something to it. It had been repaired down the side and was bigger than our Shiraz. On the end fringe was threaded a blue maşallah bead; this was a symbol to keep off the evil spirits. Neriman had given me one such bead telling me to put it on the camera when we wanted to take photographs of Turkish peasants, to reassure them that the camera wasn't going to bring them bad luck. I remember in southern Turkey we came across a woman spinning cotton and, by sending Anslow back to the car and showing her the bead, she uncovered her face and allowed me to photograph her. Anyway we bought the kilim for the equivalent of £3. I think when we were bargaining, it helped that we spoke Turkish; although it was obvious that we were foreigners, at least we weren't naive tourists. When we showed our kilim to an expert years later, he said that we had done very well and that we should hang it on the wall so that the embroidery would not wear out.

By the time that we got back to Ankara we had been away for over two weeks.

Chapter IX

Sorties, Sorrows and a Royal Visit

ACK IN ANKARA, WE PICKED UP THE REINS AGAIN, and launched ourselves into the ever changing routine. There were a number of public holidays which very often meant military parades which went on for as long as four hours, as we sat in the stadium watching thousands of troops goose-stepping their way past our eyes. In the evenings of these special days there were usually large receptions and dinners held at the Ordu Evi, the Turkish equivalent of our Officers' Mess. These were also fairly drawn out affairs when one sat through a floor show of belly dancers, Turkish singing, and male Cossack-style dancing. Another annual engagement was the Attaché Ball, which we held in the main hotel in Ankara. As Anslow was the Doyen of the Corps of Attachés, he and I hosted this event, when senior generals of the three services and their wives, and many other officers and friends were invited to attend. It was a very enjoyable evening, and the highlight of the evening was when seven Hungarian violinists came on to entertain the guests with some amazingly talented playing, and accompanied our dancing.

At home, we continued to fulfil a heavy programme of entertaining. Soon after our arrival, I had instituted what I called Attaché Wives' Lunches, when I entertained six to eight foreign wives at a time. This was in order to get to know them and find out what languages they spoke, so that when the time came to have them with their husbands, one would know who best to have them with. Language was often a problem, especially with the Eastern European wives, but it is amazing what one can achieve with sign language and photographs, and a judicious choice of other wives to help me out.

There was a constant flow of visitors to the country; for instance Dame Ninette de Valois came out regularly and on one occasion we entertained her to dinner. She was dainty, petite and good looking as one might expect a ballet dancer to be, and her dress was exquisitely-tailored and made mine feel somewhat second best. Her thank you letter the next day started 'Dear Mrs Anslow Garrett', perhaps she thought we had a double-barrelled surname! I also remember a reception at one of the Warsaw Pact countries' Embassy, when Alexander Dubcek had just been appointed Czech Ambassador to Turkey. He was a man of quite modest stature and like all those from communist countries never wore anything more formal than a lounge suit. I was introduced to him, and started a conversation with him in French, when his 'minders' moved in and quietly steered him away. When Sir Alec Douglas-Home, as he was then, was staying at the Residence, Anslow and I were asked to come over after dinner to meet him. He was such an easy natural person to talk to, and seemed like the typical Scottish laird that he was, and yet had that elder statesman air about him which foreign politicians used to admire in the British. I sat on a large comfortable sofa talking to him, and answering his questions about the country asked in a casual conversational way, but all the time I felt a shrewdness threading its way through the words which he spoke. Some other visitors to Turkey were perhaps less welcome. These were the ill-equipped young students who arrived by various means every summer and sometimes failed to take advice on how and where to travel safely in Turkey, and became a liability to our Consul.

Amidst all this, Anslow and I slipped away for a weekend to an area some hours drive west of Ankara, which was on an earthquake belt, and where there had been a tragic loss of life a few months before. The town we went to was called Kuthaya and was famous for its pottery. This was an earthenware product painted in traditional patterns and colours and made into a great variety of objects, such as plates, tiles, cups, jugs and quite large items for domestic and decorative use. We went to the factory where they were making the pottery, and watched young women working in very bad light, doing the intricate hand-painting sitting at dusty benches lighted by very dim bulbs and probably paid a pittance for their skills. We had been told that these workers often lost their sight after a few years of working in these appalling dusty and badly lit conditions. We bought several large flat serving plates which we thought were very attractive.

As Kuthaya was not a tourist area, the sight of a European woman was quite unusual to the local Turks, and having found a room in a so-called hotel for two nights, Anslow and I went to find a restaurant for our evening meal. All we could find was a place frequented entirely by working men. In these very rural out of the way places, local women would not be seen in such a public place, but nothing daunted we sat down at a table, and a menu was brought to us. Fortunately we knew enough Turkish to be able to cope with this, but then the waiter asked us if we wanted some wine. We thought this would be a good idea, and our attention was called to a wall which was covered from floor to ceiling with bottles of liquor of every conceivable kind. As we didn't think we could get through a whole bottle of wine, we scanned the shelves for a half bottle. There at the very top were some smaller bottles, and we pointed to them and made our selection of one called Kanyak. Mine host looked somewhat surprised, but got out some steps and climbed up to bring down the chosen bottle. This was duly opened and some poured into our glasses, and under the gaze of the waiter, I took a mouthful. My goodness, I wondered what had hit me. It was the rawest, strongest brandy one could imagine. It then dawned on us that Kanyak was the Turkish for Cognac. No wonder they had looked at us askance, especially me, at our choice. We simply couldn't drink it, but took it back to Ankara to put in the next Christmas pudding I made!

The other thing that we did this weekend was to buy some lovely alabaster eggs. It was a completely new mauvy-pink colour which until recently had never been found in that area, and I couldn't help wondering if the recent earthquake in the region had thrown up a seam of this attractive rock. The Turks told us that these eggs used to be used by rich Turkish women to hold in their hands to keep them cool and for them to exercise their fingers to make them slender and beautiful. Also such women always had long hair which they would spend hours having brushed and then dressed up on their heads; this was to show the world that they were ladies of leisure and had time to indulge in such luxuries.

When Lizzie and John came out that summer, we planned a trip to a very interesting and yet strange area some hours' drive south east of Ankara. This time we decided to stay in a hotel rather than camp as it was an area which we did not know and which certainly wouldn't have had any mocamps. During this journey we deviated to take in one of the finest Seljuk caravanserai in the country at Sultanhani. It had been built in the 13th century and was very impressive, with porticoes round the inside of the outer walls and a mosque in the centre. The camel trains and travellers would spend the night with their animals in safety, and there were at one time even shops and hammams (baths) within the porticoes, while the animals were housed in a vaulted area at the end of the courtyard. The whole place had been obviously and necessarily well fortified in those days, as the walls had been reinforced with small towers. We were rather glad to get back into the car after this, as a somewhat aggressive Turkish woman tried to waylay us, and even started to throw stones at us when she saw our cameras. I am afraid that Neriman's maşallah bead did not placate her, so we beat a hasty retreat while we were unscathed and the car was still undamaged, and returned to our main road.

We were making for Cappadoccia. It is difficult to describe what we saw in this quite large area, but I will try. Through extraordinary erosion, there lay out before us a valley full of cones, columns, towers and other strange shapes, some as much as 100ft high. It looked almost like a moonscape or a strange fairyland where goblins and imps might live. Some of these shapes had windows and doors, and had been hollowed out into little dwellings in which real people lived. I say this because one almost expected to see a little hobgoblin come out of the opened door. Some of the doors opened into lovely cool stores for such things as apples, while others had sheep or goats in them at night. We were able to explore the deserted dwellings and Lizzie and John were as enchanted as we were. The area was so extensive that we only saw a fraction of it. There was more to come, because we had still to see the early Christian churches also in carved-out caves. There are supposedly 365 of them, one for every day of the year. We looked at the main ones in one area only. They all had frescoes on the walls and ceilings, some very mutilated and pock-marked, but because of their being in caves, the colours had not faded, in spite of some of them being 7th and 8th century AD. Even after this, there were further surprises in store for us, and this was when we went to another part of this valley, and went down to an underground city. This was a labyrinth of passages and rooms quite deep underground into which the early Christian communities fled when threatened. They were self-sufficient for an extended period, having their own wells, and considerable storage down there to support a large number of people.

30. Strange erosion at Cappadoccia.

At certain points in the passages there were enormous carved round stones which were rolled into position to protect themselves from the enemy without. We heard after we left Turkey that two more of these underground cities had been found in this valley.

We had had a very full day, and went to the town of Ürgüp nearby, to find an hotel for the night. We found somewhere suitable and very simple, and took two rooms. In the evening we went out to find a small restaurant for our evening meal. Again we found a very simple eating place frequented by the locals and had a feast of delicious tender lamb chops, lots of lovely vegetables cooked in olive oil, and chunks of crusty Turkish bread. The children had some fresh lemonade and Anslow and I indulged in a bottle of local red wine. The pudding was crème caramel, a great Turkish standby, and we rounded the meal off with Turkish coffee. The bill was the equivalent of £3 for the lot!

The next day we decided to go a little further afield, so we drove through more of this strange land, wondering as we went. We were going to make for a place called Kayseri, as we had heard it was a place where one could ski in the winter, and we wanted to see if it had any facilities. On our way there we drove through a place called Avanos, which was a rug-making district, so we kept our eyes open, and sure enough we hadn't gone far before we saw a woman making a rug outside her house. We had seen rug-making in villages before, but never quite like this. She was sitting on the ground with her feet in a hole about 2 ft square, and lying across the hole and over her knees, was the loom. She was dressed in typical Turkish attire with a scarf over her head, and a longish dark dress and even in the heat of the summer, thick dark stockings covering her legs. We watched her for a little while and then asked her if they had any rugs for sale, so she took us into her house and showed us another rug in the making, set up on an upright loom, with a long very low stool in front of it, with three of her daughters sitting and working at it. We thought the colours very garish and not to our taste, and anyway we really wanted to buy an old rug which had mellowed in colour and yet had many years of wear in it still. Eventually we found a little rug dealer, and looked at his wares and found one which we liked. It was quite a good size, being about 8ft by 5ft, though even this one, on turning it over, had some fairly violent colour on the back where the colour had not faded. We paid £6 for this one and it is in our drawing room to this day.

31. Carpet making in a village house in Avanos.

Another thing we did on this trip and in the same area, was to see how the alabaster and marble was turned into lamps and all the other things which they made so beautifully. This was done on a lathe under a constant stream of cold water, to stop the rock getting too hot. There were lovely colours, which intensified when the rock was wet. The objects were then passed on to the man doing the polishing, also on a lathe, but dry this time. As well as my alabaster egg collection, I collected a few beautifully crocheted Turkish purses, and pocket-watch bags. One would see the women standing at their doors in the village, working away at modern versions of these little gems, in bright coloured cottons with a particular design which identified them with that region. Working men out in the fields would sometimes have a pocket-watch in a little gem of a bag, or a few coins in a beautifully made purse. My purses were antique and equally attractive and I was always on the lookout to increase my collection.

By the end of the children's summer holidays, the time had come for their return to England and school, while we continued our duties in Ankara and elsewhere. One of the things which I had taken a particular interest in was the Blind School in Ankara, and I visited them regularly, and spent one afternoon every fortnight with them. I arranged fund-raising functions from time to time. I hope it did something to encourage the young as well as their teachers, to know that someone from outside their world took an interest in them. These blind children used to play football with a ball which had a bell tied to it, and I was amazed at the skill which these children showed doing this. Another organisation which I went to on more than one occasion was the Olgunlaşma Institüsü. This was the School of Needlework, where young girls were taught the art of wonderful embroidery, such as has been done tradi-tionally for years. They learnt gold thread work and how to repair antique costumes. I watched them learning to make silk roses exactly like a particular variety, in this case Peace. They had special shaped tools which they heated in a gas flame and then ironed the silk into shapes and curves to represent the petals. The end product was so realistic one would be forgiven for thinking that they were the real thing. Later I was presented with a bouquet of these beautiful works of art.

Later that year, I had disturbing news from Mother that she was having heart problems and had even had a spell in hospital, which for her, who was seldom ill, must have been a traumatic experience. She kept me informed of how things were going for her. All my sisters were married by now and had families of their own so had left home, but were all fairly near her and able to keep an eye on events. I also had been struggling somewhat with a health problem of my own, and had been over to Cyprus several times to the RAF Hospital at Akrotiri, but in spite of copious tests, nothing more could be done for the time being, so I soldiered on, and hoped that those outside the family didn't notice that all was not well.

Anslow had another liaison visit coming up, and this time it was to Beirut. This was of course in the golden days of that city, and I went with him to have the chance to see a little of the Paris of the Middle East, as it was sometimes called. We had a short visit of three days only, and we were wined and dined handsomely, and while Anslow was talking shop during the day, our hostess took me round to see the sights and to meet some of the diplomatic community. The shops made one's mouth water, especially coming from Turkey, where some things were impossible to buy. On one of my visits to Cyprus, Anslow had come with me, and had brought back lengths of English wool cloth, to be made up into suits in Ankara, by a very good tailor he had been introduced to; this was the sort of thing that some people did when going to Beirut.

In December of that year, Anslow and the American Military Attaché decided that they would go to Eastern Turkey to see whether they could get through a certain area in spite of the snow and bad weather. When I heard of this plan, I was naturally a little apprehensive and reminded Anslow that the children were coming out on the 17th of the month. He promised to back in time for their arrival. I was rather dubious. They set off in a new Land Rover which had been sent out from England, and of course I heard nothing nor did I expect to. Imagine my surprise when true to his word, he walked into the house on the morning of the 17th. Apparently all had gone well for them in spite of the conditions being fairly ghastly at times. In one area, there was so much snow that only the tops of the telegraph poles showed them where the road was, and they had to dig themselves out frequently. On another occasion they had a puncture and had to change the wheel, only to find that the spare wheel had been welded on to the vehicle for security for its journey out from UK. Darkness fell, and they were still struggling. Finally they succeeded in getting the wheel free, and Anslow changed it while Bill stood guard with a shotgun in case of wolves, which were a very definite hazard. The delay meant that they had to break the golden rule of not driving after dark. I am glad I didn't know all this was going on.

As Christmas loomed, so did the season of parties. One of the foreign attachés gave a fancy dress party for a large number of people from different countries. The German Air Attaché was a jolly sort of fellow who entered into the spirit of the party. He decided to dress himself up as an Arab in all the suitable regalia he could lay his hands on, complete with a Yassar Arafat style headdress of chequered cloth. He then instructed his driver to take him to the address of his fellow attaché. Somehow, and we none of us knew how it could have happened, his driver lost his way, and on seeing a large official-looking building with a guard on the gate, Pieter stopped the car, wound down the window and was about to ask the guard the way when he was nearly lynched. It turned out that the building was the Israeli Embassy! When Pieter finally arrived at the correct venue, he looked decidedly shaken. We were all very amused by this incident and thought it typical that it had happened to Pieter of all people.

When the children arrived for Christmas, as always we decorated the house, and I had noticed that on the empty hillside near our house, there was quite a lot of mistletoe growing in some scattered trees. I called Hami, explained to him the custom of the English to hang up a sprig of this plant in the house, and told him to go out and cut me a piece. Well, we realized after a time that he had been gone for absolutely ages, and we looked out of the window to see if we could spot him. There in the distance we saw Hami actually up a tree and the whole thing was shaking as he sawed away at a branch the size of my wrist, on which the mistletoe was growing. He was using my saw-edged bread knife, which has never been the same since. I really couldn't blame him, as it was probably my bad Turkish which was at fault. Another little problem I had with him, was that there had been a certain amount of internal terrorism in parts of Turkey from time to time, and we had been warned not to accept strange parcels at the door in case it were a bomb. This was explained to Hami, and also that we had two buckets outside the front door, so that any suspicious package could be plunged into sand or water. Towards Christmas, along came a chauffeur-driven car with four stars on the front to show that it was the car of a senior Turkish general, and the driver, who was known to Hami, delivered a gift-wrapped box. Without using any imagination but acting strictly to the letter of the what I had said, he dowsed a box of marrons glacés in the bucket of water!

After Christmas, a whole lot of us went up to Uludağ for a week's skiing again, and then it was back to school for the children, and back to work for us. We heard that later in the year the Queen was coming out to Turkey on a State Visit, so it was going to be a busy time of preparation for many in the Embassy. Anslow was going to be personally responsible for the Gallipoli part of her tour, and so when we did our annual pilgrimage to this area in the spring, he wanted to spend a little time down there making early plans and co-ordinating with the War Graves Commission representative, as well as looking at the lie of the land and how HM would best see all there was to see. The year before, there had been a rampant fire over the whole area. The scrub was tinder dry in the hot summer and anything might have set it off, but it had the effect of exposing the old trenches from the campaign fought so fiercely so long ago. In many ways it made Anslow's task easier. Anyway on that spring visit the planning was in its infancy, and we were to go down again purely to make detailed arrangements later on.

Back in Ankara, I was making my own plans to go back to England with Anslow, who had to go to a conference in London. I wanted to go and see Mother and to see a consultant at an Army hospital in Aldershot to sort out my health problems. The next thing on our calendar was the Queen's official birthday in June. Anslow during his tenure of office had been able to arrange for a British Army band to come out to play on this occasion every year. This time the Parachute Regimental Band came out for a few days to play at the Ambassador's garden party in Ankara, and for the Beating of Retreat. Then they were to go down to Istanbul to play at a garden party in the Consulate gardens. Anslow, in the absence of the Ambassador, and I were to host this event. Back in Ankara, we managed to get to bed by midnight in preparation for the six hour journey to Istanbul early the next day. The phone woke us at four a.m., and it was the Embassy to say that a telegram had come in to say that my mother had died. I was numbed and stunned, and dreadfully upset that I had missed seeing her by two weeks. How I got through the next twenty-four hours I shall never know. I must have sent messages to my sisters but I honestly can't remember doing so.

We didn't sleep much after that, and so as soon as Özturk arrived with the official car, we set off for Istanbul. On this particular visit, we stayed in the famous old hotel called the Pera Palace. I don't know what it is like now, but it was an Edwardian time capsule in our day. It has been used in many film sets and really has to be seen to be believed. Normally when we went to Istanbul officially, if we couldn't stay at the Consulate, we went to the Hilton hotel on the Bosphorus, but as we had never stayed at the Pera Palace, we thought we would like to do so. It was very sad that it should be under such circumstances. My mind was in a haze that day, but I do remember at the garden party feeling as though I was an onlooker separated from what was happening, and I was feeling pretty ill too. When it was all over and we had said goodbye to the last of the official guests, we went back to the hotel to decide what we should do. As everything was arranged for our visit to England in so short of time, we decided to leave those arrangements in place. Mother was cremated, and there was to be a small memorial service at a later date when I could be there. We asked the schools to tell the children what had happened, and we let the family in Norfolk know of our plans. The next day Anslow was busy making arrangements to get the band back to England, and so I decided to go and see my dear friend Niğar, the wife of the Army Commander in Istanbul. She was a great comfort to me as I knew she would be. Then it was back to Ankara to make plans for our departure to UK.

This was to be a ten day trip. On arrival I went to Aldershot and saw the consultant, who said that I would have to come home for a major operation at a date to be arranged. I then went to Norfolk to see my sisters and to attend the service for Mother. We all had heavy hearts that day. I felt it was the end of an era, and apart from an aunt there was no one left from Mother's generation. Before leaving for Turkey again, I decided, and Anslow reluctantly agreed, that I should delay enough to see the Queen's visit through in October, and then come home to hospital.

Back in Ankara we barely had time to prepare ourselves before the children came out for their summer holidays. We decided to go off to the south coast again in August, as it might be the last chance we would have to do this. We went south through Konya, some four hours drive from Ankara, where we stopped for a break and a meal. We went to a small restaurant, if you can call it that. There was no menu or anything as grand as that, and we were invited into the kitchen to choose from some large cauldrons on a very hot stove. It was difficult to know what to choose as everything looked the same, but after making our selection we went and sat down and waited to see what came. Chunks of bread were always served with the meal, and often the main course had a salad with it but one had to be very careful that there were no little hot green peppers hidden among the leaves. On this occasion we drank what the Turks called 'lion's milk' which was mostly yoğhurt with one or two other additions which made it runny. It was really very refreshing on a hot day. Fazilet, Neriman's sister, had given the children a bag of sunflower seeds to munch on the journey. She was convinced that it was a certain cure for car sickness. The result of this was that the car filled with all the seed cases, and it looked as though we had confetti everywhere!

As we went south we came to a little place almost beside the road, where there were the remains of an early Christian church. While we were looking round, an elderly Turk with stubble on his face and wearing baggy black breeches appeared with his donkey. On the donkey's back was a beautifully woven bag about 2ft 6ins square and filled with manure which he was bringing down from a cave to spread on his little patch of land. Apparently he kept his sheep and goats in the cave in the winter, and in the summer months he cleaned out the cave and put the contents to good use. The yastık, for that is what it was, was a work of art and made in an intricate pattern in dark reds and indigo blue with a little gold thread running through some of the motifs, as well as touches of lighter colours. I was captivated by it and wondered if he would sell it to us. At first he was very reluctant, but after further conversation and persuasion we won the day, and bought it for the equivalent of £3. Of course it was very niffy, and we washed it copiously when we got back to Ankara; and although after that it smelt sweet to us, many years later Juno's successor always showed a great interest in it. An expert, on seeing our yastık, said it was a very fine one and the gold thread told him that it came from an area near the Syrian border. This may be an appropriate moment to say that the Turkish servants used to clean rugs in the winter when the snow was on the ground, by taking them out in the garden and putting them face down in the snow, and then dragging them along. The first time I saw them do this, I was surprised to see how much grubbiness came off on the dry powdery snow.

Our destination this time was the mocamp at Alanya, and to get there we hit the coast at Silifke and turned right. The road hugged the coast and we always liked to do this stretch of road from east to west because it meant we were on the inside of the road, and not pushed perilously near the edge when traffic came the other way. We passed Side where we had camped before, and stopped at a place called Anamur, where there was a spectacular castle practically on the beach. It was very extensive and consisted mainly of the outside walls, but I think it was its size which captured the imagination. When we got to Alanya, we climbed out of the car with empty sunflower seeds blowing all over the place. We were getting quite expert at getting the tent up quickly, and then it was the luxury of a cool swim in the hot sun.

While we were in this area we joined up with some friends who were staying on the south coast, and we took a boat out to Kızılkale. This was Maiden's Castle on an island not far from the coast. We found a young man who had a motor boat and he agreed to take us. We spent a while on this island exploring the castle and had a picnic looking out over that blue Mediterranean sea, and then the young man called us back to the boat by blowing into a large conche shell. It made a very effective and charming summons. It was also while we were near Alanya, that we explored the lower reaches of a steep wooded hill, with caves half way up. We had been told that there were bears living in this area, but we didn't see anything, and am not sure what we would have done if we had come face to face with a wild bear!

By the time that the children returned to school, the Royal visit was not far away, and Anslow said he must go down to Istanbul and out to the Gallipoli area to finalize his part of this visit. One of the things he had to do was to take down from Ankara, where they had arrived, the waxed poppy wreaths which HM and others would be laying on the various memorials. They had to be stored in Çannakkale on the other side of the Dardanelles, and he had arranged to meet the War Graves Representative there. They found a place to store them in a lock-up shed, but all the time Anslow was worried that it might not be rat proof, and that when they were produced a month later they might have been devoured! The next task was to decide where HM should stand to see certain salient points. This meant on one occasion that a small tree had to be cut down and the root dug up and got out of the way. In doing this, a human skull was revealed. Here were problems, for it if was British or Commonwealth then the War Graves chap would have to see that it was given a decent burial. If not, it was a Turkish problem. The WGR was with us on this occasion, and he picked up the skull and said 'It is a Turk.' Anslow asked him how on earth he could tell, and the answer came back 'because it has a flat back to the skull.' I think it was a case of trying to pass the buck. A compromise was reached and they reburied it.

The final knotty problem which had to be resolved was the matter of a road. Anslow had been in touch with the relevant Turkish authorities that a road must be made for the entourage to gain access to the area where the Queen was going to be told about the campaign. They had made the road and put a lot of black sticky tar on it, but a third of the stretch had no top gravel because they had run out. Our minds conjured up visions of the Queen in white high-heeled shoes treading her way through the black sticky morass. To rectify this meant a journey back to Istanbul to sort it out. So much in Turkey was left to Allah and all we could do was to hope for the best.

The Turks wanted to make a little museum on the battlefield so that the Queen could go and inspect it and make suitable comments. Anslow and I thought we had better go and look at it and see what they had found to put in it. We noticed a collection of Army trouser buttons, and what really did amuse us was an empty Shippams meat paste jar possibly left by a recent tourist in the area!

October dawned and the Royal Visit was upon us. The airport was suitably decked out for her arrival, with stretches of red carpet, a dais and the inevitable flagpole, but too late we realized that the Union Jack was upside down. The Queen shook hands with all the Turkish dignitaries, and then among others, Anslow and I were presented to her. She was accompanied by Prince Philip and Princess Anne. HM was given a wonderful reception by the Turkish people on her drive from the airport into Ankara, which I am sure must have heartened and bolstered her for this visit.

She had several days in Ankara, and a heavy schedule of engagements, some of which we attended. After seeing the Union Jack at the airport,

Anslow took the precaution of having some drawing pins in his pocket, so that any future mistakes could be rectified. We were honoured to attend the State Banquet given by our Ambassador and his wife at the Residence. The table looked splendid with wonderful silver and silver gilt adorning it. After this banquet when the Turkish guests had left, a few of us stayed on to talk to the Royal Party. It was a delightful informal interlude, which perfected a memorable occasion, when the Queen talked to me about Prince Andrew and our son John who were very close in age. I remember saying to her that the sword was mightier than the pen among the men in my family, to which she replied 'And very right and proper in an Army family.'

The Queen and her entourage then went to Izmir, to carry out engagements there, and to join the Royal Yacht Britannia which was waiting there to take her eventually to the Dardanelles. Anslow and I meantime got ourselves together for the long journey by road to the same area, as we weren't involved in the Izmir part of the visit. We spent a night in the Hilton in Istanbul. I had always thought that such an hotel would be without atmosphere and rather Americanized until we stayed here for the first time some years before. It was in a lovely position on the Bosphorus, and inside had a truly Turkish feel to it. The food was very good and we especially enjoyed the restaurant where we had breakfast, and although the shops in the foyer were expensive, they had a very good range of luxury goods, which included leather coats and jackets, alabaster, embroidery, and lots of rugs. It was also fun to sit in the foyer drinking Turkish coffee and watch the cosmopolitan world go by.

We set off for the Gallipoli peninsula the following day. It was a long, rather boring drive, and we were making for a small place on the north side of the Dardanelles called Kilitbahir, where we were booked into a tiny little basic hotel, if one could call it that. It was really the only place where we could stay so it had to do. I should think that the inhabitants of this small community must have wondered what hit them when all this activity took place. The importance of it was that it had a little jetty where the Royal launch could come in to land the Royal party on terra firma. When we got there the night before the great day, Anslow was alarmed to see that there was no sign of those Turks responsible for the flag pole and the Union Jack, but mercifully the War Graves representative

32. Fishing boats in the Dardanelles.

had delivered the poppy wreaths. On inspection they looked in good order and un-nibbled!

When we woke the next morning, it was all hustle and bustle as we dressed in our finery. Anslow, as always, looked splendid in his uniform. I suppose we had breakfast but I don't remember it. The Royal Yacht looked resplendent as she lay off-shore and at anchor not very far away. At least the most important actors on the stage had arrived. As the time passed and the hour of the Queen's arrival approached, there was still no sign of the Union Jack, but there was nothing we could do at this eleventh hour. Then suddenly a motor boat roared up to the jetty, and out jumped a Turkish soldier with the Union flag, which was run up a makeshift pole. Allah had come up trumps just in time! Hardly had this been done before the Royal Launch came into sight and the visit we had been waiting for, began.

The Queen and the other members of the Royal Family went to a number of the memorials, attended by the Australian and the Canadian Ambassadors as well as ours, of course. Anslow was part of this party while I stayed on the sidelines, taking photographs on every possible occasion, on both ours and John's cameras. I should say here that the memorials in the form of rows of gravestones with flowers at the bottom of each, were most beautifully kept on all occasions by the War Graves Commission. The inscriptions on the stones were simple which made them the more poignant. Whenever I found standing about too much, I took refuge in the Australian Ambassador's car, which had been put at my disposal if I felt unwell. The grand finale of the day, after Anslow had shown HM the layout of the area and explained a bit of the campaign to her, was to go aboard the yacht. We had been invited to have lunch, which was attended by a few senior Turkish officers, as well as the entourage. One of the first things that the Queen said when we arrived was that there was to be no formality on board. I certainly think that she felt much more relaxed when she was on her own territory. She asked Anslow and me whether there had been any funny incidents in the run up to her visit, and we told her about the roadmaking and finding the skull. After the meal, we had coffee and then I was told that a cabin had been prepared for me to lie down. All along, I was touched by the consideration for me and my imminent visit to hospital in England, when there were many more important things for her to think about at this time. After about twenty minutes a message came that HM wanted me upstairs. As I arrived the Queen smiled at me and Anslow was invited to step forward and she invested him by making him a Companion of the Royal Victorian Order, (CVO) while Prince Philip said 'You might like to have one of these.' It was a signed coloured photograph of the three Royal Guests in a lovely blue leather frame. It was a proud moment and something to be treasured, along with the very human and caring face behind the Royal panoply.

There was to be no slowing down now that this visit was nearly over, as we had to get back to Ankara, a two day journey, to prepare for my return to hospital in a few days time, and to attend the departure of HM by air from the capital. For this she wore a striking daffodil yellow outfit, which meant that even those some distance away could spot her. It had been a great experience to have been part of this memorable visit. I was glad this time had come, and although I wouldn't have missed the Queen's visit for anything, I really did feel ill. An RAF VC10 from the Far East was diverted to Ankara to pick me up. I went on board on a stretcher and was thankful to be able to finally relax. One thing about this trip home which amused me was that when we were flying over France, an RAF steward on the plane came to me and said 'Heathrow or Lyneham, Ma'am?' The decision had to be made a long way from my destination. I replied 'Heathrow' and almost imagined the pilot putting out his indicator and turning half right! A car met me on the tarmac, and soon I was safely tucked up in bed in Aldershot.

After having a major operation, a lovely bouquet of flowers were sent from Windsor. It put the hospital on their toes and certainly touched me greatly. I was starting to make a good recovery, when I had a rather alarming telephone call from John's school. This was to tell me that he had been involved in a car accident and was lying in Worcester Royal Infirmary with concussion. This was not the sort of thing I wanted to hear in my rather weak state, so I immediately got on to our friends, David and Jill, from Zambia days, who had agreed to be his guardians while we were away, and they, bless them, went down to see how things were. Mercifully they were able to reassure me that with a little break from school he would be fine. He went to stay with them, and while I was convalescing with friends later on, he was brought to see me. All was very well. The whole of this episode was not made any easier by there being another postal strike, and I had difficulty in contacting Anslow by phone, letter and signals. After six weeks, I was allowed to fly, and was taken to Brize Norton in Oxfordshire, where I caught an RAF flight to Cyprus. Anslow came over to meet me, and we had a few days there before returning to Ankara. I was back in time for Christmas and the children's arrival at the end of term.

While I had been away, one of the things that Anslow had done was to go on an exercise with the Turkish Army. As it was getting towards the middle of the winter, he dressed himself up in the cold weather clothing which had been issued to him in England. He set off, and on arrival at the appointed place, he found that all the senior Turkish officers were sitting in a large tent, which had a picture window set into one side of it, strategically placed so that they could watch the mock battle to be enacted in front of them. Chairs were lined up inside and he was invited to take his place by the officer commanding the whole thing. Then to his horror a hot air blower was put under his chair. He was soon boiling hot, and although he could take off some of his outer layers, there was a limit to how much he could undress.

All through the year there had been sporadic outbursts of internal strife by a group calling themselves The Red Army Faction. This had hotted up at times to a point when I had to go shopping in the official car instead of driving myself; I had to keep the doors locked and let Anslow know where I was going and that I had got back safely. It was all very tiresome and made life difficult. Then a day came when we went out to lunch with friends, and there was shooting in the road outside. A Turkish officer whom we knew was badly injured in front of our eyes. We couldn't leave and go back to our house, because it was thought that one of the terrorists was on the run, and was hiding on the hill near our home. I was concerned that Hami would be alright too. Anyway it all resolved itself, and for a while we had a guard on our house. The result of all this was that we decided that we wouldn't bring the children out for the Easter holidays. We made arrangements with kind friends to have them.

We were also in the last few months of our time in Turkey, and this entailed a particularly busy programme of official duties and many farewell parties. At the Easter weekend when the Ambassador was away, there was another outbreak of terrorism when some British radar technicians were murdered in a remote part of Turkey. Anslow was immediately flown to this area by the Turkish Army, while they tried to flush out the perpetrators of this awful act. Meanwhile I was trying to comfort distraught families back in Ankara. It justified in our minds our decision to keep Lizzie and John in England.

Towards the end of our time, we were given many farewell presents as well as parties. An Iranian General gave us a large antique steel engraving of the Duke of Wellington on Horseback receiving the French Eagles from Scots. He had found this picture in a shop in Istanbul. We also were presented with a large watercolour by a well-known Turkish artist of our favourite mosque in Istanbul. Anslow was presented with a silver salver by his fellow attachés, and there were a number of other very generous and much appreciated gifts of glass, alabaster and Turkish silver. Özturk gave us two alabaster ashtrays and an alabaster egg, but soon after this, he took us to a drinks party which we had to attend, and when we got back to the car, we found him crying. I asked him what on earth was the matter, to which he replied 'It was so small.' Well we couldn't make head or tale of this but finally he produced an alabaster egg the size of an ostrich's egg in a lovely shade of apricot and honour was satisfied. It was very touching.

When Anslow's successor came out, I took his wife out shopping to introduce her to all the tradesmen who had been good to me, and asked them to look after the new madam. Imagine my surprise when I did this, to be given further gifts. Dear old Rhami Bey gave me an antique yastık, and when I took Jan to my little leather shop, I was given a whole suede lambskin in the most lovely soft shade of pale leaf green. The pastahani produced an enormous box of different flavoured Turkish delight, and one of the alabaster shops gave me a pale blue marble egg, which was a very unusual colour to find. At the last minute when all our 2¼ tons of heavy baggage had gone off, I bought from this shop a lovely piece of pink mottled alabaster which had been made into a table top. It was nearly two feet in diameter and was very heavy. Anslow was horrified as it would have to be hand luggage on the plane.

After handing over our house to the new incumbents, we said farewell to the faithful Hami, who touchingly wept openly when we left. Finally through the generosity of our Ambassador and his wife, we moved into the Residence, and had three large farewell parties to say goodbye to the many friends we had made in the four years we had spent in this fascinating and hospitable country. I think we both left a little bit of our hearts behind.

Epilogue

T WAS A STRANGE FEELING TO KNOW that our enforced travels and moves were to come to an end with Anslow's retirement later in the year. Although he had enjoyed his time at Sandhurst and his career of 35 years in uniform, I think he felt, as I did, that we were ready for a more static life. Our house and garden were waiting for us, and in the ensuing 26 years since then, we have improved and maintained the house and made and enlarged the garden. At last we have all our possessions under one roof, and have been able to spread our Turkish rugs on the floors. It is a nice feeling to know that everything we do now is for keeps and we are no longer nomads.

As for the family, Lizzie and John did well at their respective schools and in their careers. They are both married and have given us five lovely grandchildren. John chose the Army as his career, and Lizzie has married into the Army, and so the cycle starts all over again. Our Ambassador and his wife have been staunch friends for all these years, until sadly the latter died not so long ago, as did my eldest sister Patti who also died of cancer recently. Anslow's mother died the year after we came home, and both my aunts have gone to their Maker. We have moved up the ladder and become the grandparents of today, with the passing of this previous generation.

On a more cheerful note, we went to stay with Neriman in Istanbul a few years ago, and saw Fazilet, Niğar and their husbands and a number of our other Turkish friends. They gave us a great welcome and all gave us that typically generous Turkish hospitality which we always associated with them. It was a most heartening and warming experience. Niğar and Kemal came to see us in our home, but sadly since then Niğar has also died. After the overthrow of the Shah, we lost touch with Mimi and her husband. We heard that he had been executed, and we dare not communicate with her in case it should endanger her. Many of our English and foreign diplomatic friends have stayed with us in our home and we keep in regular touch with many others, including Margie and the Collings from Cyprus days. I am in contact with several of my old pupils from Westminster Abbey, and go to a Reunion at the Abbey most years. My old school friend Harriet has recently died and we occasionally see Anslow's and my cousin, who gave me away at our wedding. Three old friends from Lusaka days now live in Knysna in South Africa, and we still correspond. I have always found letter writing to be the most satisfactory and rewarding way of keeping in contact, and gain much pleasure in receiving and sending news this way. I find it sad that letter writing is a neglected pastime. Of those that I knew best of the Llanmorris family, only Meg and one brother are left; after all, 65 years have passed since I first met them.

As for ourselves, retirement has proved to be almost as busy as our hectic times abroad, but we wouldn't have it any other way. We are involved in local politics, charity work and the pursuit of our various hobbies, as well as the enjoyment of our many friends. We have a lovely home, many happy memories and each other. What more could we ever want?

1998.